SLAVERY AND RACE RELATIONS IN THE AMERICAS

D0988636

*the text of this book is printed
on 100% recycled paper*

Crosscurrents in Latin America
Edited by Joseph S. Tulchin

Roberto Cortes Conde — THE FIRST STAGES OF MODERNIZATION IN LATIN AMERICA

Tulio Halperin-Donghi — THE AFTERMATH OF REVOLUTION IN LATIN AMERICA

Jorge Hardoy — LATIN AMERICAN CITIES

Harmannus Hoetink — SLAVERY AND RACE RELATIONS IN THE AMERICAS

Jay Kinsbruner — CHILE: A HISTORICAL INTERPRETATION

Anthony P. Maingot — PERSONALISM IN LATIN AMERICA

Gilbert Merkx — TWENTIETH-CENTURY LATIN AMERICA

Hobart P. Spalding — ORGANIZED LABOR IN LATIN AMERICA

Joseph S. Tulchin — LATIN AMERICA IN WORLD AFFAIRS

SLAVERY AND RACE RELATIONS IN THE AMERICAS

COMPARATIVE NOTES ON THEIR NATURE AND NEXUS

H. HOETINK

HARPER TORCHBOOKS
Harper & Row, Publishers
New York   Evanston   San Francisco   London

A hardcover edition of this book is available from Harper & Row, Publishers, Inc.

First HARPER TORCHBOOK edition published 1973.

LIBRARY OF CONGRESS CATALOG CARD NUMBER: 76–181526

STANDARD BOOK NUMBER: 06–131710–1

Designed by Ann Scrimgeour

To J. J. Fahrenfort
Emeritus Professor of Ethnology, University of Amsterdam

CONTENTS

PART I
SLAVERY VERSUS
RACE RELATIONS

1

THE SLAVE AND THE FREEMAN

THE TANNENBAUM POSTULATE: A CRITIQUE

Since the publication of Frank Tannenbaum's *Slave and Citizen*,[1] much, maybe too much, has been written about the supposed differences among the slavery systems of the Western Hemisphere. However, less critical attention has been given to Tannenbaum's underlying hypothesis—the character of a society's race relations outside the system of slavery and after its abolition is determined by the peculiarities of that system of slavery. Those systems of slavery that both permitted the slaves to preserve their moral personality and facilitated their integration into society through frequent manumissions produced conditions after abolition under which the chances of freemen to be accepted as social equals would be enhanced.

This postulate, which directly and even causally connects the conditions of slavery with the present-day socioracial structure and relations, has gained more popularity in recent years. The growing literature and number of conferences, especially in the United States, on comparative slave systems are not only the result of a legitimate need for further insight into the contributions and experiences of the black population in North American history but also the product of the belief that the present tragic racial situation in the United States can be explained by studying the tragic history of slavery. Thus, not only historians but also sociologists, who usually adhere to the ahistoricism so deeply embedded in North American culture, surprisingly genuflect before a methodology that in my view is unacceptable.

The phenomenon is not limited to the United States, nor to

[1] Frank Tannenbaum, *Slave and Citizen* (New York: Alfred Knopf, 1947).

adepts of conservative ideologies. The Brazilian sociologist Florestan Fernándes thinks that the still-observable racial prejudices in
Brazil have their origins in slavery; therefore, these prejudices are
"anachronisms," and will gradually disappear. While he ably
analyzes recent developments in Brazilian social structure, he
prefers not to functionally dissect racial prejudice and explains its
presence by referring to the past. (See pp. 107–108.) In *The
Growth of the Modern West Indies,* Gordon K. Lewis writes with
some irritation about present-day Guianese who, like Barbadians
or Jamaicans, "continue to refer to a slave past abolished over a
century ago as if it were a continuing factor in their present dis-
contents; as if, in Dr. Raymond Smith's apt phrase, one were to
attribute Britain's balance-of-payments problems to the Napoleonic
Wars."[2]

Tannenbaum's postulate may be simply stated as follows:
Where master-slave relations were "good," race relations outside
and after slavery would be "good"; on the other hand, where
slavery developed in an unfavorable "moral and legal setting,"
there "the very nature of the institution of slavery . . . in turn
shaped the political and ethical biases," which in Tannenbaum's
view "manifestly separated the United States from the other parts
of the New World in this respect."[3]

Eric Williams, Sidney Mintz, and others who criticized Tannenbaum's ideas did not explicitly attack his postulate that links the
conditions of slavery with race relations. Rather, they proposed to
show that slavery in the plantation colonies of the Western Hemisphere was also, and possibly more than anything else, an economic institution. Therefore, the character of master-slave
relations and the frequency of manumission directly responded to
such factors as the supply and demand for tropical products on the
world market. Where the economy was predominantly autarchic,
as in Cuba and Puerto Rico in the early eighteenth century, slavery
tended to be more benign than in a later period in the same terri-

---

[2] Gordon K. Lewis, *The Growth of the Modern West Indies* (London:
MacGibbon and Kee, 1968), p. 259.
[3] Tannenbaum, *Slave and Citizen,* p. 42.

tories when sugar became the main agricultural product. Similar observations can be made about Jamaica, Trinidad, or the United States in different periods of their economic history.[4]

This economic critique significantly undermined—correctly in my view—two other assumptions of Tannenbaum: First, that for noneconomic reasons, slavery in the United States (and by extension in the Anglo-Saxon colonies of the Western Hemisphere) was more cruel and damaging to the personality of the slave than in Brazil (and by extension in Latin America); second, that the benign or harsh character of master-slave relations was a permanent factor in any plantation colony in the Western Hemisphere. More recent research in which Brazilians also participated has generally confirmed this criticism.[5]

However, although the inconstancy of master-slave relations may hamper the empirical verification of Tannenbaum's postulate, its theoretical plausibility has not yet been questioned. Did not the future development of race relations have to profit from a generally benign system of slavery where manumission was frequent?

Before answering this question directly, it will be helpful to compare two different slave systems.[6] By comparing two colonies controlled by the same metropolitan power, the Dutch slave

[4] Eric Williams, *Capitalism and Slavery* (Chapel Hill, N.C.: University of North Carolina Press, 1944); Sidney W. Mintz, "Labor and Sugar in Puerto Rico and in Jamaica, 1800–1850," *Comparative Studies in Society and History* 1, no. 3 (March 1959). "In the mid-nineteenth century, Cuban slavery dehumanized the slaves as viciously as had Jamaican or North American slavery" (S. W. Mintz in his review of Stanley M. Elkins, *Slavery: A Problem in American Institutional and Intellectual Life* [Chicago: University of Chicago Press, 1959], *American Anthropologist* 63, no. 3 [1961]).

[5] See Octavio Ianni, *As Metamorfoses do Escravo* (São Paulo, Brazil: Difusão Europeia do Livro, 1962). See also David Brian Davis, *The Problem of Slavery in Western Culture* (Ithaca, N.Y.: Cornell University Press, 1966).

[6] H. Hoetink, "The Free Black and Mulatto in the Slave Societies of the Netherlands West Indies," in *Neither Slave Nor Free: The Freedman of African Descent in the Slave Societies of the New World,* eds. J. Greene and D. Cohen (Baltimore: The Johns Hopkins University Press, 1972).

colonies of Curaçao and Surinam, several complicating cultural and political variables are eliminated.

During a long period preceding the abolition of slavery in 1863, Curaçao, a tiny island off the Venezuelan coast, was a society in which the relations between master and slave were decidedly "mild." Economic and demographic conditions caused such relative "mildness." The island was not a conventional plantation colony, but a commercial center; the small number of slaves per master did not inspire fear; and the small size of the island made slaveholders susceptible to whatever social control emanated from the local political and religious representatives of the metropolitan power.

During the same period, however, Surinam, a real plantation colony, had very severe master-slave relations, so severe, in fact, that they gave the Dutch throughout the Western Hemisphere a reputation as harsh and oppressive slaveholders.[7]

The economic and demographic conditions in Surinam were antithetical to those in Curaçao. The large number of slaves per master induced a permanent fear and led to sadistic punishments; the large size of the country and its sparse settlement sufficiently isolated many plantations from the corrective social control of the capital. The geography of the country that enabled rebellious slaves to withdraw as Maroons into the jungle plus the difficult communication among plantations may explain why, in spite of the generally cruel conditions of slavery, Surinam did not witness a general slave rebellion, whereas such a rebellion arose in Curaçao in 1795—showing that the causes of rebellions were neither exclusively economic nor always due to the severe treatment of slaves. In Curaçao, the ideological influences of the Haitian Revolution, which stretched far into South America, were clearly discernible. In turn, the Curaçao revolt inspired a slave rebellion in the nearby Spanish American Coro area.[8]

---

[7] See J. G. Stedman, *A Narrative of a Five-Years Expedition Against the Revolted Negroes of Surinam*, 2 vols. (London, 1813); see also Tannenbaum, *Slave and Citizen*, p. 65.

[8] See Pedro M. Arcaya, *Insurrección de los Negros de la Serranía de Coro* (Caracas: Instituto Panamericano de Geografía e Historia, 1949); and

According to Tannenbaum's postulate, the experience of slavery in each of the Dutch colonies would result in the following: In Curaçao, with mild relations between slave and master as well as early and frequent manumissions, Negroes and coloreds (two social categories that outside the United States must be carefully distinguished) both outside of and after slavery would have been socially accepted by the rest of society and would have achieved increased mobility toward higher social strata. However, in Surinam, unfavorable master-slave relations and the small number of manumissions (excepting those immediately preceding abolition) would have produced very tense relations between whites and Negroid groups, and the latter hardly would have penetrated the more prestigious occupational strata of society.

Yet, precisely the reverse took place! In Curaçao, the appointment of nonwhite civil servants to high-ranking positions only hesitantly started in the second quarter of the twentieth century, and today the different racial groups maintain a certain social exclusiveness. The highest prestige and power remained in the hands of white groups, even though already in the eighteenth century a small nucleus of "respectable" coloreds, mostly merchants, had been formed. But, in Surinam already in the early nineteenth century, there existed a group of prestigious coloreds, several of them academically trained, who served in a number of the highest posts both in government and in plantation agriculture. Some of them had close social contacts with the upper stratum of white families. This nonwhite professional elite preserved and strengthened its dominant role after abolition and Negroes were gradually integrated into it.

This brief comparison at least seems to deny the general validity of Tannenbaum's postulate and even suggests its very antithesis: During a prolonged period where master-slave relations were "good" and manumission frequent, white attitudes would be more unfavorable toward the manumitted than toward the slaves; conse-

---

Miguel Acosta Saignes, *Vida de los Esclavos Negros en Venezuela* (Caracas: Hespérides, 1967), pp. 277 ff. Compare further the causes of Jamaican slave revolts in H. Orlando Patterson, *The Sociology of Slavery* (London: MacGibbon and Kee, 1967), pp. 273–283.

quently, the chances for the manumitted's social acceptance and mobility would be less than in a slave society where master-slave relations were unfavorable and the number of manumitted and their descendants small.

The logic of this antithesis is clear: Where a master's relations with his slaves are "good," he need not fear them; where there are simultaneously too many freemen both whose social behavior is unregulated and whose subsistence is uncertain, the master's fear will be directed more toward them; and, if some of these freemen acquire a certain prosperity, the whites, especially the poorer among them, will perceive this as a social threat and rationalize it in racial terms and prejudices. Conversely, where the masters severely treat their slaves and perceive them as menacing, the whites will form a favorable opinion of freemen, as long as their number is small, and try to involve them in a social alliance against the slaves.

Historical reality in Curaçao and Surinam corresponded to these alternatives. Observers from the early nineteenth century, comparing both societies, concluded that in Curaçao the colored (freeman) was more despised and feared than the Negro (slave), while in Surinam the situation was the reverse. Here at the end of the eighteenth century, when the number of freemen was minimal, white opinion about them was predominantly favorable. When the number of urban poor gradually increased, this general opinion took a turn for the worse, although it was always more favorable toward the colored elite in Surinam than it was in Curaçao.

Yet, general validity cannot be attributed to this counterpostulate, for that would again suggest a causal link between slavery and race relations, albeit in a sense opposite to Tannenbaum's. The exceptions to this counterpostulate are easily discernible: In the Spanish and Portuguese colonies, frequent manumissions and "good" master-slave relations over a long period of time coincided with a remarkable degree of social acceptance of the free colored, thus contradicting the Curaçao alternative; in the French colony of Saint Domingue, however, unfavorable master-slave relations accompanied the phenomenon of a considerable and prosperous group of freemen, who were often slaveholders themselves, but the initial alliance between this group and the whites was substituted in the course of the eighteenth century by an ever more virulent discrimination against the prosperous free colored, thus contradicting the Surinam alternative.

FACTORS INFLUENCING THE POSITION OF FREEMEN

This comparative exercise makes clear that a variety of factors, operating outside the institution of slavery and related to the total social and economic structure of society, were of crucial importance for the social categorization, integration, and mobility of the ex-slaves both during and after the period of slavery.

Numerical Proportions and Security

The comparison between Curaçao and Surinam showed the importance of numerical proportions among whites, freemen, and slaves.

Where the number of slaves was relatively large and the other two groups were relatively small, the chance of a more tolerant attitude of the whites vis-à-vis the freemen was greater than in societies where the freemen were seen because of their numbers as a greater menace than the slaves themselves. The collective sensation of being threatened, however subjective and dependent on many factors, often is related to numerical group proportions. (See chapter 5, pp. 166–192.)

Racial Differentiation and Resulting Social Stratification

Donald R. Horowitz, in an interesting essay, is even of the opinion that the recognition of the colored group as a separate social category in the British West Indies, and its absence in the United States, was in great part determined by the whites' need for security:

The very elevation of the mulattoes [in the British West Indies] was largely intended to facilitate and perpetuate the brutalization and degradation of the blacks [for] in the British West Indies, the presence of a massive slave population gave rise to a serious security problem and reinforced the tendency to distinguish brown from black. In the Southern United States, a lesser security problem made the initial distinction less compelling for the whites, and the growth of such a problem later made it all the more imperative in their eyes to reduce the privileges of all free non-whites. . . .

Racial differentiation [in white, colored, and black] and the presence of a large class of free non-whites, it has been thought, were reflections of tolerance or flexibility manifested concretely in frequent manumission and inconsistent with the harshest form of chattel slavery. The British West Indian data make it clear that such inferences are not necessarily justified. . . . Manumission—even of blacks [as distinct from coloreds]—cannot be used uncritically as an indicator of either the master's view of the slave or the general atmosphere of the slave society. Differentiation bears no necessary relation to degradation.[9]

In his essay, Horowitz mostly limits himself to a comparison between the three-tier stratification of the British West Indies and the two-tier sociracial distinction of the United States. It is useful, however, to make clear that in all American multiracial societies outside the United States (and, historically, also in French or Spanish influenced enclaves in that country, such as New Orleans or Charleston) there existed and exists a stratification of white, mixed, and Negro. And in all these societies, the feeling of security of the whites vis-à-vis the slaves could not always have been less than in the Deep South. Both in Curaçao, where certainly before 1795 the whites felt secure, and in Surinam, where the whites always felt insecure, the distinction between coloreds and blacks both administratively and socially was very early established.

Therefore, it seems more correct and prudent not to link the degree of security of the whites directly to the origin of the three-tier stratification, but rather to suggest that there existed a positive relation between this need for security and the generally prevailing attitudes—of tolerance and social encouragement or of discrimination and repression—of the whites vis-à-vis the coloreds or the freemen.[10]

[9] Donald R. Horowitz, "Color Differentiation in the American Systems of Slavery" (1969), unpublished manuscript quoted by permission of the author.

[10] This does not diminish the importance of Horowitz's observation that in the Deep South after the two-tier stratification was already firmly established voices sometimes were heard "often from areas where large numbers of slaves made the comparatively few whites insecure" in favor

Miscegenation and Social Stratification

There is another factor that Horowitz considers important for the emergence of the colored group as a separate social category in the British West Indies. He is of the opinion that in the southern colonies of the North American mainland "most of the earliest white-black unions seem to have been between servants and slaves" so that "any claim of mixed offspring to special treatment on account of white ancestry was blunted by the low status of the white ancestor." This "initial low status of children of mixed origin and the stigma that attached to them affected even the mulatto progeny of high-status whites."

In Horowitz's view, in the British West Indies—where, in contrast to the United States, the ratio of white females to males remained low in the major territories, especially so in Jamaica— "planter concubinage was nearly universal," so that the group of free coloreds came to include a "substantial portion of privileged sons of high-status fathers," sufficient in number "to elevate the status of the rest." In this fashion, Horowitz believes, the basis was laid "for the perceptual differentiation of the group as a whole from the free blacks."

Similar considerations would, according to Horowitz, account for the origin of the mulatto social category in Latin America; he notes in this context that "the compensatory function of money or education in elevating the status of dark-skinned mulattoes seems very likely a latter-day surrogate for the high status paternity which was initially responsible for both of those advantages. In the United States, by contrast, the advantaged mulatto was so excep-

---

of "a distinct group of free and privileged mulattoes [who] would be an asset in case of a slave revolt."

After the Haitian Revolution, the southern states took severe measures against the free coloreds and tried to diminish their numbers, but the British West Indies started to lessen the restraints on this group. This is understandable in view of the already established differences in socioracial structure with their corresponding differences among whites' expectations of coloreds. In the United States, the fear of freemen and mulattoes identifying with the slaves was more widespread than in the British West Indies or in the rest of Afro-America.

tional that the depressed status of the great majority was imputed on a color basis to the group." This line of thought is original and attractive, like Horowitz's earlier one. But both need to be applicable to the whole Caribbean in order to acquire validity as two of the original causes of the separate status of the mulatto stratum.

In Haiti during a part of the eighteenth century and in Surinam especially since the last quarter of the same century, conditions were present similar to those depicted by Horowitz for the British West Indies: A scarcity of white women led to regular unions, very rarely marriages, that were called *"plaçage"* in Haiti and "Surinam marriage" in Dutch Guiana.

Not infrequently such unions involved rich planters or high public servants and Negro or colored women. The offspring of these unions were often sent to the father's country for their education and upon their return came to form an influential part of the group of "respectable" coloreds. Also, in Martinique and Guadeloupe such unions took place, which strengthens Horowitz's argument. Yet, one may ask whether the numerical proportion of these "educated and reasonably prosperous" coloreds (who in Jamaica around 1760 are estimated by Horowitz to have amounted to no less than 44 percent of all freemen)[11] was in all Caribbean colonies sufficiently large "to elevate the status of the rest." The available data suggest rather that in many Caribbean slave societies the majority of the coloreds were very poor; mostly urban, the majority of them had to make their living as artisans, peddlers, and the like.

It was further not the scarcity of white women per se that can have led to the social recognition of an intermediate colored group, for in Curaçao, where a considerable number of white families came to live permanently, pre- and extramarital relations of white men with nonwhite women did produce a socioracial intermediate group carefully distinguished from the blacks.

Then, the only question that remains is whether in all Afro-American societies, except the United States, early interracial

---

11 Horowitz, "Color Differentiation" based on data in Edward Long, *The History of Jamaica* (London: T. Lowndes, 1774), vol. 2, bk. 2, p. 337.

unions were more frequently characterized by high social status of the white partner. Further research on this question seems necessary, but the plausibility of this thesis is not overwhelming, considering that also in several British and French islands white indentured laborers were introduced early, who must have been no less eager to establish sexual relations with Negro slaves than their counterparts in the United States.

Even assuming that Horowitz's thesis is correct with regard to the Caribbean and Latin America, it must be noted that it does not explain the related phenomenon of the decidedly greater frequency of marriages[12]—as opposed to concubinates or sexual liaisons—between whites and light coloreds in the Spanish and Portuguese speaking countries as compared with the British, French, and Dutch areas. Even when in the latter areas there existed a temporary scarcity of white women, marriages with local coloreds did not occur with any sociologically relevant frequency. In Curaçao, for example, a marriage with a South American woman from the nearby mainland was preferred to that with a daughter from a local, prosperous colored family.

For the moment, it seems advisable to dilute somewhat the Horowitz thesis by merely suggesting that those coloreds whose white fathers occupied a socially prestigious position in society generally were more favored economically and educationally than the offspring of poorer whites or of visiting sailors.

Any explanation for the absence of an intermediate colored stratum in the United States must be based on the fact that in the British, Danish, Dutch, French, Spanish, and Portuguese slave colonies such an intermediate group did emerge. It is the North American situation that in this context has to be understood as a deviation. Would not the normal initial situation have been one in which the social preference of the white was directed toward the coloreds—as opposed to the blacks—the more so when they were

---

[12] The term "marriage" here and elsewhere refers to a union which, even when not legalized or approved by the church, was sufficiently acceptable not to prevent recognition of the offspring by their father and society at large.

his own children and when, as certainly was the case initially, no fear against too large a colored group could complicate his feelings?

Rudolf van Lier, in his study of Surinam society, as a matter of course, states that "the coloreds considered themselves socially superior to the black group. They were not only closer to the white masters but the latter showed them preferment so that they occupied a better social position than the free blacks."[13]

POOR WHITES, WHITE IMMIGRANTS, AND THE DEVELOPMENT OF A TWO-TIER SOCIORACIAL STRUCTURE IN THE UNITED STATES

A factor that may explain the unique deviation of the North American socioracial structure has been indicated elsewhere:[14] Nowhere, but in the North American mainland, did the number of extremely poor whites always exceed the number of slaves. Nowhere, but in the South, were special police forces predominantly manned by poor whites found. They were established in the early nineteenth century when "the attempts at insurrection were frequent enough to keep the South in constant fear."[15] "They had a very definite part in keeping the slaves confined to their own plantations and properly intimidated. Negro hunting, Negro catching, Negro watching, and Negro whipping constituted the favorite sport

[13] R. A. J. van Lier, *Samenleving in een Grensgebied: Een Sociaal-Historische Studie van de Maatschappij in Suriname* (The Hague: Martinus Nijhoff, 1949), p. 103.

[14] H. Hoetink, *The Two Variants in Caribbean Race Relations: A Contribution to the Sociology of Segmented Societies,* trans. Eva M. Hooykaas (London: Oxford University Press, 1967).

[15] Maurice A. Davie, *Negroes in American Society* (New York: McGraw-Hill, 1949), p. 45. Elsewhere in the Caribbean and Latin America, it was mostly Negro and mulatto regiments, often under white command, that were allotted similar tasks, although in Cuba in the mid-nineteenth century landless whites engaged in "brutal hunting excursions after runaways" (Franklin W. Knight, *Slave Society in Cuba during the Nineteenth Century* [Madison, Wis.: University of Wisconsin Press, 1907], p. 70).

of many youthful whites."[16] These poor whites "had nothing to sell except their labor, and the market for that was closed to them almost completely by the presence of Negro slaves. . . . They had just one distinction to gratify their vanity—they belonged to the dominant white race."[17]

In the fifteen states comprising the South in 1860, only 3 percent of the white population belonged to the genuine planter class (those with more than twenty slaves),[18] and a very considerable part of the white population lived in economic circumstances similar to those of the free blacks and coloreds. These whites were eager to undertake police functions, which in a visible way elevated them above the Negro, colored, and slave, all of whom they saw as a permanent economic and social threat. Thus, poor whites detained the process of social recognition of the coloreds as a separate social category and undid it in the few areas where it initially existed.

The plantation system in the South, advancing rapidly since the end of the eighteenth century, robbed the small farmers of their good land so that the number of poor whites increased continually. The slave became an instrument in the agricultural competition between planter and smallholder, just as the artisan slave or freeman was a competitor in another field. "The net effect was to impoverish the mass of the [white] Southern people. A devastating picture of the injury done to the great mass of white Southerners by the institution of slavery was presented in a book published in 1857 entitled *The Impending Crisis of the South,* by Hinton R. Helper, who came from a smallholder family in North Carolina. The volume created a tremendous sensation, and there is reason to believe it alarmed the slaveholders more than did *Uncle Tom's Cabin.*"[19]

In this context it is useful to remember that, in the southern

---

[16] J. Winston Coleman, *Slavery Times in Kentucky* (Chapel Hill, N.C.: University of North Carolina Press, 1940), p. 97, cited in Davie, *Negroes in American Society,* p. 37.

[17] Davie, *Negroes in American Society,* p. 62.

[18] Ibid., p. 59.

[19] Ibid., p. 60.

states between 1790 and 1860, the number of slaves increased more than threefold and that, in addition to the states where slave labor had been used for a long time in the cultivation of sugar, rice, or tobacco, there were extensive areas where slavery first was introduced on a large scale as a result of the spread of cotton production since the end of the eighteenth century. In this sense, slavery in its largest and most capitalistic dimensions was a new and short-lived institution in large parts of the South.

As the socioracial structure was formed under this new impact, it was probably not so much influenced by remnants or reminiscences of specific situations in the older slavery areas as it was by the direct effects that the more recent, massive increase in plantations and slaves had on the social and economic condition of the "great mass of white Southerners." These effects must have decisively influenced the latter's social perception and contributed to the prevention of the emergence or the continued existence of a separate grouping of coloreds. There is no distinct "great mass" of poor white Jamaicans, Trinidadians, or Surinamese to disclaim the historical uniqueness of this factor.[20] Yet, even if it is true that no other slave society in the Western Hemisphere had to undergo a similar process whereby such a large, white, traditional, agricultural class was pauperized rapidly as a result of the large-scale introduction of an economy based on plantation slavery, the fact remains that in Spanish and Portuguese slave colonies great numbers of whites also lived on an economic level comparable to that of the Negroes and coloreds. Why did not this fact in itself produce a socioracial stratification similar to that in the United States in islands such as Cuba, Santo Domingo, and Puerto Rico? This question has two answers.

First, these white peasants (the *guajiros* of Cuba, the *campesinos* of Santo Domingo, the *jíbaros* of Puerto Rico) lived in a different ecological environment than did the population clusters of

[20] A possible exception is Barbados, where the poor whites ("Redlegs") were particularly numerous and where, according to some authors, the mulattoes were not recognized as a separate class. Cf. Philip Mason, *Patterns of Dominance* (London: Oxford University Press, 1970), pp. 281 ff.

the comparatively recently imported slaves and their descendants; the latter lived predominantly in the coastal plains where sugar production was located; the former were small tobacco growers or coffee workers in the mountainous interior of their countries. Second, in none of these countries had these whites lived in absolute racial endogamy. Even though large-scale plantation production of sugar and its concomitant slave importations were predominantly nineteenth-century phenomena in Cuba and Puerto Rico, in both countries as well as in Santo Domingo and Brazil, a process of racial amalgamation with the group of much earlier imported slaves and their descendants, operating partly on the basis of sexual liaisons and partly on that of marriage, had been evolving for generations.

This amalgamaton produced a continuum of subtle gradations in physical traits, which made it impossible to establish rigid racial dividing lines. Though a light skin and Caucasoid features enjoyed a high social prestige also in these countries, these poor white groups were hindered in presenting themselves as a distinct racial category by the family ties of loyalty that linked many of them to the darker skinned. But, maybe, the most important element in this matter is still the fact that the Iberian poor whites did not suffer from a corrosion of their economic bases on a scale and a pace remotely comparable to that of the white southerners.[21]

In speaking of the poor whites and their relations with the Negroes in the South of the United States, it is necessary not only to think of the impoverished white, traditional farmer but also to pay attention to the new white immigrants and their impact on the socioracial structure.

Recent research indicates a gradual worsening of the position of the urban Negro artisans and workers, both freemen and slaves, since the second quarter of the nineteenth century. This deterioration resulted from the growing number of Irish, German, and other European immigrants. Genovese reports data of Herbert Gutman

---

[21] According to Knight in *Slave Society in Cuba,* those Cuban *guajiros* that were uprooted by the sugar revolution in the mid-nineteenth century developed "a strong racial prejudice."

about Mobile, Alabama: In 1860, the Negroes constituted only 4 percent of the free male productive population, and southern whites no more than 18 percent. But 55 percent of this working population were from the North, 62 percent of which were European immigrants.[22] The influx of Irish immigrants in the 1840s and 1850s especially brought about "a bitter confrontation between the negroes and the immigrants," a confrontation that was used by "racist rural politicians as well as urban businessmen." Even without their instigation, European immigrants were "quick to seize upon white racism as a way of forcing themselves into the job market." The autochthonous poor white southerner, because of his economic plight, tended to classify free Negroes and mulattoes as one socially despicable category. This perception was strengthened by the newly arrived, poverty-stricken immigrants who competed with the Negro artisan and laborer, resented him, and used color to distinguish and socially elevate themselves above the former slaves.

The waves of immigration that swept over the United States from the 1850s to the 1920s gave the above process a historical length, not to say quasi-permanence, which in itself further supported and confirmed the exceptional rigidity of the socioracial structure. Each wave of immigrants (at least into the North) may have found its direct economic competitors among the immediately preceding immigrants; yet, all of them could always compensate socially for their impoverished immigrant status by their awareness of "superiority" to the group of ex-slaves and their descendants. As many investigations into the social perceptions of the different white ethnic groups have indicated, the prestige of the blacks remained constantly at the nadir whereas that of more recent immigrant groups was subject to positive changes.

A country such as the United States, of which the socioethnic composition shows only a minimal continuity with the British colonial past and of which the sociological base line—as far as the

---

[22] Eugene D. Genovese, "The Free Negro in the Slave States of North America," in *Neither Slave nor Free,* Greene and Cohen.

attitudes and general sociopsychological make-up of the large white masses are concerned—ought to be located around the middle of the nineteenth century, has adopted a social perception of the Negro group as a monolithic category. Whatever historical causes there may have been for this categorization, it completely responded to the sociopsychological needs of the poor immigrant and his immediate offspring, who were and are able to diminish the insecurity about their own social and cultural position and identity with the help of the consoling conviction that there will always be one group whom they can look down upon.

Of course, such convictions are not limited to the United States, but the peculiar and recent formation of the North American people has given special force to this conviction, which made it impossible to debilitate the two-tier socioracial structure, once it had been formed, in either the North or the South. Seen from this perspective, it becomes irrelevant whether Marvin Harris is right in stating that the antagonism between poor whites and Negroes was continually stirred up by the southern planter class,[23] nor would it be more than a historical curiosity if Nathan Glazer were correct in assuming that "Southern attitudes . . . have been brought North—physically—by black and white; they have become an integral part of this country's history through the power of the white South as reflected in national policy; and [that] models were available—through the history of colonialism—that made it possible for intellectuals, social scientists, blacks, and others to

---

[23] Marvin Harris, *Patterns of Race in the Americas* (New York: Walker, 1964), pp. 92 ff. In this respect, Max Weber's opinion is interesting: "The 'poor white trash,' the propertyless whites of the southern states of the Union who, given the lack of opportunities for free labor, often lived in miserable conditions, were in the slavery period the real 'carriers' of race antipathy, which was completely foreign to the planters themselves, because precisely and simply their [the poor whites'] social 'honor' depended on the social degradation [*Deklassierung*] of the blacks" (Max Weber, *Grundriss der Sozialökonomik*, Band 3, *Wirtschaft und Gesellschaft* [Tübingen: Mohr, 1922], p. 211). See also C. Vann Woodward, *The Strange Career of Jim Crow* (New York: Oxford University Press, 1959).

apply the southern model to the whole country."[24] At first both opinions seem plausible. But the important point rather is that this southern model also could maintain itself outside the South, without further encouragement of a no longer existing plantocracy, because it continued to respond to the functional needs of U.S. society; in other words, the same precarious economic line between poor whites and Negroes that is responsible for the origin of this model persisted until the present day and led to the same socio-psychological responses.

It is precisely this consideration, though it is not the only one, that makes it so difficult to compare the present situation of the blacks with that of more successful immigrant groups in their earlier stages. Actually, the "Negroes in Northern cities" are not "the worst off [of the major ethnic groups],"[25] but rather they are worst off because of the immigrant groups.

For a century, the United States geographically and economically underwent the convulsions of an unrestrained capitalistic expansion that was effected and made possible by the massive importation of a European proletariat which simultaneously prevented, or at least slowed down, the formation of a stable (in the sociopsychological, rather than in the sociomorphological, sense) national elite. However, if the U.S. social structure as it existed during the middle of the nineteenth century had been permitted to adapt itself to both a gradual exploitation of the country's resources and a gradual industrialization, then more interstitial positions undoubtedly would have been allotted to Negroes. In this sense, Harris's thesis that the poor whites in the South monopolized the interstitial positions—and, I would add, began to do so in the first quarter of the nineteenth century in the urban areas—seems to be correct *grosso modo* for not only that region and that period but also the entire United States and the present.

---

24 Nathan Glazer, "Negroes and Ethnic Groups: The Difference, and the Political Difference It Makes," *Key Issues in The Afro-American Experience,* Vol. II., eds. Nathan I. Huggins, Martin Kilson, and Daniel M. Fox (New York: Harcourt Brace Jovanovich, Inc. 1971).
25 Ibid.

THE DEVELOPMENT OF A THREE-TIER SOCIORACIAL STRUCTURE

While the large and growing number of lower-class whites in the United States is the principal factor for the origin and the continuation of the two-tier system there, as Harris states,[26] it is necessary to disagree completely with the complement of his explanation that the three-tier system in Brazil (or elsewhere in plantation America, as Harris suggests by implication) can be explained out of the economic and demographic necessity to have the interstitial positions occupied by mulattoes.

"The white slave-owners [in Brazil]," writes Harris, "were compelled to create an intermediate free group of half-castes to stand between them and the slaves because there were certain essential economic and military functions for which slave labor was useless, and for which no whites were available. One of these functions was that of clearing the Indians from the sugar coast; another was the capture of Indian slaves; a third was the overseeing of Negro slaves; and a fourth was the tracking of fugitives."[27] He mentions further the raising of cattle and the growing of food for the urban areas as interstitial types of activities for the "half-caste type of men."

There is no need to dwell extensively here on the validity of these factors for Brazilian society. Let it be sufficient to observe that they definitely are not applicable to all Caribbean societies.

From the beginning in Surinam, the government distinguished between colored and black freemen. In 1770, a military corps of blacks (as distinguished from coloreds) consisting of freemen and slaves, which was to deal with the capture of runaway slaves, was established. Before that date there already existed separate Negro

[26] "Because the influx of Africans and the appearance of mulattoes in the United States occurred only after a large [I would say poor as well as large] intermediate class of whites had already been established, there was in effect no place for the freed slave, be he mulatto or Negro, to go" (Harris, *Patterns of Race*, p. 89).

[27] Ibid., pp. 86–89.

and colored guards regiments. Several governmental decrees limited the overseeing of slaves to whites.

In his social historical study of Surinam, Van Lier begins the chapter "The Free Coloreds and Negroes and the Position of the Manumitted" with the following significant paragraphs:

The free "coloreds" and Negroes formed in a society, which had the plantation system as its economic basis, an element for which, economically speaking, there was no place. There was not much to do for a class of freemen in a society, where a small number of whites in leading positions, in combination with a large mass of slaves, produced agricultural products mainly for a foreign market. In such a society a middle class can only play a limited role; there did exist some need for artisans and clerks.

In the early period of the colony, the artisans were whites, but the unfree mulattoes and Negroes learned a craft on the plantation and it became a rule that a plantation owner had artisans among his own slaves so that the number of freemen practising a trade, remained small until the early nineteenth century.

Van Lier further points out that clerical work in Surinam was done mostly by Jews. Nor was it attractive for the manumitted to specialize in small farming in order to produce foodstuffs for the white urban dwellers, because most of the latter had their own slaves to work in garden plots, which often produced enough to allow for some selling on the side. Moreover, most of the manumitted had been house or artisan slaves, and were not accustomed to work in agriculture. In 1830, only one-twelfth of the free coloreds and Negroes lived outside the capital Paramaribo.[28]

It is clear that Van Lier's description does not leave much room for the idea that economic and demographic factors would have caused the formation of a separate social category of coloreds in Surinam. And many of his data apply even more strongly to the Caribbean islands, where a prolonged struggle against the Amerindians did not exist at all, where cattle raising rarely occurred on any large scale, where local food production was also mainly in the hands of slaves, and where the coloreds also mostly lived in the urban areas. As Horowitz observes for the British islands:

[28] Van Lier, *Samenleving*, pp. 52, 57, 96–98, 104.

In the pre-emancipation period, West Indian browns were occupied in a wide range of positions. In the countryside, they were sometimes landed proprietors, petty merchants and occasionally estate artisans. But they far more usually congregated in the towns. They were mainly clerks and tradesmen (butchers, shopkeepers, tailors, shoemakers, grog sellers) and domestic servants. A minority were professionals or affluent men of leisure. When this occupational pattern is put in the context of a cost-benefit analysis, it renders economic arguments for differentiation [in blacks, coloreds and whites] unpersuasive in the [British] West Indies. The striking characteristic of the occupations of the vast majority of the free colored population is their marginality to the needs of the plantations. . . . The occupational interstices most valuable to the estates were . . . filled by whites.[29]

Elizabeth remarks that in the French islands during the slavery period the freemen never played "a decisive economic role." But, the mulatto slaves were "considered as being closer to the European than to the African which seemed to assure them in the beginning a 'vocation for liberty.' " Therefore, in the seventeenth century, they were declared free at an early age. Only when their growing numbers caused fear among the whites, measures were taken to restrain the free mulatto group numerically and economically.[30] In this case, economic and demographic factors again operated against the colored group. However, once this social group had evolved because of other factors, it proved impossible to invalidate its intermediate position in the socioracial structure.

When in (Spanish) Santo Domingo in 1784 a local commission was working on proposals for a *código,* instead of stressing the economic demand for mulattoes to occupy intermediate positions, the commission complained that mulattoes deprived many whites of their subsistence: "The white population does not have any useful occupations because the mechanic trades and retail commerce are in the hands of free Negroes and *pardos.*" Hence, they proposed to reserve "the mechanical arts and professions" for the whites.

The commission also criticized those slaveowners who instead

---

[29] Horowitz, "Color Differentiation."
[30] L. Elizabeth, "The Free Black and Mulatto in the Slave Societies of the French West Indies," in *Neither Slave nor Free,* eds. Greene and Cohen.

of employing their slaves in agriculture made them earn a daily wage in "factories, construction works, transportation, or in the processing of tobacco . . . in which activities ought to be employed white persons or those of medium color (*de color medio*)."

The interesting point here is that, on the one hand, the commission wished to reserve the most privileged and prestigious occupations for the whites, while, on the other, it wanted to economically protect persons of mixed racial traits against the competition of the slaves. In fact, the commission considered the "mulattoes and *pardos* the real people of the Island of Española," and added, "The intermediate classes provide the equilibrium between Negroes and whites and they never mingle with the Negroes, whom they hate."[31] But this latter observation was a complacent ex post facto sociological observation; it was not the cause of the origin of the colored group as a separate social category; nor did this category, once it was formed, occupy itself willingly with those activities that the white planters deemed most preferable and necessary. The coloreds came to occupy an intermediate position in the socioracial structure outside the United States, but this did not necessarily imply that the socioeconomic structure of the plantation society demanded such a position. In fact, the wide variety of their occupations as well as their widespread poverty might lead to the opposite conclusion. In other words, the recognition of an intermediate social status on the basis of intermediate physical characteristics (in which paternal sentiments vis-à-vis the illegitimate child, or notions about greater reliability, converged with implicit considerations of greater somatic proximity and hence less social inequality) may very well have preceded the rational need, if any, for such an intermediate stratum on economic and demographic grounds.

At first, there appears to exist a surprising parallel between the situation in Santo Domingo at the end of the eighteenth century (as analyzed by the Código Commission of 1784) and the South of the United States during the same period—at least in the sense

---

[31] Carlos Larrazabal Blanco, *Los Negros y la Esclavitud en Santo Domingo* (Santo Domingo: Julio D. Postigo e Hijos, 1967), pp. 122–123.

that in both areas the poor whites felt economically threatened by the free Negroes and coloreds as well as by the slaves and ascribed their poverty in great part to their competition.

In Santo Domingo, this led to a proposal to reserve certain occupations for whites and, further, to the suggestion that "the public schools which so far have been open to all without distinction, from now on will be closed for the Negroes and for *mulatos primerizos* (of the first grade or generation) who will be destined for agricultural work."[32] In the United States, it led to, or at least strengthened, the tendency to relegate socially the free colored to the same position as the free Negro and to treat both as groups of slaves unless the opposite could be proved.[33]

The Spanish American colony primarily differed from the United States in that the proposed measures (which, incidentally, were never put into practice), as far as they indicated social preference, involved both whites and light coloreds in that order, and, as far as they purported repression or discrimination, involved the Negroes and the darkest coloreds. The economic threat per se to the poor whites did not differ in both areas; what differed was the whites' perception of the social position that specifically the light coloreds ought to occupy in society.

Again in this context, the greater frequency of socially recognized family ties between whites and light coloreds in the Spanish and Portuguese colonies than in the other areas of the Western Hemisphere must be mentioned. In the former region, the dividing lines between whites and light coloreds (as well as between the latter and the contiguous gradations in the black-white continuum) were weaker and vaguer than elsewhere. Thus, not only somatic ambiguities but also kinship loyalties made legislative discrimination against the coloreds (as distinct from the blacks) virtually unworkable.

In the non-Iberian societies outside the United States, there existed also social gradations within the group of free coloreds, and in a few of these societies the lightest colored and most pros-

[32] Ibid., p. 122.
[33] Genovese, "The Free Negro."

perous among them—often called *mustee, mixties,* or *métis*—were even distinguished administratively and socially from the others.[34] But intimate social-sexual relations (marriage) between whites and light coloreds did not occur there in sociologically relevant numbers.

During the eighteenth century in the French colonies, several repressive measures were taken against the group of freemen, but no attempt was made to distinguish the different racial subgroups of the "free colored people."[35] This difference between the Iberian colonies and the non-Hispanic Caribbean might seem to be related to numerical proportions since, in the former area, the group of freemen was often larger than that of the slaves and the whites whereas, in the latter region, it was smaller—implying that in the Iberian area the coloreds were socially more influential and powerful. But such a generalization would be unacceptable if only because in a society like Curaçao since the early nineteenth century the number of freemen was also larger than both that of the slaves and that of the whites.

It is undeniable that all Caribbean societies from their colonial beginnings considered the coloreds as a separate social category, although no clear economic, demographic, or military needs for such a distinction can be found.

Adverse economic, demographic, or political considerations at a later stage were unable to tear down the three-tier stratification. In the Iberian-American countries, such stratification endured because of the special ties that existed between whites and light coloreds. In the non-Hispanic Caribbean, its endurance is attributed to the absence of a sufficiently large number of poor whites undergoing unfavorable economic experiences of the type described for the U.S. South.

Thinking back once more to the adverse factors in the United

---

[34] In Curaçao at the end of the eighteenth century, the *mestiezen* were incorporated into the white military guard, though they were still carefully distinguished from the whites in other respects. See H. Hoetink, *Het Patroon van de Oude Curaçaose Samenleving: Een Sociologische Studie* (Assen: Royal Van Gorcum, 1958), p. 82.

[35] Elizabeth, "The Free Black."

States that inhibited the development of whatever incipient three-tier structure initially existed in different areas of that country,[36] it is useful to keep in mind that the poor whites or European immigrants in that country were not necessarily in an objectively more favorable position than the free Negroes to occupy the interstitial positions in the industrializing and urbanizing society. Large numbers of these whites did not have any urban or industrial experience. On the other hand, among part of the Negro group there did exist a tradition of responsible craftsmanship.

"As a matter of fact," writes Genovese, "the notion that Negroes were incapable as craftsmen grew up during the late Antebellum period in the face of overwhelming evidence of the contrary. . . . It grew, along with a broader sentiment for racial exclusiveness, as two major trends unfolded in the Old South: the first being the perfection of the pro-slavery argument which . . . included a stronger racist component than ever before; and the second being a marked influx of Irish and other immigrants who sought to capture the labor market of the large towns and cities."[37]

Therefore, the process of social selection by which the white was preferred over all those who were defined as Negro (a process that in all multiracial societies under discussion results from the existing socioracial structure in which the whites are the dominant group) had not much to do with objective economic and demographic factors but, rather, with subjective ones based on racial preference. Seen in this light, the demographic factor, which, as Harris explains, is the cause of the two-tier system in the United

---

[36] In addition to such incipient structures in New Orleans and Charleston, attention may be drawn here to the "isolated racial islands of Indian-White-Negro hybrids" such as the "Brass Ankles of South Carolina; the Cajains or Cajuns of Alabama, Mississippi, and Louisiana; the Croatans of North Carolina, South Carolina, and Virginia; the Jackson Whites of northern New Jersey and lower New York; and the Melungeons of the southern Appalachians. . . . The members of these various mixed-breed communities have this in common: a social status intermediate between that of whites and blacks"; economically "they all present a mixture of extreme poverty, ignorance, and social decay" (Davie, *Negroes in American Society,* pp. 393–394).

[37] Genovese, "The Free Negro."

States, is not so much an objective and technical factor as it is one in which the antagonism and competition between the two racial groups is already included: The demographic factor was unfavorable for Negroes, not because so many equally or more able craftsmen and industrial workers were already in the country or beginning to enter it, but because the latter were white. Race put the Negroes in a progressively and irrevocably disadvantageous position, and they were excluded from the type of free competition in which capacity is the predominant criterion. And precisely because the irrationality of the racial argument made it so hard to refute, it was manipulated *à outrance* by both autochthonous and immigrant whites. Also, this argument affected, maybe especially, those who elsewhere in the Western Hemisphere would have been considered coloreds, as distinct from Negroes.

A racist society may be defined as one in which the above mentioned selection process operates. In such a society the ascriptive somatic traits of the dominant racial group exert an important—and for the members of that group, favorable—influence on social and economic mobility.

Seen in this light, the thesis that all multiracial societies are racist needs little qualification. (See chapter 6, pp. 192 ff.) Without any doubt, the racist selection principle operates also outside the United States, in the multiracial societies of the Western Hemisphere. (See, for example, p. 106.)

Therefore, social and economic mobility of nonwhites was everywhere in these societies dependent on the degree of competition from whites for the vacant positions. Thus, Harris's thesis in the more general sense is applicable to both North and South America. Open positions, for which whites either did not compete or hardly competed became available to members of nonwhite social categories. In the case of higher-ranking positions, such a lack of competition from the whites was mostly due to their numerical weakness, or even absence. However, this was not the origin of the social group of coloreds as a group distinct from blacks.

The high positions in the governmental bureaucracy, which members of the Surinamese colored elite began to fill in the early nineteenth century, had become available after the exodus of whites caused by the serious economic crisis in the wake of the Amsterdam Exchange debacle of 1773,[38] but the social distinction between the colored and black categories dated back to the early colony. Already in the early eighteenth century a small group of "respectable" coloreds existed in Curaçao. They consisted mostly of protégés of rich Sephardic merchants and occupied positions in their businesses, but the social distinction between the colored and black categories dated back to the early colony.

In Guadeloupe and Martinique in the 1720s, legal measures were taken to diminish the number of manumissions in order to slow down the increase of the group of freemen. Some ten years later, however, freemen in Martinique again started to increase rapidly in number; but in Guadeloupe as late as 1775, their number only just equaled that of 1730. This difference between the two islands appears to be related to the number of whites. In Martinique after 1738, the number of whites decreased; this created a number of vacant positions that freemen filled; in Guadeloupe, however, the number of whites kept increasing.[39] But in both islands, the social distinction between the colored and black categories dated back to the early colony.

In Saint Domingue, where the number of freemen increased from 500 in 1703 to 3,000 in 1755, the colonial authorities showed a preoccupation with this increase in 1745 but noted that mulattoes were manumitted more frequently than blacks since the former were "enemies" of the latter.[40] The distinction between both social categories dated back to the early colony.

Herbert Klein observes that, in Brazil in the first quarter of the eighteenth century, the boomtowns (especially in the gold mining area of Minas Gerais) had many open positions that were taken by mulattoes:

[The Provincial Governor] charged that white men were leaving their families in Europe or on the coast to work in the mines and were living

---

[38] Van Lier, *Samenleving,* pp. 40 ff.
[39] Elizabeth, "The Free Black."
[40] Ibid.

in open concubinage with Negro slave women and in turn were bequeathing all their holdings to their mulatto children. To prevent the mulattoes from gaining complete domination over all the mines in the region he went so far as to ask the Crown to deny mulattoes, even if they were exclusive heirs, the right to inherit property, an act which the Crown held to be completely against all the laws of the Kingdom.[41]

In this example, those elements that influenced both the creation of the mulatto group as a separate social category and the occupational mobility of this group converge.

To the first category belongs the paternal preference for his extramatrimonial children born out of semipermanent, and often institutionalized, sexual relations with nonwhite women. Although this type of relationship occurred in all multiracial societies including those where there was no pronounced scarcity of white women, it is clear that such scarcity mitigated or prevented opposition from the legal wife, so that the man's support of his partner and her children could be more open and generous ("Surinam marriage," Haitian "*plaçage*"), though it is useful to stress that such support was by no means absent in societies where white women were more plentiful.

This paternal preference was based on such factors as genuine affection, notions of greater reliability of, and confidence in, his "outside" children, and the more general idea of a lesser physical distance between white and mulatto as compared to the Negro. This preference could lead only to a socially recognized distinction between coloreds and Negroes as far as their potential rights and obligations were concerned. This preferment, partly on ascriptive somatic grounds, was in fact identical to the previously mentioned racist selection principle that operates in favor of the dominant racial group. Whether the preferment allotted to the mulattoes as a socioracial category manifested itself in their occupational mobility depended, of course, on the overall socioeconomic structure and on the competition they would have to meet from the whites who preceded them in order of social preferment.

Therefore, the primary reason for the coloreds' occupational

[41] Herbert S. Klein, "The Colored Freedmen in Brazilian Slave Society," *Journal of Social History* 3 (Fall 1969):30–52, 41.

mobility is the absence or weakness of a dominant white group consisting of both males and females, and thus incapable of numerical self-preservation. Its absence meant that the highest positions in the region were given to those who in "line of succession" came after the white children. The protests and complaints of the provincial authorities indicate that such an absence of a white dominant group was rather uncommon in Brazilian society at large: the absence of white females and its social consequences were apparently not so typical and acceptable as some historians would argue.

THE JORDAN THESIS: A CRITIQUE

The above examples indicate that vacancy of interstitial economic positions did not cause the formation of the colored group as a distinct social category, but did cause considerable occupational mobility of members of this group outside the United States. To what extent is this reasoning compatible with that of Winthrop D. Jordan? This author states: "The attitude toward interracial sex was far more genial in the [British] islands than in the [British] continental colonies";[42] by "interracial sex" he means sexual relations between white men and nonwhite women outside or without marriage. Jordan does observe that only one of the British islands formally prohibited interracial marriages, but this cannot be interpreted in the same way as the absence of decrees against interracial cohabitation outside or without marriage. The latter was such a generalized phenomenon "that to legislate against the practice would have been merely ludicrous"; interracial marriage, on the other hand, was so rare that to legislate against it would have been utterly superfluous. Where such legislation existed (for example, in the French Code Louisiane of 1724), it was based

---

[42] Winthrop D. Jordan, "American Chiaroscuro: The Status and Definition of Mulattoes in the British Colonies," *William and Mary Quarterly* 19, no. 2 (April 1962):183–200; reprinted in *Slavery in the New World: A Reader in Comparative History,* eds. Laura Foner and Eugene D. Genovese (Englewood Cliffs, N.J.: Prentice-Hall, 1969), p. 196.

on only a few but epoch-making cases, where a poor white immigrant male married a prosperous nonwhite female.[43]

What Jordan maintains for the British islands—that there was gradual, silent, and general acceptance of nonlegalized interracial sexual relations—can be generalized for the remaining Caribbean area. However, one important qualification is necessary: It would be incorrect to assume that official decrees against such relations existed in only the United States during the first half of the eighteenth century. As Van Lier makes clear, Surinam had similar ordinances: "In the first Plantation Regulation of 1686, designed by Van Sommelsdijck, the tenth article emphatically prohibited all sexual contact between [white men, and black and Indian women]: 'All Inhabitants are severely prohibited to have carnal conversation with the Negresses and much more so with the free Indian women, under Penalty of two pounds of Sugar.' " In the later versions of the Plantation Regulation in 1725 and 1749, this stipulation remained unchanged. In the proclamation of 1761, the penalty for such misdemeanors was put at 200 Guilders (Article IX). However, no attention at all was paid to this prohibition, and in the new version of the Regulation in 1784, the article was amended in such a way that a penalty of 200 Guilders was to be paid by those engaging in sexual relations between "whites and female slaves," if these "were to create any disorder on the Plantations." In 1818, this article was eliminated.[44]

Since the number of whites in Surinam never amounted to more than 7 percent of the number of slaves during the seventeenth and eighteenth centuries,[45] Jordan's idea of a "close connection between a high proportion of Negroes and open acceptance of miscegenation,"[46] insofar as such open acceptance or its absence can be deduced from the existence of legal decrees, must be rejected. Both Surinam and the United States, irrespective of the

---

[43] Elizabeth, "The Free Black." For a similar exceptional case in Surinam, see also Van Lier, *Samenleving,* p. 65.

[44] Van Lier, *Samenleving,* p. 74. The Spanish *Recopilación* (1680) also attempted to prohibit intermixture among Spaniards, Negroes, or Indians.

[45] Ibid., p. 51.

[46] Jordan, "American Chiaroscuro," p. 199.

numerical proportions of whites and Negroes, in their early history as colonial plantation societies legally prohibited even informal cohabitation between blacks and whites. These prohibitions in Surinam gradually became ever less stringent and were finally abolished in the early nineteenth century, whereas the United States was the only multiracial society in the Western Hemisphere where these prohibitive regulations eventually included an ever greater number of states and also became applicable to interracial marriage.

In comparing the British colonial mainland and the British Caribbean islands, Jordan further pays attention to the numerical ratio between white men and white women; on the mainland, he believes, this sex ratio was normal by 1750, except in the frontier region. However, this was, as Jordan observes, also the case in many British islands at that time, especially the smaller ones (Barbados even had a surplus of white women). Earlier, both the mainland and the islands had a white male surplus.[47]

These data make it impossible to consider the white sex ratio as a cause of the formation of a colored class as an intermediate social category in the British West Indies, since this ratio apparently showed the same early characteristics in both areas. Moreover, in some societies outside the United States where a white group came to settle permanently (as in Curaçao, and in Surinam prior to 1775), this group virtually from the beginning had a rather balanced sex ratio; yet, the colored group there was early recognized as a distinct social category. Then, a high sex ratio of the white group was no condition for either the "acceptability of miscegenation" or the "acceptability of mulatto offspring," although it is probable, as Jordan postulates for Jamaica, that it contributed to such an acceptability.

As stated earlier, such a high white sex ratio could increase the occupational mobility of the coloreds because of the numerical weakness of the white group as a stable population component. The lack of white women made it difficult to keep the white group intact, so that higher economic positions could become occupied

[47] Ibid.

by coloreds. But this greater occupational mobility fell to a group that had already been recognized as a separate social category. Because of these considerations, Jordan's observations can be amended as follows: Formal disapproval of interracial sexual relations can be observed already or especially at an early stage in the history of more than one plantation colony (of course, such formal disapproval does not provide any information on the actual frequency of such relations); there is no clear and direct nexus between the high proportion of Negroes and the open acceptance of miscegenation; and it is in only the United States that this formal disapproval expands and intensifies in the course of time. This expansion and intensification cannot be explained by a balanced white sex ratio, since several Caribbean societies show parallels with the United States, either in the development of the white sex ratio or in the length of its stability. Since this phenomenon is unique to the United States, it is necessary to find an equally unique explanatory factor in that country.

There are no data available to show that the expansion and intensification of legislative prohibition of interracial sexual relations in the United States had anything to do with an increasing frequency of such relations either outside or within marriage. The frequency of interracial marriage was always very small, and the extramarital relations or unions were, I suppose, not more frequent in the United States than elsewhere in the Caribbean area. In addition, in the United States, and in the South as a separate region, the percentage of Negroes was smaller than in most other plantation societies of the Western Hemisphere, so that there was, objectively speaking, less reason for United States whites to fear a numerical domination by nonwhites or mulattoes; and it would seem more logical to have expected such an expansion and intensification of prohibitive regulations in the Carribbean islands, with their small white populations, than in the United States.

Applying Jordan's remark on the North American white colonist to the permanent white settler of these islands: "He remained firm in his rejection of the mulatto [as a social equal]. . . . It was an unconscious decision dictated perhaps in large part by the weight of Negroes [and mulattoes] on his society, heavy enough to be a burden, yet not so heavy as to make him abandon all hope of maintaining his own identity, physically and culturally."[48] For it would be a serious error, which Jordan commits by implication, to believe that the creole whites of the Caribbean islands, living for generations in a multiracial society, ever abandoned the wish of maintaining their own physical identity. In fact, they succeeded in preserving it without needing an expansion and intensification of the legal prohibitions on interracial sexual relations. The social control on the range of positions and status available and considered permissible for their "outside" children was generally strong enough so that government did not have to enact additional decrees.

Even through such a process of elimination of certain factors, one inevitably has to confront again the groups of old and impoverished whites and poor immigrant whites unique to the United States. In 1948, Arnold Rose wrote of the lower-class whites in the South—but much of his observation is equally valid for the North:

They need the caste line for much more substantial reasons than do the middle and upper classes. They are the people likely to stress aggressively that *no* Negro can *ever* attain the status of even the *lowest* whites. . . . [They] have been the popular strength behind Negro disenfranchisement. . . . They create the popular pressure upon Southern courts to deny Negroes equal justice. They form the active lynching mob; they are responsible also for most of the petty outrages practiced on the Negro group. They are the interested party in economic discrimination against Negroes, keeping Negroes out of jobs which they want themselves.[49]

It would seem logical, although perhaps painful, to add to this list of indictments the suspicion that the expansion and intensification

[48] Ibid., p. 201. This remark applies more, as will be shown throughout this book, to the non-Iberian than to the Hispanic Caribbean; in the latter area, many of those defined as mulattoes in the non-Hispanic area were considered social equals in the Hispanic area and were acceptable as marriage partners without the notion, however, that this would mar the whites' physical identity. See further pp. 197 ff.

[49] Arnold Rose, *The Negro in America* (London: Martin Secker and Warburg, 1948), p. 200.

of the prohibitions against interracial sexual relations in the first place served to please the feelings of socioracial superiority of the lower-class whites. As a result of the character of immigration to the United States and this country's political system, the numerical and political importance of this group in its society was not matched elsewhere in the Western Hemisphere, nor can a demographic factor that exerted such a long and penetrating influence upon social relations be found there. As Genovese's data cogently demonstrate, Rose's remark, which applies to the mid-twentieth century, is just as valid for the mid-nineteenth century.[50]

SUMMARY

In summary, the above discussion has divided itself into three subjects: (1) the causes of the nonemergence of the colored group as a distinct social category in the United States; (2) the factors that influenced the socioeconomic positions of the free nonwhites, especially the mulattoes, in the slave colonies; and (3) the nature of the connection between the institution of slavery and the position of ex-slaves and their descendants during and after the period of slavery.

In all but one of the Afro-American multiracial societies, a group of coloreds with its own internal social differentiation came to occupy an intermediate rank between blacks and whites in the socioracial structure—as distinct from the socioeconomic structure. This was a normal phenomenon in these societies and occurred very early in their existence. Among its causes was the paternal preference for the "outside" child, based on affection, ideas of reliability and trust, and the general notion of greater physical proximity between mulatto and white as compared to black and white. However, in the United States such a three-tier socioracial structure did not develop,[51] mainly because of the

---

[50] Cf. Genovese, "The Free Negro."

[51] This, of course, does not mean that in the United States white fathers always isolated themselves from their mulatto children. See A. Davis, B. Gardner, and M. R. Gardner, *Deep South* (Chicago: University of Chicago Press, 1941), pp. 6, 37, 39, 40; cited in Davie, *Negroes in American Society,* p. 393.

socially downgrading influence always exerted by the numerous groups of poor whites, who had been impoverished in the South since the end of the eighteenth century, and to whom were added the influx of poor white immigrants after the middle of the nineteenth century.

The attitudes of the dominant white group vis-à-vis the freemen and—in the societies outside the United States—especially the colored among them were determined by the following factors:

1. Where slaves outnumbered both whites and freemen, the chances for a tolerant and encouraging attitude of the whites toward the freemen were great. Where the freemen were larger in number than the slaves, in the Western European (British, French, Dutch, Danish) colonies, the chances were that a tense relation between whites and freemen would develop. In the Iberian (Spanish and Portuguese) colonies, these chances were distinctly less because of the less rigid endogamy of the whites with regard to those who in the West European colonies would have been considered (light) coloreds. The line of tension in the Iberian colonies ran between the whites and light coloreds, on the one hand, and the darker coloreds and blacks on the other, but, precisely because of this, the division could be neither as rigid nor as potentially explosive.

2. Scarcity of white women possibly increased the number of institutionalized sexual relations between white males and nonwhite females (but not necessarily the number of interracial marriages in the West European colonies) and enhanced the chances for socially tolerated demonstrations of affection and economic and educational protection for the offspring of these unions.

3. Where a considerable part of the white male elite maintained such unions, there were more chances for the formation of a socially prestigious layer within the colored category.

4. Where, for whatever reasons, the white group was not or no longer capable of occupying all or some of the positions in the

administrative or economic sector, it was probable that coloreds would occupy them.

5. The occupational mobility of the freemen was hindered by the presence or immigration of whites, especially a large number of poor whites, who monopolized lower and middle positions and legalized discriminatory actions.

6. Where, because of factors 2 and 3, an economically prosperous and socially prestigious layer within the colored stratum evolved, social tensions subsequently might arise between coloreds and the whites, especially the poorer whites whose possible initial scarcity was not necessarily permanent. Also, belated discriminative legislation might then be enacted, such as could be observed on the French islands. (Haiti is an example where an explosion was triggered by such a development, and Martinique and Guadeloupe are cases where an "accommodation" with coloreds took place). For reasons explained under 1, such tensions were less likely to develop in the Iberian colonies.

Thus, those factors that exerted an unfavorable influence on the attitudes of the whites vis-à-vis the freemen clustered around two elementary needs of the white dominant group: the need for physical security (fear of a numerical excess of freemen in the West European colonies) and the need for economic security for itself and its white offspring, where present.

Those factors that favorably influenced white attitudes vis-à-vis the freemen also centered about the need for physical security (fear of a numerical excess of slaves; hence also the enhanced chances for freemen's military careers) and the need to fill vacant positions (which can be distinguished as either social-sexual, caused by a scarcity of white women, or economic and administrative, caused by a scarcity of white men).

In the above list of six factors that determined the attitudes of the whites toward the freemen and the latter's chances for mobility in the slave societies in the Western Hemisphere, the word slave occurs only in factor 1. This means that, if we are correct, the institution of slavery as such only influenced these attitudes insofar as the numerical force of the slaves did or did not affect the whites' sense of physical security. It would not be correct, however, to thus limit the influence of slavery on the chances for freemen to increase their social status and occupational mobility, because these depended not only on the attitudes of the whites but also on the economic repercussions that slave labor had on the freemen's chances. In all slave societies, it was especially the artisan and hired slaves who seriously limited the freemen's field of fruitful economic activities, so that many of them and especially the urban majority among them, could blame their very unfavorable economic circumstances on slave competition. But even if this factor is accounted for, the prospects for economic betterment of freemen and coloreds and the whites' social attitudes toward them were determined before abolition to a great extent by factors that did not relate to master-slave relations per se but, rather, to the total social structure, such as it existed outside the institution of slavery, and, more directly, to the number of available positions in that structure—to a situation, in short, that also in contemporary multiracial societies determines the economic perspectives of socially subordinated racial groups.

Authors like Mintz, Williams, Ianni, and Davis criticized the idea that predominantly cultural elements determined the supposed differences in severity between the slave systems of Latin and Anglo-Saxon America. They further demonstrated that in one and the same slave society considerable fluctuations in the nature of master-slave relations could sometimes be observed.

Also, freemen in a society that had known mild slavery for even a considerable time would not necessarily come to occupy favorable economic positions; on the other hand, a cruel slave regime did not exclude the possibility of an early formation of a colored elite. In addition, frequent manumissions were not necessarily an indication of mild master-slave relations nor a guarantee for socioeconomic mobility of the manumitted. If mild slavery is defined as a relationship between masters and slaves that was characterized—at least during a considerable period—by the absence of frequent and cruel punishment and by reasonable material care, measured against the prevailing criteria of the period, and if mild race relations are defined as a relationship among the different socioracial groups (slaves excluded) during and after the slavery period, characterized by the absence of severe legalized discrimination, the attainment of middle and high positions by freemen, and the paucity of open conflicts verbalized in racial terms, again measured against the then prevailing criteria, then no causal link exists, nor does historical continuity always have to be expected, between a mild or harsh slavery, on the one hand, and mild or respectively tense race relations on the other.

MASTER-SLAVE RELATIONS AND RACE RELATIONS: A CRITIQUE OF VAN DEN BERGHE'S THESIS

This means a rejection of the admirable pioneer work of Tannenbaum, who *did* postulate a link or at least such a continuity between the condition of slavery and race relations and of the work of others, such as Elkins,[52] insofar as they have parted from several of Tannenbaum's postulates. It also means that we cannot accept certain arguments in Pierre L. Van den Berghe's interesting and important *Race and Racism*.[53]

At first, this author's assumption is plausible: ". . . If abrupt qualitative changes in race relations can be shown to coincide with structural changes in the society at large, it is reasonable to accept that basic aspects of the social structure exert a considerable degree of determination on the prevailing type of race relations."[54]

However, Van den Berghe considers master-slave relations to form a part of race relations. Of his two ideal types of multiracial society, he sees the paternalistic type characterized by slavery or serfdom (an aristocracy versus a "servile caste"); the race rela-

---

[52] Stanley M. Elkins, *Slavery*. It would not be difficult to prove the existence of the "Sambo" type of slave and free black also in Latin America; this is apart from the question whether this type is to be interpreted in terms of fixed role behavior or as a personality type. For a Cuban slave's comment on the *dulones de amo* and other slave types, see Miguel Barnet, *Biografía de un Cimarrón* (Barcelona: Ariel, 1968).

[53] Pierre L. Van den Berghe, *Race and Racism: A Comparative Perspective* (New York: Wiley & Son, 1967).

[54] Ibid., p. 26.

tions produced by this structure he describes in such terms as accommodation, paternalism, and benevolent despotism.[55] The opposite type he calls competitive.

Apart from the question whether, even on the level of an ideal typical abstraction, the slave systems of the colonial plantation societies in the Western Hemisphere could be labeled paternalistic and benevolently despotic—given both the modern organizational aspects and the cruel punitive sanctions on many of these societies' plantations—it seems incorrect to assume that basic aspects of the social structure would exert their influence in an identical or at least similar direction both on master-slave relations and on race relations outside of slavery.

The position of freemen and slaves could be affected quite differently by the same sociostructural factors. For example, in the United States from the second quarter of the nineteenth century "the South . . . in a variety of ways . . . tried to render the condition of the slave materially and spiritually more acceptable, and . . . one of the ironic corollaries of this . . . development was the attack on the status of the free Negroes."[56] And in a slave colony such as Surinam, the important structural change that caused an exodus of whites and the introduction of absentee plantation ownership led to a deterioration of the already harsh master-slave relations, on the one hand, and to an improvement in the position of the colored elite, on the other. When Van den Berghe summarizes the results of his comparison among the premodern phases of Mexico, Brazil, the United States, and the Union of South Africa, he concludes:

the system of race relations developed in . . . the four societies examined showed great similarities despite great differences in the culture of both dominant and subordinate groups: In all instances a typically paternalistic system united in symbiotic interdependence a servile or quasi-servile labor force . . . the stereotypes of subordinate groups were similar . . . the dominant group rationalized its position by virtue of cultural and racial superiority. . . . The paternalistic regimes were all characterized by two social processes . . . physical intermixture or

[55] Ibid., pp. 31–33.
[56] Genovese, "The Free Negro."

miscegenation [and] . . . the extensive and relatively rapid assimilation of the subject groups to the culture of the dominant group.[57]

There is, however, a dramatic difference between Anglo-Saxon and Latin societies, which profoundly influences their socioracial structure as well as their race relations. For, while it is true that physical intermixture is not absent in any multiracial society, it is necessary for sociological reasons to distinguish clearly the offspring of: (1) incidental interracial sexual relations; (2) more stable interracial sexual relationships that, however, are not considered completely acceptable by the dominant group (principally indicated by the nonacceptance of the female partners as social equals by the white married women); and (3) the interracial stable relationships, often in the form of legal marriages, that do not encounter social ostracism from the racially dominant group.

Relations of the first and second type can be found in all multiracial societies. The frequency of the second possibly is in part determined by the white sex ratio. However, in the third type of relationship, there is a difference between Latin and other societies of the Western Hemisphere. The racial endogamy of the white group was and is less rigid in the Latin societies, as far as the social acceptability of a partner is concerned who, in the non-Iberian societies, would be classified as light colored. One of the consequences of this difference was that the social alliance between whites and light coloreds in the Iberian societies became ever more solid in the course of time and made it impossible to openly discriminate against the group of coloreds as a whole.

This difference has proved to be constant in the sense that the transition from a paternalistic to a competitive type of society in the United States or in parts of Latin America has not exerted any discernible influence on it. Precisely the fact that structural changes in the society at large had no apparent impact on this essential difference (with its many ramifications) makes us assume that the causes of this difference are of another order than commonly investigated by sociologists.

However great the admiration may be for the careful ways in

[57] Van den Berghe, *Race and Racism*, pp. 122 ff.

which Van den Berghe has elaborated his typology, the objections against a dichotomy of the type he proposes remain firm. For there is the danger that author and reader, because of the description and names of the two ideal types, might become caught in a new evolutionism—a simpler one even than its nineteenth-century predecessor—that presupposes that the paternalistic stage must be succeeded by the competitive one. In this fashion an inevitability is suggested both in the social process and in the development of race relations that is methodologically untenable.[58]

The creation of polar ideal types implies that all multiracial societies have to find their place on what is called a continuum, a suggestive but misleading term, in which concept a similar kind of evolutionistic notion sometimes is hiding. For it is not difficult to find societies—for example, in the Caribbean region—that are competitive qua economic traits, paternalistic qua division of labor (along racial lines). They have paternalistic patterns of mobility and social stratification; a paternalistic numerical ratio (the dominant group being a small minority) with competitive value conflicts; paternalistic race relations, roles, and statuses; intermediate types of etiquette (definite, yet simple); paternalistic forms of aggression (generally from lower caste, not directly racial); paternalistic miscegenation; paternalistic patterns of segregation, but a competitive psychological syndrome, which stereotypes lower castes and intensifies prejudice alternating between the two types, but with both competitive forms of government (restricted or pseudodemocratic) and competitive legal systems. Such a society probably would be said to be moving toward a competitive destination but still would be showing some paternalistic traits, which are becoming more and more dysfunctional, or—to use an old evolutionist term—which are on their way to becoming survivals.

Such a judgment parts from the idea that the variables of each of the two types ideally have to interconnect as pieces of a jigsaw puzzle; by definition, a mixed form cannot be a type, since stability and mutual functionality of its competitive and paternalistic vari-

---

[58] Cf. H. Hoetink, "The New Evolutionism," in *Structure, Function, Process,* ed. A. J. F. Köbben (Assen: Royal Van Gorcum, 1973).

ables are supposed to be lacking. But this latter premise becomes doubtful if, as in parts of Latin America, paternalistic traits have been preserved in strongly urbanized and industrialized environments. Patron-client relationships, extended kinship, and ritual kinship (*compadrazgo*) have proved to be sufficiently elastic to function under drastically changed economic and ecologic conditions.[59] Their significance for the nature and atmosphere (as distinct from the structure) of race relations is clear. Instead of one, more models of modern types of society ought to be designed; the differences among them would be determined more by deeply rooted cultural-structural traits than Van den Berghe apparently is willing to concede.

The Northwest European culture type, which inspired the dominant groups in the United States and the Union of South Africa, is markedly different from the Iberian or Mediterranean culture variant, which so deeply influenced Van den Berghe's two other cases—Mexico and Brazil. If we add to these cultural differences those in acceptability as marriage partners of members of the racially mixed intermediate strata in the Anglo-Saxon and Iberian societies in the Western Hemisphere, then some of the essential ingredients for the design of two basically different models of modern multiracial societies are disposed of. Because these ingredients show such a remarkable resilience and resistance to structural changes in the society at large, the influence of the economic structure on the prevailing type of race relations, though it certainly cannot be dismissed entirely, does not seem to have the considerable degree of determination that Van den Berghe ascribes to it.

There are three basic ingredients that, in their specific configurations, determine the nature of every concrete racial situation, and whose connections with the prevailing economic structure are not always direct. There are the cultural ingredients, which in the context of the Anglo-Saxon–Iberian contrast have to be defined mainly in terms of religious differences, variations in culturally imposed images of social structure, and differences in vertically

[59] Ibid.

structured channels of cultural communication; there are, further, the numerical ingredients, similar to those that determined the occupational mobility of freemen in a slave society, whose objective and subjective consequences can also be observed in present-day multiracial societies; finally, there are the somatic ingredients of race relations, which manifest themselves most clearly in the extent to which dominant racial groups use different socioracial criteria in their manipulation of social selection. The cultural ingredients determine mainly the character of race relations; the somatic ones, mainly the socioracial structure; but the numerical ingredients influence both relations and, though rarely, structure. In the later chapters of this book, these ingredients will be more closely investigated.

2

RACISM AND SLAVE LABOR

First, it is necessary to explore a few more aspects of the concept of slavery and its all too easy association with race relations. So far, the argument has been that there is hardly any causal connection or even historical continuity between a given character ("mild," or cruel) of a slave system and the character of race relations outside slavery in the same society.

Based on empirical investigations of concrete historical situations, this conclusion does not, of course, preclude on another level of abstraction the existence of a number of similarities between slavery and horizontally layered multiracial structures—similarities that, most probably, have given origin to the idea of a causal link between both.

In both structures a dominant and subordinate group exist. As far as the Western Hemisphere is concerned, masters and slaves were mostly of different races, but this, of course, is not a general characteristic of slavery. In the multiracial societies outside the United States, the free racially mixed group soon came to occupy an intermediate position of its own in the socioracial structure. In the United States, however, the dominant-subordinate dichotomy was preserved in the socioracial structure outside and after slavery, thus making its similarity to the master-slave structure much more striking. This is why many consider the system of slavery as part of, and inseparable from, the multiracial system in the United States.

The dominant-subordinate relationship in both systems produced further parallels in the complementary patterns of behavior in the groups involved. The symbiosis, condescension versus submissiveness, was symbolized and communicated in many diverse ways.

The slave and the member of the lowest subordinate group also have in common a very limited range of mobility. Within the system of slavery the Negroes perceived a difference in social status between the slave recently arrived from Africa (who was often, though not always, considered as socially inferior) and the "creolized" slave; there was further some social differentiation linked to slave occupation in ascending order from field slave to artisan slave to house slave. In contemporary multiracial societies the chances of mobility for the immense majority of the subordinate socioracial groups are equally scarce and limited: from plantation laborer to unskilled industrial, harbour, or mine workers to low-paid occupations in the service sector.

If not economically, at least sociopsychologically, the slave obtaining freedom underwent a transformation comparable to that which the Central American Indian undergoes from the moment he is considered a ladino, or that experienced by the North American Negro who loses his social stigma by the mechanism of "passing." Within both systems certain cultural and social accommodations finally take place that give the behavior of dominant and subordinate groups a certain degree of predictability, while sexual contacts between men of the dominant group and women of the subordinate group tend to make, conversely, the general social relations between both groups psychologically more complex.[1]

In short, slavery and multiracial, horizontally layered structures are both special forms of what used to be called *Herrschaftsüberlagerung* in German sociology; a stratification consisting of at least two layers of which the upper layer has, as it were, moved over the

---

[1] The role of slave women in revolts deserves more investigation. In the Curaçao revolt of 1795, female slaves exerted a moderating role, which was explained by contemporary observers as the result of their function as wet nurse or mammy of the master's children and of the sexual relationship that some of them had with their masters. See H. Hoetink, *Het Patroon van de Oude Curaçaose Samenleving: Een sociologische Studie* (Assen: Royal Van Gorcum, 1958), p. 130.

lower one (by military conquest, colonial usurpation, and so forth) or the lower layer has been pushed under by the upper one (by subjugation, the importation of forced labor, and the like).

Neither slavery nor racial diversity is a necessary condition for a *Herrschaftsüberlagerung* (one need only think of the Roman domination over large parts of Europe); nor is it necessary for a multiracial dominance system always to be accompanied by slavery, or slavery by multiraciality. The similarities in distribution of power, limitation of mobility, and peculiar forms of social intercourse among the social strata, common to all systems that fall into the *Herrschaftsüberlagerung* category, make it possible, on a high level of abstraction, to compare, for example, nineteenth-century Dutch East Indies, twentieth-century South Africa, tenth-century Moorish Spain, and eighteenth-century Brazil; or even, on that level, a comparison can be made between slavery as a social system and society at large in Jamaica during the eighteenth century, as a multiracial system excluding slavery and only focusing on free whites, coloreds, and blacks.

Wherever in Afro-American societies both a multiracial system and a slavery system coexisted together for a protracted period and contained the above mentioned similarities, which caused each to crudely reflect the other, the continuation of the multiracial *Herrschaftsüberlagerung* after the abolition of slavery was considered a prolongation of the structural elements of slavery—the sociological causes of the contemporary socioracial structure were sought in that vanished institution.

Yet, the contemporary socioracial structure is historically linked to the total socioracial structure, such as it was formed outside slavery. Of course, it is not denied that in most plantation societies of the Western Hemisphere the first imported Negro slaves were, strictly historically speaking, also the ancestors of the subordinate group in the local socioracial system, but this latter system as such only was created at the moment that the first Negroes or coloreds found themselves outside the institution of slavery, yet within society (the Maroons, therefore, were not part of it).

Postulating a causal link between contemporary socioracial structure and slavery can be rejected as a maneuver in historicism since it does not trace the parallels in historical continuity to corresponding structures in the past but has them converge toward a much more limited past structure. An analogous situation would exist if a contemporary family type were explained, not by analyzing the historical processes that link the present family structure to an earlier one, but merely by focusing on the past institution of child labor.

SOCIORACIAL STRUCTURE OUTSIDE SLAVERY

In all multiracial societies of the Western Hemisphere, a socioracial structure was formed outside slavery in which positions were allotted to all recognized socioracial groupings. Once slaves were manumitted or slavery was abolished, the ex-slaves were placed in this already-existing color stratification; as far as Afro-America outside the United States is concerned, the colored ex-slaves and their descendants thus found their positions in the intermediate strata—the blacks, on the lower rungs of this scale.

As already noted, for analytical purposes this socioracial stratification has to be distinguished from the socioeconomic stratification in which such criteria as prosperity and occupation are used. The correlation between both stratifications is not at all perfect in multiracial societies. In each of these there are some blacks who are more prosperous than some coloreds and some blacks and coloreds who are higher on the socioeconomic scale than some whites.

But each multiracial society is racist in the sense that membership in a socioracial group prevails over achievement in the allotment of social position. An affluent black doctor in the United States is considered a black first; his professional qualities and economic achievements only serve to determine his position on the socioeconomic scale within the black group.[2] This prevalence of socioracial over socioeconomic stratification is an essential trait of all multiracial societies. However, in a very differentiated socio-

---

[2] See M. G. Smith, "Institutional and Political Conditions of Pluralism," in *Pluralism in Africa,* eds. Leo Kuper and M. G. Smith (Berkeley: University of California Press, 1969), p. 49.

racial stratification, such as in Afro–Latin America, it is sometimes difficult to immediately place a person on the basis of his somatic traits in one of the many subtly graded socioracial categories. In such cases, obvious wealth or education or the lack of it may influence a person's socioracial categorization. It is these rare ambiguous cases that have led some observers to deny the validity of the general predominance of socioracial stratification. The members of the dominant racial group owe their position, of course, to the economic, social, and cultural power that, as a group, they already possessed at the moment of the inception of the multiracial society and that they have preserved since. But this observation, which often is taken as the explanation of socioracial structure and mobility in such a society, is not that at all. It is neither more nor less than an a priori condition for the formation of a horizontally layered, multiracial structure. To state that such a structure (or, for that matter, any hierarchical stratification) can be explained by a difference in power is a tautological exercise since the definition of such a structure already presupposes a power differentiation. What really matters is with which attributes this power is being associated. In multiracial societies ascriptive, somatic attributes are of such an importance in the mechanism of social selection that Shibutani and Kwan even reached the conclusion that competition among the ethnic groups is eliminated or at least greatly reduced once a system of ethnic stratification is stabilized.[3]

From the moment that such a stratification is formed, racist principles of selection predominate over nonracist ones in such a manner as to preserve this stratification. It is in this sense that the prevalence of socioracial over socioeconomic stratification exists.

If this line of analysis is acceptable, then it is difficult to see how, as long as the dominant racial group preserves its dominance and thus its mechanisms of selection, changes in the collective socioeconomic position of a racially subordinate group can lead to changes in the socioracial structure.

[3] Tamotsy Shibutani and Kian M. Kwan, *Ethnic Stratification: A Comparative Approach* (New York: Macmillan, 1965), pp. 146 and 235.

A massive migration of poor black rural workers from one part of the country to another and their successful transformation into better paid industrial workers may be seen as an impressive socioeconomic rise, and will lead to a sense of considerable enhancement of social prestige within their socioracial category; but their relative position vis-à-vis the dominant racial group does not basically change because their economic ascendancy falls within the limits of what the dominant group considers tolerable within the socioracial framework. It is precisely the irrationality of social preference and selection, based on somatic traits, that makes the socioracial structure virtually unsusceptible to the impact of economic and educational changes within the racially subordinate group, as far as the latter's position in the overall socioracial structure is concerned and as long as these racist preferences prevail.[4] It may be noted in passing that even the dethronement or disappearance of the racially dominant group in a particular society does not automatically lead to the abolition of its somatic preferences, which may be maintained even by the nonwhite groups in power. Such a paradoxical state of events is clearly linked to and explained by the international, even global, multiracial stratification.[5]

If economic and educational changes within the racially sub-

---

[4] To maintain, moreover, that differences in occupational structure between Negroes and whites in the United States can be fully explained by differences in education would be in conflict with available data: "According to a Special Labor Force Report of the Department of Labor, while young white males with 9 to 11 years of schooling had an unemployment rate of 11.3%, the rate for young non-white males, with *the same amount of education,* was 22%. . . . Over a lifetime, a male Negro college graduate will earn only 47% of the income of a white college graduate. . . . *A Negro college graduate* [can] look forward to earning during his lifetime *less* than a *white high school* graduate (Frank J. McVeigh, "The Life Conditions of Afro-Americans," in *Afro-American Studies* 1, no. 1 (May 1970):48 ff.). For racist factors limiting occupational mobility in Brazil, see p. 106.

[5] See H. Hoetink, *The Two Variants in Caribbean Race Relations: A Contribution to the Sociology of Segmented Societies,* trans. Eva M. Hooykaas (London: Oxford University Press, 1967), p. 141, on "the world as a segmented society."

ordinate group—short of a *détournement de pouvoir*—do not change the overall socioracial structure, this does not mean that such changes do not influence the character of race relations. However, it may be safely stated that the attitudes of the dominant group will be more benevolent and milder to the degree that the distribution of positions among the racial groups in the socioeconomic stratification is more closely commensurate with the socioracial stratification, as originally imposed by the dominant racial group. Viewed from the socioracial frame of reference, the more inconsistencies there are in status the greater the chances of resistance from the racially dominant group.

RACISM AND WHITE IMMIGRATION

Where there are great numbers of poor whites or where the relative position of white blue-collar workers has been worsened or where members of the subordinate racial groups have penetrated in considerable numbers, not as mere tokens, the middle and higher economic strata, where they, viewed from the white socioracial structural image, do not "belong," conditions for racial conflict, initiated by white resentment, are clearly present. Earlier, it was shown that the widespread presence of poor whites in the United States over long periods represents such a status inconsistency, which helps to explain its deviating—more rigid—socioracial structure and other anomalies, such as lynching, in its development of racial relations.

To the extent to which inevitably the black North Americans will attack and try to undermine the irrational socioracial structure, the countless white immigrants and sons of immigrants—because they are insecure in their economic status (or, conversely, clinging to a newly achieved economic security), insecure in their social status, and insecure in their cultural identity and therefore eager to affirm themselves within the national structure—will vehemently defend the priorities and superiorities that the socioracial structure offers them. The peculiarities of the actual position of the white lower and middle classes explains the acuteness of the North American race problem. This is not to say that in any multiracial society the members of the dominant racial group will ever on their own initiative give up their vision of the socioracial structure and the mechanisms of selection inherent in this vision— too many obvious interests as well as irrational and subconscious motivations are at play. But the character of race relations becomes more unfavorable and the potential or actual conflict more dramatic if for an important part of the racially dominant group, as in the United States, the psychological effects of what are viewed as status inconsistencies are compounded by psychological complexities of its (ex-) immigrant status.

When the government through far-reaching social legislation would try to ameliorate the deplorable economic and social conditions in the black ghettoes, on the one hand, and, on the other, try to increase the feeling of personal economic security of the lower-class whites, a considerable improvement in the socioeconomic structure would result, which might have some effect on the character of race relations. However, the relative positions of the groups in the socioracial structure would not change, and the belated emergence of a distinct intermediate colored group would seem doubtful.

Brazil: A Case Study

What became a national phenomenon in the United States during the nineteenth century could also be observed in Latin America.

Florestan Fernándes writes about São Paulo since the end of the nineteenth century: "As he climbed the social ladder . . . the [white] immigrant did not have enough social prestige to face the demands of his newly acquired social level, while at the same time maintaining seemingly spurious connections with the past. Such connections aroused in him the fear of social degradation, as if the visibility of the Negro affected and spread to those who were seen with him. . . . The immigrant and his descendants wound up building a world in which there is no place for the Negro. Neither of the effects mentioned were the products of his cultural tradition. They derived, rather, from the complex tensions created by social climbing in a class society." The idea that the immigrants introduced race prejudices into São Paulo is rejected by Fernándes. Their presence might temporarily aggravate the general character of race relations, but they did not introduce any innovations in this respect: "The immigrant simply absorbed attitudes and behavior patterns previously incorporated in the Brazilian race relations system."[6] Nor did this immigration cause changes in the long-existing Brazilian socioracial structure, as distinguished from the economic stratification: The division of races into whites, coloreds, and blacks with characteristically Latin American vague transitions between whites and light coloreds, and their mitigating influence on racial relations, was kept intact.

However, Fernándes perceives white immigration clearly as "one of the accelerating factors in the economic growth and social development of the community. . . . In fact, since the structure of the race relations system excluded the 'Negro' from [the opportunities to participate in these two processes], the whites practically monopolized the advantages which derived from them." Elsewhere, he reiterates that white immigration did not cause changes, on either short or long terms, in the structure of "the pre-existing race relations system" but did indeed contribute to "the collapse of the servile regime." Here, again, an explicit and essential distinction between the socioracial and the socioeconomic order is made and our argument supported that changes in the latter do not necessarily influence the former: "The rapid and intense changes that affected the development structure of São Paulo did not have any repercussions on the position of the Negro in the social system or on race relations patterns."[7]

RACE RELATIONS AND THE SOCIORACIAL STRUCTURE

In the foregoing pages there has been an attempt to show that it is necessary to distinguish clearly between the *character* of race relations and the socioracial *structure*. The character of race relations is subject to varied cultural, demographic, and economic

[6] Florestan Fernándes, "Immigration and Race Relations in São Paulo," in *Race and Class in Latin America,* ed. Magnus Mörner (New York: Columbia University Press, 1970), pp. 140–141.

[7] Ibid., pp. 142, 136.

influences. The structure, however, once it has taken historical roots in a particular society (whereby such anomalies as the North American socioracial dichotomy may very well be caused and maintained by particular economic and demographic factors), is being influenced much less by such factors, and shows a remarkable resiliency or resistance to change. This resistance exists because the hierarchy of socioracial groups in a multiracial society is a function of the interests and preferences of the racially dominant group. These interests and preferences, rooted in the need for maintenance of power, for economic and physical security, and in not always conscious somatic preferences, virtually by definition have a permanent character; only their rationalizations adapt themselves to the fashions of the times. Within each of the socioracial groups, changes in the positions of their members may be observed (the formation of an elite group within the colored category, a black intelligentsia, or a white proletariat). Such changes are caused by the vacancy or disappearance of positions and by the configuration of factors that determine the attitudes of the racially dominant group toward the subordinate one(s); but these changes have no influence on the total interracial structure, that is, the relative positions of the main socioracial groups as they are viewed as normal and desirable by the dominant racial group.

RACISM IN SLAVERY

Now, while in the multiracial society as a whole the socioracial structure is predominant over the socioeconomic one (caste over class, white over black), so that economic factors and considerations, though not excluded, are subordinated, the opposite is the case within the institution of slavery. There economic considerations predominate in principle although in the slavery systems of the Western Hemisphere—where, during the greatest part of their existence, the master-slave distinction coincided with a racial distinction—"racist" elements in their internal differentiation certainly were not absent.

Racist considerations manifested themselves in at least two ways. First, privileged slave positions, especially those of house servants, were often given to mulattoes instead of blacks; and manumission, especially that of an affective, noneconomic type, was more often extended to coloreds than to Negroes. Such racist mechanisms of selection often made the slave plantation a reflection of the total society, as far as its internal stratification was concerned: the field slaves, mostly black; the artisan and house slaves, disproportionately colored; the masters, predominantly white.

Second, on the North American mainland and in several Caribbean islands, initially both whites and Negroes had a servile status, but in the course of the seventeenth century, while Negroes were enslaved in larger numbers, white servants gained increasingly liberal terms of indenture and ultimate freedom.[8] Moreover, according to Degler, from the beginning the Negroes occupied a lower position than any white, bound or free, in the United States. Thus, if it is correct that chattel slavery developed there in the course of several decades in the seventeenth century, the socioracial structure in that country was developed and fixed earlier than the institution of slavery. This adds a chronological objection to our previous criticisms of explaining the present socioracial structure as a result of slavery. As Degler observes: "The important point is . . . the fact that discriminating legislation regarding the Negro long preceded any legal definition of slavery."[9]

Noel attributes the difference in treatment of white and Negro bondsmen, "ultimately indisputable and probably present from the very beginning," to "differences in ethnocentrism and relative power"; with regard to the latter he points out, as does Marvin Harris, that the British government protested against the enslavement of British subjects, while the Negroes lacked such prestigious and powerful spokesmen. Further, the need for more immigrants may have led to improvement of the conditions of the white servants, so that the potential migrants in England and Scotland would not be deterred by unfavorable reports on their treatment.[10]

8 Donald L. Noel, "A Theory of the Origin of Ethnic Stratification," *Social Problems* 16, no. 2 (Fall 1968):157–172.
9 Carl N. Degler, *Out of Our Past* (New York: Harper & Row, 1959), p. 35; cited in Noel, "Theory."
10 Noel, "Theory," pp. 168–169.

With the term ethnocentrism, Noel wants to point to the greater physical and cultural differences between the Negroes and the white dominant group, which made the latter more easily disposed to keep Negroes as slaves than whites. This means, of course, that through the racist selection principle that prevailed in the multiracial total society the white indentured servant was spared the fate of formal slavery. The dominant racial group by furthering free white immigration could not only ease a shortage of labor but also strengthen itself as a socioracial category; the Negroes, however, became slaves, and their increased immigration only served economic goals. This same selection mechanism, which privileged the white servant over the Negro, would later within the institution of slavery privilege the colored over the black.

Because of all this, the stratification within slavery could become even a more perfect reflection of what the white dominant group viewed as a desirable socioracial structure than was the case in the free multiracial society. In the latter there existed, during long periods, incongruencies such as extremely poor whites subsisting on an economic level similar to that of many Negroes. Such anomalies were absent in the later slave plantations, where the masters could wield the power of the proprietor in order to create an internal stratification, which coincided with the ideal position of the racial groups in the society at large.

But the essential point here is: Only gradually did American slavery become the reflection of the total socioracial structure; it adjusted itself to it and was not its forerunner or model.

In Spanish America the first involuntary immigrants must have been white. In 1497, five years after the discovery of Hispaniola (Santo Domingo), the Catholic kings ordered that all delinquents in their kingdoms condemned to expulsion be sent to that island.[11]

Only in the instructions of 1501 to the newly appointed Gover-

---

[11] For the following see José Antonio Saco, *Historia de la Esclavitud de la Raza Africana en el Mundo Nuevo y en Especial en los Países Americo-Hispanos,* 4 vols., Prólogo por Fernando Ortiz, ed. (Habana: Cultural S. A., 1938). (These 4 volumes contain Books IV and V of the original edition, published in Barcelona (Jaime Jepús) 1879, and Havana (Revista Cubana), 1883, especially I, 91–128, 245, and II, 24 ff.

nor of Hispaniola, Nicolás de Ovando, was permission given to introduce black slaves, but on the condition that these had been born among, and were still property of, Christian owners. Already in 1503, one year after his arrival on the Caribbean island, De Ovando requested the Spanish government not to send any more black slaves, because they were apt to flee, joining the aborigines and teaching them bad customs; it proved virtually impossible to capture them.

His request was granted by Queen Isabel: a brief interruption in the legal introduction of black slaves ensued, but upon her death the next year the trade was resumed. During this brief interlude, a man like Alonso de Ojeda was, indeed, not allowed to take black slaves with him from Spain. He had to be content with five white slaves. The early instructions to introduce only *Christian* slaves to the new colonies were clearly not complied with. In 1506 the government was ordered to expel all *esclavos berberiscos* from Hispaniola and in an interesting Royal Provision on February 25, 1530, the prohibition to introduce non-Catholic slaves (*berberiscos, de casta de moros, o judíos*) was not only repeated, but a new racial element was introduced: special mention was made of mulattoes and *loros* (dark-skinned mulattoes). Anyone who tried to introduce any of these categories of slaves without permission would have to return them on his own expense to the *Casa de Contratación in Seville,* having to pay in the case of *moriscos* an additional fine of one thousand gold pesos. By implication, illegal introduction of black Christian slaves, although punishable, did not lead to their deportation from the colony. It is tempting to speculate on the reasons for the singling out of special racial categories of unwanted slaves. Maybe their role in slave rebellions (the first of which occurred in 1522 in Hispaniola) had something to do with it.

In this early period the contraband slaves were often imported from Spain itself "where slaves of various races and creeds abound," many of them being brought there from Africa by way of Portugal. Others came from the Mediterranean islands of Mallorca, Menorca, and Cedeña and possibly also from the Canary Islands, from where slave expeditions to Africa seem to have been organized at an early date. While the prohibition against Islamic and Jewish slaves stayed in force, the introduction of pagan slaves directly from Guinea was allowed since 1511.

On the American continent the first Negro slaves arrived in Darién (Panamá), where their presence was noted as early as 1513. Soon they were brought to most other Spanish American colonies, where their relations with the Amerindians, as had been the case in early Hispaniola, caused preoccupations among the Spanish authorities. Complaints were made in the fifties that in Peru—as well as elsewhere—Negro men and women, both freedmen and slaves, made use of the aborigines, keeping them as sexual companions (*manceba*) or treating them badly and oppressing them. Of course, the white colonists themselves certainly did not abstain either from humiliating treatment or sexual relations with Indians and Negroes.

It was for this reason that the king in 1512 ordered the *Casa de Contratación* to send white Christian female slaves to the colonies. There being a great need for women, the king observed, these white slaves would not only serve the Spaniards better than the Amerindian women did, but, moreover, the Spaniards could take them as their wives, instead of associating themselves with the indigenous women, as some had already done. Curiously enough, Governor Diego Colón and his officials in Hispaniola objected to the king's plan, writing him that actually there were on their island many *converted* Castilian young marriageable ladies, who would be looked upon with disdain by the Spaniards, as soon as unequivocally Christian females, be they slaves, would become available as marriage partners. The king's order, however, was carried out.

In the same year we also learn of a royal permission to a Hernando Peralta to introduce in San Juan de Puerto Rico two Christian white female slaves. These cases of white, predominantly female, slavery which apparently had to serve sociosexual rather than economic purposes seem all to have been confined to the early colonization period and are not dissimilar to efforts of the Dutch and other colonizing powers to increase the white population by such devices as the forced introduction of female orphans in their American colonies. They do show, however, that the concept of slavery in early sixteenth-century Spain was much more familiar and socially accepted than it was in the England or Holland at the time of the latter's colonial expansion in the Americas.

An Iberian system of white indentured labor, similar in scope to that in British North America and in the British and French Caribbean never did develop. The later contracting of white immigrants in the Iberian Peninsula or the Canary Islands, though not without its onerous aspects, mainly served to people the American colonies with free agricultural colonists, rather than with serfs.

Thus, after the first decades of the colonization process had passed, also in Iberian America the status of the unfree laborer came to be associated ever more closely with people of African descent (slaves) or of aboriginal origin (who, though not legally slaves, were submitted to different forms of compulsory labor also, as we shall shortly see). It is useful to keep in mind, however, that also in Iberian America, this identification of race with compulsory labor was not present from the start. It evolved in the course of time, thereby making the systems of forced labor an ever more perfect reflection of the social stratification in the society at large. The social structure in Indo-America, in turn, where initially small sectors of the native population had continued to enjoy some of their pre-Conquest social prestige in the eyes of the European colonizers became increasingly adjusted to the new colonial criteria of stratification, according to which cultural and somatic likeness to the dominant stratum was of more importance than previous rank in the native society.

Slavery in plantation America, like all social institutions, did not exist in a vacuum: It continuously exerted and underwent influences upon and from its wider sociocultural environment. The cultural characteristics of the society at large, such as the prevailing religion, and other culturally conditioned patterns of thought and behavior had positive or negative influences on master-slave relations. In the same way, slavery absorbed structural elements from the prevailing multiracial system. But this did not mean that slavery in the Western Hemisphere was primarily a cultural, religious, or socioracial system. However much noneconomic influences came to bear upon it, introducing manifold irrationalities from an economic point of view, slavery was in its origin, its intention, and its continued *raison d'être* an economic system.

SLAVERY AS AN ECONOMIC SYSTEM: NIEBOER'S THESIS

Seventy years ago, the Dutch ethnologist H. J. Nieboer published his seminal study on slavery as an economic system.[12] Using what he called the inductive-comparative method, he researched the literature on hundreds of peoples belonging to what was known at the time as the savage stage of cultural development. Nieboer came to the conclusion that slavery essentially has to be understood in terms of division of labor. "The function [of slavery] is a system of compulsory labour, and slavery is the absorption of the whole personality to this end. As this absorption is properly expressed by the word 'property' or 'possession,' we may define the slave as a man who is the property or possession of another man, and forced to work for him."[13]

Nieboer then proceeded to simplify this definition for, as he stated, "when one man is the property of another, this implies compulsory labour." By describing slavery as "the fact that one man is the property or possession of the other," he was able to elude much ambiguous information in ethnological literature; the definition further was similar to that of many theorists, and "it lies within the limits of current speech."[14] Nieboer has been rightly criticized for this simplification. By emphasizing the property or possession aspect of slavery, he introduced the danger of a never-ending debate about the legal limits of these concepts, the sociological relevance of which is not always clear, whereas the concept of compulsory labor does have such a relevance. Nieboer himself was not entirely clear about this matter, since in his first chapter he

[12] H. J. Nieboer, *Slavery as an Industrial System: Ethnological Researches* (The Hague: Martinus Nijhoff, 1900). As far as I know, in the United States only Sidney W. Mintz has recently pointed out the importance of this work.

[13] Ibid., p. 7.

[14] Ibid., pp. 7–8.

did not consider serfs to be slaves (because they are not their master's property, in the sense of Roman law),[15] while later he changed this opinion. Also, he defined pawns or debtor-slaves as real slaves, because "sociologically a system of pawning performs the same function as a slave system. . . . The same system of compulsory labor, the same subjection of the entire person exists, whether the subjected are perpetually slaves or temporarily pawns."[16] As can be seen from this quotation, the author did not consider duration an essential criterion for slavery: Temporary compulsory labor does not fundamentally differ from slavery.

Nieboer's painstaking survey of slaveholding primitive peoples led him to the general conclusion that "slavery, as an industrial [i.e., economic] system, is not likely to exist where subsistence depends on material resources which are present in limited quantity." He therefore divided all societies into two types. In one, "the means of subsistence are open to all," and "a man who does not possess anything but his own strength and skill, is able to provide for himself independently of any capitalist or landlord." In the other, "subsistence depends on resources of which the supply is limited, and therefore people destitute of these resources are dependent on the owners," be they capitalists or landowners.[17]

The first category Nieboer called peoples with open resources; the second, those with closed[18] resources. "Only among peoples with open resources can slavery and serfdom exist, whereas free labourers dependent on wages are only found among people with closed resources."

Nieboer was keenly aware of the influence of secondary factors limiting the universal applicability of his main contention. In this connection he paid due attention to the position of free women (who in some cases perform slave labor, thereby rendering real slavery unnecessary); to the influence of external trade on a slave-

[15] Ibid., p. 37.
[16] Ibid., p. 39.
[17] Ibid., pp. 387, 420.
[18] In the first edition of the book, used here, the word is consistently misspelled as "close."

holding agricultural society (slavery becomes more useful economically, and external trade may even cause slavery to develop);
to the relation between warfare and slavery (in the higher stages of
agriculture, where there is an elaborate division of labor, it is no
longer dangerous to enlist the slaves in the inferior ranks of the
army); to slavery as an economic luxury (some slaves may be kept
for luxury, "but then there must be other slaves who, by perform-
ing productive labour, provide for their master, their fellow slaves
and themselves"—while warfare and luxury may lead "to the
keeping of a larger number of slaves than would otherwise be
required, [they] have not probably ever given rise to slavery").
Nieboer even takes the *vis inertia* into account, which may explain
why slavery does not exist in all primitive societies where the
keeping of slaves would be profitable and where only the introduction of the slave trade may serve as the external cause of the
establishment of slavery.[19]

In spite of these secondary considerations, the general empirical
rule holds that the chances for slavery are not great where there
are closed resources. Poor people will offer themselves as wage
laborers, and, even if there are no poor people—because all participate in the exploitation of the closed resources—the use of
slavery cannot be widespread; for, whereas with open resources an
increase in the number of slaves means an increase in the wealth of
their master, in a closed resources situation, where a man only
possesses a limited piece of land or capital, he only can use a
limited number of laborers. "Moreover," writes Nieboer, "as soon
as in a country with closed resources slaves are kept, they form a
class destitute of capital, or land, as the case may be; therefore,
even when they are set free, they will remain in the service of the
rich, as they are unable to provide for themselves."[20]

The rich, in such a situation, are not interested in keeping their
laborers in a state of slavery. It can even be more profitable for
them to set them free as their wages will then be determined by the

[19] Ibid., pp. 391–418, 420.
[20] Ibid., p. 421.

law of supply and demand, instead of by custom, with the result that the rich classes will receive a greater part of the economic product than before.

Although Nieboer initially wished to limit his research to the "savage" tribes, he did consider his conclusions valid for all societies; and in the chapter of his book entitled "Transition from Serfdom to Freedom in Western Europe," he confirms his principal thesis. In this chapter he abandons his earlier legalistic objections to identifying serfdom as a form of slavery. He now states that between slaves and serfs, on the one hand, and modern laborers and tenants, on the other, there exists one crucial difference: The former groups are under personal compulsion—the slave is property of his master; the serf is bound to the soil, astricted to the estate, and not permitted to leave his work and living area.[21] Nieboer apparently now adheres to Spencer's dictum that he had rejected earlier: "As the distinctions between different forms of slavery are indefinite, so must there be an indefinite distinction between slavery and serfdom, and between the several forms of serfdom. Much confusion has arisen in describing these respective institutions, and for the sufficient reason that these institutions themselves are confused."[22]

In this chapter Nieboer concludes: "[The] difference between countries with open and with closed resources goes far to explain why slavery (and serfdom which is also a form of compulsory labour) has gradually disappeared in civilized Europe, whereas in thinly peopled countries it maintains itself much longer, and even now is sometimes introduced under some disguise ('labour trade,' convict labour, and similar expedients in the tropics)."[23]

COMPULSORY LABOR AND SLAVE LABOR: KLOOSTERBOER'S THESIS

As far as can be ascertained, Nieboer's work, though written in English, hardly influenced the international scholarly community,

---

21 Ibid., p. 351.
22 Herbert Spencer, *Industrial Institutions* (New York), p. 472; cited in Nieboer, *Slavery*, p. 36.
23 Nieboer, *Slavery*, p. 36.

but in The Netherlands it remained an object of debate and study.

In 1943, J. J. Fahrenfort published an article[24] in which he, though admiring Nieboer's methods and sharing his conclusions, criticized the author's ambiguity with regard to the legal definition of slavery. The concept of property or possession is rarely exact or absolute, and may be applied in very different instances and gradations of control and personal domination. On the basis of several case histories of involuntary labor, Fahrenfort concluded that Nieboer's argument was equally valid for compulsory labor outside the legalistic definitions of slavery. This point of view was further elaborated by Fahrenfort's student W. Kloosterboer, in her *Involuntary Labour Since the Abolition of Slavery: A Survey of Compulsory Labour Throughout the World.*[25]

Koosterboer defines compulsory labor as that from which withdrawal is generally considered a criminal offense, so that it engenders penal sanction, "and/or for which [the laborer] has been accepted without his willing consent."[26] In her survey of compulsory labor Kloosterboer gives considerable attention to the Western Hemisphere. She discusses the apprenticeship system and the vagrancy laws that were introduced in the British West Indies after abolition and the compulsory aspects of the British Indian migration to Trinidad and British Guiana as well as to Surinam (Dutch Guiana). In the latter country, there also took place immigration of contract laborers from Java, and "even in 1915 complaints were still being heard of unprovoked savagery and brutal treatment on the part of overseers, especially against Indonesian labourers."[27] The British consul in that colony warned in 1911 against migration of East Indians to Surinam, considering their working conditions as "veiled" slavery.[28] Among the laborers of the balata (rubber) in-

24 J. J. Fahrenfort, "Over Vrije en Onvrije Arbeid," *Mensch en Maatschappij* 19 (1943):29–51.

25 W. Kloosterboer, *Involuntary Labour Since the Abolition of Slavery: A Survey of Compulsory Labour Throughout the World* (Leiden: E. J. Brill, 1960).

26 Ibid., p. 2.

27 Ibid., p. 35.

28 Ibid., p. 36.

dustry in the Surinam jungle, debt bondage was common in the early twentieth century.

In the United States, several forms of compulsory labor persisted for considerable time after the abolition of slavery. Vagrancy laws in several southern states in combination with legal or customary obstacles for Negroes to acquire land of their own had the predictable effects. Debt bondage was not uncommon both in the South and the North and among both Negro and white laborers. Kloosterboer mentions the case of the Maine lumber companies around the turn of the century whose laborers mostly came from the Boston area. The state of Maine passed a law similar to those of several southern states, whereby deserting workers could be legally sued for accepting monies under "false pretenses." Also in mining and industry such debt relations occurred. The illegal migrant Mexicans could at that time—and probably still can—be forced into compulsory labor in a similar fashion. "The Negroes in the South, however, were still being treated even more atrociously. In the season in which many labourers were needed, the planters simply rounded up Negroes and put them to work on their plantations, claiming that they were in debt to them; and there they had to work from 12 to 16 hours a day, as a rule without wages, till the busy season was over."[29] Collaboration with the judicial authorities provided another source of labor in the South whereby convicts were sometimes hired out to the highest bidder and subsequently tied to more and more debts. Conditions in the convict camps were horrible; in some camps the convicts had to sleep chained to each other and were locked up during the weekends.[30]

The debt-slavery aspects of the sharecropping system are also dealt with in vivid detail by Kloosterboer. In 1934, the average interest on farm implements, etc., lent by the landowners to the sharecroppers was no less than 37 percent. The sharecroppers' work generally was done under the direct supervision of the plantation owner and sometimes took place in labor gangs. "The

[29] Ibid., p. 61.
[30] Ibid., p. 63.

owner by padding the account of the Negroes to the point where the balance due always exceeds the value of the crop can assure his labor supply for the following year. The result is a virtual system of peonage, which is a Federal offense," Maurice Davie observed as recently as 1949.[31]

In the 1920s and 1930s, advertisements still appeared in southern newspapers such as: "Notice—I forbid any one to hire or harbor Herman Miles, colored, during the year 1939, A. P. Dabbs, Route 1, Yanceyville"; or "Negro boy Runaway: A small colored boy about 14 years old ran away from his home. . . . Anyone seeing him will please notify me and hold him till I arrive. I will pay reward. I object to anyone using him—Roy Haines, Stapleton, Ga., Rt. 1, Box 16."[32]

In *Negro Labor: A National Problem,* Robert C. Weaver wrote of "instances of peonage [that] occasionally remind us that forced labor still exists in our Southland."[33] In 1960, Kloosterboer considered compulsory labor in the United States a thing of the past, a statement which, of course, in no way wants to deny the otherwise sordid conditions of many Mexican and Puerto Rican migrant workers.

In Latin America after the Conquest, initially the encomienda system prevailed, whereby a Spanish colonist or religious functionary received power over the labor force or the production of a certain number of Indians in exchange for which the encomendero was supposed to enhance the Indian's cultural and spiritual well-being. The judicial apparatus stayed in the hands of the Crown, and—initially at least—the encomendero was not considered ipso facto owner of the land on which his Indians lived.

The duration of such an allotment of Indians was, in the beginning, short (a few years); but later it acquired hereditary traits. As was the case with real slavery, the living and working conditions of this involuntary Indian labor differed from area to area and from

---

[31] Maurice A. Davie, *Negroes in American Society* (New York: McGraw-Hill, 1949), p. 67.

[32] Ibid., p. 68.

[33] Robert C. Weaver, *Negro Labor: A National Problem* (1946), p. 4; cited in Kloosterboer, *Involuntary Labour,* p. 65.

owner to owner. The benevolent decrees issued in the mother country had, as was the case with Negro slavery, little effect. The efforts to concentrate the Indian labor reserve in *congregaciones*— inspired partly by economic, partly by civilizing, arguments— meant to numerous Indians an uprooting from their local environment, which qualitatively differed very little from the transplantation of the Negro slaves; and their dwellings were burnt down, so that the Indians might lose their attachment to their traditional habitat. They were exchanged, hired out, and sold by their encomenderos. "In this respect the position of the encomienda Indians *hardly differed at all from that of the slaves*" and "the conditions in the first period of colonization were probably worse than slavery was anywhere at any time."[34] The formal abolition in 1785 of the encomienda system, which had already gradually degenerated, was partly the result of ethical and political considerations. As for the latter, the Crown clearly felt irritated by the power of some of the encomenderos.

But there was also an economic cause, as Kloosterboer points out. The Indians that were fit to work were distributed among a limited number of colonists: Consequently, newly arrived Spaniards were hard pressed to find laborers. Therefore, already in 1622 the Crown legalized a new system of compulsory labor, which became known under different names (in Mexico it was called repartimiento, or *cuatequil;* in Peru, *mita*). This system took the form of a levy imposed by the colonial authorities on the Indian communities, whereby a certain number of laborers were to work for a particular institution or landowner.

The laborers were to be selected by their own Indian chiefs in such a way that no one would have to work more than a limited number of days and no more than an established maximum would be absent from the village at a given time. But again the good intentions of the metropolitan authorities could not prevent the colonial opportunists from circumventing the rule and abusing terribly the Indian laborers. Especially in Peru the Indians often

---

[34] Kloosterboer, *Involuntary Labour,* pp. 84–88, and the literature cited there; my italics.

had to work long distances from their place of origin; their mortality, due to the hardships of forced travel and work, was exceedingly high. Their wages were often paid in valueless goods. Next to the *mita* there existed other forms of compulsory labor, which further laid a claim on the productive time of the Indian. Kloosterboer concludes that especially in Peru the *mita* system in combination with other legal or illegal systems of forced labor were "just as hard for the Indians to bear as the encomienda system had been when personal services still formed the principal element of it."[35]

At the end of the eighteenth and the beginning of the nineteenth century, the repartimiento or *mita* systems were abolished. And again there were not only political and ethical motives that caused their abolition but also forceful economic arguments. On the one hand, newly developed mining and industrial enterprises were not greatly interested in a labor force consisting of rotating gangs of unskilled workers, which actually hampered industrial development. On the other hand, more and more Indians lost their own agricultural lands (sometimes, however, an Indian community simply abandoned their village and escaped to areas as yet not exploited by the Spaniards, see p. 84). This made the available free labor reserve at least somewhat larger, though still insufficient to prevent the use of force in recruiting Indians and intimidating them to extend the length of their work period. But, in the course of time, this compulsion no longer came directly from the government, which for political and ideological reasons became more and more reluctant to intervene directly in these matters. Now the employer with the approval and assistance of government began to directly exert compulsion, which took the form of debt peonage. This type of involuntary labor, though known in Latin America already in the seventeenth century, developed in the nineteenth and twentieth centuries into a massive quasi-slavery in the agricultural and mining areas of Central and South America.

In the beginning of the twentieth century in the southern Mexican tobacco districts and on the agave plantations of Yucatán (to which the Yaqui Indians were deported), "the debt slaves were far

[35] Ibid., p. 95.

more badly off than the Indians in colonial times"; and the same could be said of the rubber workers—debt slaves in the Amazon basin during the rubber boom in the early twentieth century. The London *Times,* on July 15, 1912, commented on a British government report about this latter area: "The bluebook shows that in an immense territory which Peru professes to govern, the worst evils of plantation slavery which our forefathers laboured to suppress are at this moment equaled or surpassed. They are so horrible that they might seem incredible were their existence supported by less trustworthy evidence." The indignation of the *Times* was perhaps the greater since the Peruvian Amazon Company was partly British property, even though local management was predominantly Peruvian. A British-American government report later commented on the "ancient, deep-rooted, and almost universal attitude of the Peruvians who, while they may not approve of cruel and inhuman treatment, generally regard the Indians as placed here by Providence for the use and benefit of the white men and as having no rights that the white man need respect. This attitude of the people has found concrete expression in the universal system of peonage, an old institution, well established, . . . which has come to be the basis on which the rubber-industry (the sole industry of trans-Andean Peru) almost entirely rests. [The system of] advancing supplies . . . has led to the establishment of what is virtually a slave trade." In the Putumayo district, murders, flogging, torture, and deliberate starvation were some of the means by which the number of Indians was estimated to have fallen from 50,000 in 1906 to 8,000 in 1911. By working a whole year, the average rubber laborer might be paid "a hammock and an ax or a gun without any ammunition." Not only Indians but also British West Indians, especially from Barbados, were engaged in the work, often as overseers (just as in an earlier age, Indians from Central and South America had been shipped to the larger Antilles and the North American mainland to serve as slaves, together with Negroes). In the towns of the area slavery was also known:

Great numbers of young Indians are held in what amounts to house-hold slavery in Iquitos and all the other towns under the style of "pupilos," or wards under age. A master applies to a magistrate stating that he wishes to take such a young Indian . . . under his protection, and he is given a legal right to the services of the child without wages. . . . This right can be enforced by law . . . and [a] runaway brought back by the police.

At the Ucagali River . . . there is a regular trade in children and young women.[36]

Although the debt-bondage system was officially abolished in several Latin American countries between 1915 and 1920, it did not disappear completely in practice. The notorious *Ley de Trabajadores,* issued in 1894 by President Reina Barrios of Guatemala, was in force until the 1940's. The law considered the nonpayment of a debt by a laborer as a criminal delict, and gave his *patrón* the right "to pursue and capture *colonos* and *jornaleros* . . . who ran away from the finca owing money or service." The law contained no proscription against corporal punishment of a worker by his employer. "The Ley also ordered government officials and local police to assist the *finqueros* in apprehending fugitive *mozos.* All expenses incurred in such action were to be added to the debt the men owed."

In 1934, President Jorge Ubico prohibited the granting of any more monetary advances by employers to Indians. Simultaneously, however, he issued a "rigid and comprehensive vagrancy law. It extended the meaning of the term 'vagrant' to cover all males of the laborer class without personal service commitments who did not cultivate their own land, and those who failed to fulfill their work obligations to a patrón."

Vagrancy was punishable under the penal code, and in 1935 landless *jornaleros* were required to carry a work certificate attesting that they worked at least one hundred days a year for a *patrón.*

A decree of 1877, temporarily revived in 1908, had stipulated that "plantation owners could request from the Jefe Político the seasonal laborers they needed, for a maximum number of 70 *mozos* at a time, and for as long as two weeks. Municipal officials,

---

[36] "U.S., Message from the President, Transmitting Report of the Secretary of State with Accompanying Papers Concerning the Alleged Existence of Slavery in Peru," *Slavery in Peru* (Washington, D.C.: U.S. Government Printing Office, 1913), pp. 3, 14, 16, 68, 432.

assisted by leaders of the Indian communities, rounded up the required number of laborers." All these decrees, the vagrancy laws, and the legalized debt peonage reinforced, as Nañez observes, "the servile status of the landless Indian peasants"[37] and virtually prolonged the repartimiento system into our day.

In the cautiously written report of the International Labour Organization on *Labour Problems in Bolivia,* published in 1943, mention is made of "promiscuous use of child labour" in the factories of La Paz and of "evidence of violations of the child labour laws" in the mines, while the "haciendas visited clearly established the widespread usage of a farm tenancy little short of feudal serfdom."[38]

The much more outspoken and better documented report of the same agency, *Conditions of Life and Work of Indigenous Populations of Latin American Countries* (1949), pays special attention to the sharecropping system, the most prevalent type of tenancy in Latin America (known as *huasipungo* in Ecuador, *aynoca, pegujar,* or *parcela* in Bolivia, *conuco* in Venezuela and other Caribbean countries, and *agregado* in Nothern Argentina), and speaks in this connection of a "position of dependence through the accumulation of debt, which often compels the Indian to remain indefinitely in the owner's service."[39]

Also, the recruiting system (known as *enganche*) is still in existence in several countries; a private recruiter (*enganchador, conchabador, cuadrillero*) delivers the required manpower against a previously agreed lump sum: "frequently the contractor uses the

---

[37] These data from Guillermo Nañez Falcón, "Paul Dieseldorff: German Entrepreneur in the Alta Verapaz of Guatemala, 1889–1937" (Ph.D. diss., Tulane University, 1970), pp. 310–316.

[38] International Labour Organization, "Report of the Joint Bolivian–United States Labour Commission," *Labour Problems in Bolivia* (Montreal, 1943).

[39] International Labour Organization, "Report on the Fourth Conference of American States' Members of the International Labour Organization," *Conditions of Life and Work of Indigenous Populations of Latin American Countries* (Geneva, 1949), p. 56.

indebtedness to secure and retain a constant supply of cheap indigenous manpower."[40]

Countries such as Peru, Bolivia, Ecuador, Guatemala, and Argentina have issued decrees meant to prevent the excesses of the *enganche* system, but as the joint Bolivian–U.S. Labour Commission dryly observed, "in some areas there are not enough inspectors to carry out [adequate] supervision."[41] Similar recruiting mechanisms serve to arrange the immigration of foreign laborers in several countries, such as the immigration of Haitian and British West Indian sugar workers into Cuba several decades ago and the continued importation of Haitians into the Dominican Republic. Continued illegal Mexican immigration into the United States can not be prevented and sometimes leads to horrible situations (as late as 1969 Texan newspapers reported on Mexican laborers recruited by fellow countrymen, who suffocated in the closed trucks that were to bring them to their U.S. destination).

Several forms of unpaid and forced labor in Latin America, although officially prohibited, are mentioned as still existing in the 1949 report. Such were the traditional tasks in the house or on the estate of his master to be performed by the Indian after his normal day of work: the *pongeaje* in Bolivia and southern Peru, the *huasicamía* in Ecuador. In Bolivia, such tasks are listed as the *cacha* or *apiri* (messenger service), spinning, weaving, *mukeo* (preparation of the *chica* ingredients), laundry, and so forth.

"In some urban centres to which the Indians go for commercial reasons, it is still the custom to require them to clean the squares and streets free of charge. There have been cases where the local police have waylaid Indians early in the morning and taken away some article of their clothing, to be redeemed only by the performance of this task." Sometimes an appeal was made to the Indian traditions of mutual help to have such work carried out.

Some Indo-American countries in 1949 still had a conscription duty for roadbuilding. The law obliged all inhabitants selected by

[40] Ibid., p. 90.
[41] Ibid., p. 91.

lottery to either work for two or three days without wages or to buy off their obligation by paying a certain amount of money to the municipal treasury. In fact, the whole system amounted to a temporary forced labor for the poorest members of the community.[42]

Although the term "plantation America" is often associated with the Atlantic coasts of the Americas, it should not be forgotten that also in several areas on the Pacific side of Latin America a plantation economy developed for which Negro slaves were imported. When, as a result of the abolition of Negro slavery or of an upsurge in the plantation economy, the traditional Negro labor reserve became insufficient, immigration of Chinese contract laborers took place. Between 1849 and 1874, Peru imported some 80,000 Chinese to work on the sugar plantations and on the guano islands. Their inhumane treatment gave rise to international scandals. In Cuba between 1847 and 1867, some 11,400 Chinese plantation workers arrived, as well as numerous Filipinos and Amerindians from Yucatán; only the activities of the Chinese in the 1868–1878 war made the Spanish colonial authorities decide to halt their immigration.[43]

After this brief description of unfree labor in the Western Hemisphere, some attention can now be paid to Kloosterboer's conclusions based on a survey of many more countries regarding the applicability of Nieboer's theory to those situations of involuntary labor that cannot be legally defined as slavery. In general terms, Kloosterboer is of the opinion that such an applicability exists but that certain modifications are in order as far as the more complicated societies are concerned, which Nieboer did not include in his research. Thus, she observes that those societies where all arable land is being cultivated need not immediately produce a labor surplus—the population increase may be too slow for that.

[42] Ibid., pp. 94–96.

[43] Magnus Mörner, *Race Mixture in the History of Latin America* (Boston: Little, Brown & Co., 1967), p. 131. For forced labor in Puerto Rico see Labor Gomez Acevedo, *Organización y Reglamentación del Trabajo en el Puerto Rico del Siglo 19* (Río Piedras: Editorial Universitaria, 1970).

In addition, migration to urban areas—absent in Nieboer's primitive societies—may cause a shortage of rural labor even in situations of closed resources.

Furthermore, the need for cheap labor in a situation of relative labor scarcity may lead to tying the worker to the soil; often this is the result of competition between several employers and is especially feasible in societies where government is not politically interested in protecting the social and economic rights of the workers and/or in societies where governmental power is generally weak.[44] Also, an artificial situation of closed resources can be created as in the United States, where Negroes in the South after abolition were virtually prohibited from acquiring land or property. In spite of these artificially closed resources, debt bondage persisted in the South. Kloosterboer ascribes this to the economic recuperation of the region toward the end of the 1870s, which created a greater demand for seasonal labor. Moreover, in the United States as a whole at that time, there were still considerable open resources. Forced labor in remote and unattractive areas—such as is known in the Soviet Union and in some cases also in twentieth-century United States (the Maine lumber companies)—which need have no direct relation with the existence of closed resources elsewhere in the same country, Kloosterboer considers atypical.

She concludes that although ethical considerations played a role in the abolition of compulsory labor "the most important motives have always been of an economico-commercial nature."[45]

This conclusion seems correct as far as the final abolition of such labor in particular societies is concerned. As far as the different *forms* of unfree labor are concerned, Fahrenfort rightly observes that "in modern times *political* considerations have also influenced . . . the form in which involuntary labor was permitted, and the moment in which it became prohibited."[46] For where slavery was abolished in the legal sense, promptly an apprenticeship system

[44] See also Fahrenfort, "Over Vrije en Onvrije Arbeid," p. 49.
[45] Kloosterboer, *Involuntary Labour,* pp. 206–215.
[46] Fahrenfort, "Over Vrije en Onvrije Arbeid," p. 49; my italics.

often was established, or foreign contract laborers were imported under penal sanctions, or debt slavery started to flourish. The economic and commercial factors persisted in those cases in favor of unfree labor. Only the forms that the labor system adopted were changed under pressure of political, and sometimes ethical, considerations.

CLOSED AND OPEN RESOURCES

Nieboer's polar distinction between open and closed resources lent itself well for the primitive societies he investigated. He applied the term resources both to land and capital, correctly assuming, furthermore, that in primitive agrarian societies the need for capital is limited—every able bodied man with some land can make a living, acceptable to the criteria of his own society.

Under those circumstances it is easy, at least theoretically, to establish whether a society has open or closed resources. Only the proportion between available land fit for cultivation and land under cultivation has to be ascertained. Hence, Nieboer concluded that "the keeping of slaves is economically profitable to people with open resources *among which subsistence is easily acquired*."[47] The case theoretically farthest removed from this would be a society with closed resources, where the inhabitants are dependent on exceptional skills and difficult-to-acquire capital for their subsistence.

In Nieboer's study, the Eskimos are presented as a people that do not have slavery precisely because of the difficulty with which food is procured. The possession of a boat and the long practice needed to use it adequately for transportation and hunting make Eskimos' labor not only exceptionally skilled but also dependent on costly capital. Men among the central Eskimos who have lost their sleds and dogs are at the mercy of their tribesmen. "A man destitute of capital cannot provide for himself, and is therefore at the mercy of the capitalist," Nieboer writes in this context. "Now the Eskimo capitalist most often allows such men to share his house and food, and makes them feed the dogs, etc., rather as a means of procuring

[47] Nieboer, *Slavery,* p. 426; my italics.

employment for them, than because such work requires hands outside the family. . . . The Eskimos have to struggle with 'unemployment' difficulties, not with scarcity of hands; therefore a slave-dealer visiting them would not find a ready sale for his stock-in-trade."[48]

This case is mentioned because its parallels, however defective, with the most industrialized societies will not escape the reader's attention. Seen from this viewpoint, the North Americans are the Eskimos of the world. With virtually closed land resources (it goes without saying that open spaces are not synonymous with open resources), with its capital concentrated in a small part of the population, with much-demanding skills in most occupations, and with much of the earlier slave work (except that in the service sector) taken over by machines, the United States among the complex societies comes very close to Nieboer's extreme case of a society with closed resources and subsistence difficult to acquire. According to Nieboer, slavery is unnecessary here:

When indispensable resources have been appropriated, the meanest labour is imposed upon those who are destitute of land and capital. *There is now no longer a personal, but an impersonal compulsion.* It may at first sight seem strange, but it is true, that generally labour is much more at a disadvantage in countries where slavery does not exist, than in slave countries. In slave countries labourers are naturally independent; therefore he who wants to make another work for him, must enslave him and resort to all possible means of retaining him in his service. Hence the strange compound of severity and indulgence that has so often been observed among slave-owners. In countries with closed resources the landlord or capitalist has a natural advantage over his labourers: he need neither use severity nor indulgence to maintain his position.[49]

It is clear that here Nieboer looks at the capitalist and laborer from an exclusively economic point of view, paying no attention to the sociopolitical actions with which an organized labor movement

---

[48] Ibid., pp. 252–254.

[49] Ibid., pp. 423–424; Nieboer's italics—note their Marcusian flavor! The author then proceeds to explain why he does not believe that a socialist system would offer better alternatives (waste of human energy, loss of spirit of enterprise, bureaucratism, stagnation, and so on).

also may force concessions from the capitalists in a society with closed resources. In such a society labor, it is true, is not scarce, but neither are all laborers dispensable as yet. Nevertheless, in such conditions of closed resources, the better skilled laborer shall want to defend his own economic gains not only against the employers but also against his unskilled co-workers to the point of wanting to monopolize these gains, thus waging both an external and an internal battle. In multiracial societies such as the United States where certain white workers' monopolies exist, the internal labor struggle may acquire special and potentially violent overtones.

Those without capital, who lack the skills for the better-paying occupations (or are excluded from these positions by racist mechanisms of selection) and by implication lack the capital needed to acquire those skills, find themselves in a situation comparable to those Eskimos who have lost their sleds and their dogs. Here, the system has to struggle with unemployment difficulties, not with scarcity of hands; they are made to feed the dogs—meaning that they are incorporated into a system that grants certain minimal social support, thus mitigating potential political upheaval, and that, furthermore, is less costly than a redistribution of land and capital.

The idea, exaggerated or not, that the United States has reached a stage of closed resources of land and capital goods (without the authors' knowledge of Nieboer's terms) also inspired Louis O. Kelso and Patricia Hetter's book *Two-Factor Theory: The Economics of Reality,* which received some publicity in 1970.[50] Before the close of the frontier, according to these authors, even the poorest worker (but not the slave nor, in the South, the freeman) could acquire virtually free capital in the form of land. This free land now no longer exists, while "5 percent of the U.S. population owns the capital—money, securities, land, and tools—that produces 90 percent of the wealth. This means that the rich have grown richer while the bulk of the U.S. workers are denied an opportunity to obtain a worthwhile share of the nation's abun-

[50] See *Time* Magazine, June 29, 1970, quoted here.

dance." The authors propose a series of government sponsored mechanisms through which a redistribution of private capital in the form of stocks would take place without changing the essentials of the present economic system.

Whether such a plan would be practical is of no concern here. But it is interesting to note that this is a proposal to artificially make the private capital resources less closed in order to create a "normal" situation in which these resources are neither open nor closed, but scarce.

Scarce resources is, of course, a term often used in contemporary sociological jargon, mostly in the context of competition among different (cultural, ethnic, racial) groupings within one social system, and implying that a good's scarcity does not exclude its attainability. The term would fit very well on an axiomatic continuum between Nieboer's open and closed resources.

Since for many innocent bystanders scarcity would seem to be socially more rejectable than abundance, it is worthwhile to realize that in Nieboer's theory open, i.e., abundant, resources tend to lead to some form of unfree labor. There is further the apparent paradox that both in a society with open resources and easily acquired subsistence and in one with closed resources and difficult-to-acquire subsistence the chances for mobility of the lowest economic strata tend to be very limited indeed: in the first case because they are slaves, in the second because they cannot acquire sufficient capital to realize such mobility. Therefore, it would seem that a situation of scarce but, in principle, attainable resources would be the most favorable for the lowest strata. However, just as a situation of closed resources can be artificially created with land (as Kloosterboer assumes was the case in the U.S. South after abolition), a similar mechanism may operate among other resources in such a way that these might be scarce but attainable for some groups, while remaining closed to others. Given the mechanisms of selection based on racial considerations, which are typical for multiracial societies, such a situation is altogether feasible in this type of society. For the dominant racial group, the resources are in principle, however scarce, attainable; for the subordinated they are all, or part of them, closed. What part is attainable and what part is closed depends on the configuration of the same, constant, factors that were mentioned earlier when the mobility of freemen in a slave society was discussed. They include: numerical relations (in society at large and in specific social strata) and their psychological impact; open positions, caused by scarcity of men or women of the racially dominant group; or, conversely, competition over available positions with, for example, immigrants belonging to the dominant socioracial group, who, over the long term, tend to be the winners. If it were true that the United States today has approached the point where (though the national myth of the open resources of course persists) the phase of the scarce but attainable resources already has given way to that of the monopolized and closed land and capital resources affecting the chances for mobility of the destitute black and poor white, then it could only be the racial antagonism between the two groups that has impeded, so far, their combined action as a sociopolitical unit. This divisiveness and antagonism have their basis in the perception of even the poorest whites of the socioracial (as distinguished from the socioeconomic) structure, who therefore believe their chances for mobility are, and must be, greater than those of the Negroes, since they belong to the dominant racial group.

It is tempting, although obviously hazardous, to try to rank the countries of the Western Hemisphere according to the present state of their resources in Nieboer's sense and to the extent to which their inhabitants' subsistence, generally speaking, is more difficult or easier to acquire (the accepted level of subsistence is, of course, determined mostly by each society's subjective notions).

The economic exactness and importance of such a schematic presentation can hardly be underestimated; its neglect of regional varieties is obvious. Yet, it has, for the purposes of our discussion, two advantages.

First, it again shows the advantage that sociological theory and analysis, especially with regard to stratification and mobility, could derive from introducing the concepts of open and closed resources at either side of the better known scarce resources; in this way the

GEOGRAPHICAL UNIT	RESOURCES	DEMANDS ON CAPITAL AND SKILLS FOR ACCEPTABLE LEVEL OF SUBSISTENCE	CONSEQUENCES FOR LABOR MARKET
United States	closed	difficult, high general level	tendency toward structural unemployment of the unskilled, except in low-paid service jobs and seasonal agricultural labor
Canada	open	difficult, high general level	tendency toward immigration of highly qualified labor, emphasis on education, some necessity for unskilled labor in the service sector
British, French, Dutch, Caribbean, Haiti, Puerto Rco	scarce to closed	less difficult, lower general level	tendency toward emigration to countries or regions with lack of unskilled labor
Central America, South America, Cuba, Dominican Republic	open to scarce	relatively easy, low general level	tendency toward compulsory forms of unskilled agrarian labor

dynamics of a given social stratification in the course of time could be more fruitfully explained and analyzed. Indeed, with certain modifications, it is possible to read the chart from the bottom up as the historical development, in not much more than a century, of the U.S. labor market, whereby the migration of the second phase of the chart would have to be seen as internal migration; its consequences for the evolution of social stratification (minus the racial complications) can easily be deduced.

The second advantage of the chart is that it shows how Nieboer's variables not only determine the existence or absence of unfree labor but also generally influence the character of the labor market from unfree labor to structural unemployment.

The chart further shows that it is the United States that is farthest removed from the conditions which, according to Nieboer, cause involuntary labor to exist; Latin America, however, is closest to those conditions. Yet, it is to the United States that the thesis of the continuity between the slavery past and present racial problems is most fervently and frequently applied. One of the reasons for this is the similarity between a society with open resources and easily acquired subsistence (where unfree labor tends to exist), and one with closed resources and difficult-to-acquire subsistence (where the lowest economic strata lack the capital needed for mobility). It is this paradoxical similarity as to limited chances for mobility that explains the success of the metaphor which compares, even equates, the present situation of the U.S. Negro with that in slavery and which sees no essential differences between the urban ghetto and the slave plantation.

In this way a society with closed resources, in Nieboer's sense, is quite often compared with a total institution such as a slave plantation, in Goffman's sense of that term.[51] Whatever the usefulness of such metaphors, it is clear that they create confusion insofar as they do not distinguish clearly between the economic and demographic determinants of slavery, on the one hand, and of a situation of closed resources, on the other. They further create confusion insofar as they tend to ignore that in the predicament that has befallen the black minority in the present situation of closed resources a much stronger racist mechanism of selection is at work than was the case within the institution of slavery, which was predominantly an economic institution.

Finally, these metaphors are confusing, because, at least in Nieboer's view, the end of compulsory labor was unavoidably

---

[51] See Erving Goffman, *Asylums* (New York: Aldine, 1961). See further R. T. Smith, "Social Stratification, Cultural Pluralism and Integration in West Indian Societies," in *Caribbean Integration: Papers on Social, Political and Economic Integration,* eds. S. Lewis and T. Mathews (Río Piedras: Institute of Caribbean Studies, 1967), p. 229.

linked with increasing population density and the consequently increasing scarcity of resources—in other words, with developments of a natural and self-explanatory nature. The present racial situation in the United States, however, asks (on the economic level) for a total and artificial, maybe even revolutionary, redistribution of resources and—beyond that on the sociopsychological level—for an abolition of collective racial prejudices, the latter being even more difficult, if not impossible, to bring about than the former. The metaphors that equate the present socioracial complexities with master-slave relations are, consequently and paradoxically, too optimistic.

Again, the chart further illustrates that the origin of race problems in a society is not causally linked to the introduction of systems of unfree labor, nor is even the persistence of such systems (where they are operating in multiracial societies such as those of Latin America) necessarily linked to the seriousness of the race problem in society at large.

Modern societies such as the North American and West European ones with closed or near-closed resources and high levels of difficult-to-acquire subsistence lack all conditions for the emergence of unfree labor. Yet, their economies, predominantly in the service sectors, are in need of the immigration of unskilled laborers. In several West European countries, a race problem now exists even though there has not been a historically contiguous period of slavery. Conversely, European Russia knew a system of unfree labor until 1861; the demographic and economic factors that had caused this phenomenon later lost their force without there being at any moment a racial division within the Russian people, coinciding with the division between masters and serfs. And the same can be said, of course, of systems of servitude that operated in Western Europe well into the late Middle Ages.

The most important effect of the work of Nieboer, Fahrenfort, and Kloosterboer seems to be that it erases much of the peculiarity of the institution of slavery and perceives it as one of many forms of unfree labor, emerging under specific economic and demographic conditions.

SLAVERY AS A MONOLITHIC CONCEPT: THE RESULT
OF RACISM

Once this perspective has been adopted, it becomes quite difficult to maintain that slavery in the Western Hemisphere was essentially different in its operation, function, and effects from any other form of involuntary labor that was also found there.

The encomienda and repartimiento caused long human suffering through separation of families, sale of humans, destruction of the traditional habitat, and forced labor at great distances—suffering of an order, as Kloosterboer judged, in some of its phases no less cruel than that of the worst conditions of slavery. All forms of unfree labor, including that of the East Indian contract laborers, led to rebellions and to efforts to escape.

The Maroons of Negro slavery, establishing their own communities in the larger Caribbean islands, the Guianas and Brazil, had their counterparts in those Peruvian Indians who disappeared collectively, from their villages, to reestablish themselves in the *páramos* where the Spaniards' exploitative influence had not yet been felt. And, in the 1870s, the East Indian indentured laborers of Trinidad, if they had a chance, fled to Venezuela,[52] just as in Cuba in the middle of the nineteenth century the Chinese forced laborers and those from Yucatán fled from the plantations and wandered around as *cimarrones*. Their treatment "was predominantly similar to that of the slaves. They could not obtain passports, transit permits, or temporary leaves, unless applied for by their own *consignatarios* or *encargados*."[53]

Both the Negro slaves and the Asian unfree laborers had a common situation in which the first generation of each group was

---

[52] Judith Ann Weller, *The East Indian Indenture in Trinidad* (Río Piedras: Institute of Caribbean Studies, 1968), p. 51.

[53] Margarita Dalton, "Los Depósitos de Cimarrones en el Siglo XIX," *Etnología y Folklore,* no. 3 (enero–junio 1967):5–31; Knight observes for Cuba: "Regardless of legal technicalities, slavery and indentured labor were synonymous" (Franklin W. Knight, *Slave Society in Cuba during the Nineteenth Century* [Madison, Wis.: University of Wisconsin Press, 1970], pp. 118–119).

transplanted into an alien environment from afar. However, Negroes as forced laborers were in a more advantageous position than the American Indians since the period of enslavement of the former was shorter than that of the latter, who still perform compulsory labor in parts of Latin America today. While it is true that from a purely legalistic point of view slavery stood in a category by itself, it is equally true that the formal legalistic aspect that distinguishes slavery from all other forms of unfree labor (i.e., the principle of human property) was often weak in its material manifestations. What is the meaning of houseslaves as property if they receive an annual wage from their masters, as was the case in Curaçao in the early nineteenth century?[54] And what, asks Juan Bosch, was the real meaning of slavery in the impoverished Santo Domingo of the seventeenth century? When new cacao plantations needed workers, the registered slaves were nowhere to be found, having apparently settled themselves elsewhere in the country. "Could it be that the general misery of the seventeenth century led to a de facto, if not de jure, liberation of the slaves, to the point where these already in 1659 behaved as free men, even though, legally speaking, they were not?"[55]

Ecological, economic, demographic, and cultural factors gave each system of unfree labor in a given time and place a historical unicity, and the variations in severity of treatment and in possibilities for individual betterment or manumission were as great within the system of unfree labor for Negroes as within that for Indians. Indeed, what gives unity to slavery as a historical concept in the Western Hemisphere is not a common experience essentially different from that of other systems of forced labor, nor is it a peculiar and unique social institution that had no equal under any other name in the Hemisphere; rather, its categorical unity lies in the simple fact that—with scarce exceptions—the subjects of slavery belonged to a similar racial group.

However varied were the experiences that slaves underwent in

---

[54] Hoetink, *Patroon*, p. 111.
[55] Juan Bosch, *Composición Social Dominicana: Historia e Interpretación,* Colección Pensamiento y Cultura (Santo Domingo: Julio D. Postigo e Hijos, 1970), p. 96.

the different American societies, because they were predominantly Negroes, the historiography of slavery for a long time tended to ascribe a monolithic uniformity to the different slave systems, which in reality they did not possess, and to postulate their incomparability with other forms of unfree labor.

The "Negro problem," as it became more visible and acute in the American multiracial societies, became explainable and reducible to a slavery past, supposed to be both unique and everywhere essentially the same, in spite of acknowledged variations in slave treatment. The question may be asked whether in reality there was not also, and maybe more so, an opposite process in operation. The race problem did not so much result out of a unique and uniform slavery past; but, rather, drastically different situations of unfree labor easily could be kept under the historic-legal umbrella of slavery because those who had suffered from it were mostly members of one racial group. Seen in this way the present Negro-white situation is not to be explained as a result of slavery, but, rather, the monolithic concept of slavery, much as it prevailed until recently, is the product of the race problem.

PART II
ON RACE RELATIONS

3
VARIATIONS AND PARALLELS

On one level of abstraction it is not difficult to analyze in common terms the recent acts of collective violence in the Caribbean area, from the Dominican Revolution in 1965 to the riots in Jamaica in 1968 and in Curaçao in 1969 and to the series of bombings in Puerto Rico and the massive disturbances in Trinidad in April, 1970. On this same level of abstraction, it is possible to classify these events as expressions of a frustrating discontent with the internal social structure and with the externally imposed patterns of domination. Local governments can be looked upon as stooges for foreign capital and interests; the higher social strata can be viewed as collaborators and middlemen of large, often multi-national, corporations.

From a different perspective, it is also possible and rewarding to analyze the anatomy, in the sense used by Crane Brinton,[1] of these conflicts as sociological processes by emphasizing a number of parallels: the role of local university members (or where there is no university, the role of teachers and academics recently returned from metropolitan countries) as intellectual stimulators and, some-times, organizers; the communication of their ideas through special periodicals (*Abeng* in Jamaica, *Kambio* in Curaçao, *Tapia* in Trinidad, and so forth); the alliance with some trade union leaders (as in Curaçao and Trinidad), with dissatisfied military (as in Trinidad and Santo Domingo), or with student groups (as in Puerto Rico, Santo Domingo, and Jamaica); the phase of mass demon-

---

[1] Crane Brinton, *Anatomy of Revolution,* rev. ed. (New York: Random House, 1957).

strations; the first martyr; the confrontation; the role of outside intervention, if any; and the aftermath of success or suppression, of absorption of ideas or personnel, or of continued tensions and struggle.

Again, it is also legitimate to stress historical continuity in these types of conflict. As Lloyd Best and other British West Indian economists maintain, there are indeed similarities between the old plantation economy and the new bauxite or oil economy: the interests of external ownership, the externally determined market conditions, the local management contracted elsewhere, the profits flowing elsewhere. In fact, some of the complaints of twentieth-century Curaçaoans against the policies of Royal Dutch Shell or against the social behavior of its personnel curiously resemble the complaints of their eighteenth-century predecessors against the West Indian Company and its hirelings. In both cases these criticisms result from the supremacy of a powerful economic organization, more supported than checked by the metropolitan power, in a small society whose own resources are too scanty to provide an adequate response.

These approaches have great appeal for the sociologist for at least two reasons. First, the social categories used in these structural analyses are universal. They can be applied to all societies where strong external economic and political influences have demonstrable repercussions on their internal economic structure and social stratification; thus, they respond to the sociologist's desire for wide generalization. Second, these approaches have ideological components attractive to many. They support the idea of basic similarities in the external relationship and internal structure of all third world societies, and they imply a structural remedy that, in principle, would be universally applicable.

These approaches are both useful and academically legitimate. What is more, several of their implications (especially of the first and third approach) can be accepted a priori, as given; they form the broadest possible framework in which the greatest number of societies or even social groups subjected to external domination can be brought together in a methodological fashion that is still acceptable. But this recognition also implies a severe limitation.

For the high level of abstraction of these analyses makes it possible to find—for example, in Haiti, Indonesia, Ghana, and the black internal colony within the United States—no more difference than Tweedledum and Tweedledee, so far as their supposedly essential structural traits are concerned. This gives some works written in such a vein the fascinating monotony of a broken record, while some of their authors are endowed with the apparent conviction: If you have seen one third world country, you have seen them all—a conviction that in more sophisticated form may even be the justification for sociology of development as a subdiscipline and for the scholarly prestige of some of its representatives.

Those societies that at their historical base line were characterized by socially relevant racial and cultural diversity lend themselves to a comparison of the ways in which their cultural and racial components have reacted to the external forces mentioned earlier. Those who attempt such an analysis must not shrink from using concepts that deal with racial and cultural cohesion and with group alignments along racial and cultural lines even if those concepts failed to receive much attention in classical sociology, based as it was on the study of more homogeneous societies.

A race problem exists where two or more racially different groups belong to one social system and where one of these conceives the other as a threat on any level or in any social context. It is irrelevant whether the groups have been brought together by military conquest, forced or free migration. One of the groups will commonly be perceived and perceive itself as dominant; the chances that two racially different groups within one society would attain an equilibrium of power, though not absent, are exceedingly small.

A racially homogeneous society, which would be characterized by the absence of any influence of somatic traits on the social ranking order, does not exist in reality. In every society somatic modalities have some influence upon selection and on the allocation of positions. These modalities are determined first by the ideals and norms, closely linked to the dominant physical type, that regulate the aesthetic appreciation of physical traits within a society: the somatic norm image.[2] Second, they are influenced by historically changing—ergo, culturally and socially determined—fashions about what is physically attractive; these fashionable opinions, however, commonly move within the limits of whatever changes the dominant physical type permits. (See p. 203.) A racial problem only presents itself in those societies where certain members are perceived by themselves and consequently or previously by the rest of society as somatically different.[3] This perception of somatic difference together with the awareness of its entailing social consequences give the aggregate of these members grouplike qualities. Such a type of society is racially heterogeneous.

A culturally homogeneous society, which would be characterized by the absence of any influence of cultural traits on the social ranking order, does not exist in reality either. In every society cultural modalities have influence upon selection and the allocation of positions. Culture conflict only presents itself in those societies where the carriers of certain cultural traits—in the cultural anthropological sense, like language or religion—perceive themselves and are perceived by the rest of society as being culturally different to such a degree that this difference entails collective social consequences, which give their aggregate grouplike qualities. Such a type of society is culturally heterogeneous.

There are several societies that are culturally heterogeneous, but that are not, nor have been, racially heterogeneous: for example, Switzerland and Belgium.[4] There are, however, at present no

---

2 For an elaboration of this concept, see H. Hoetink, *Caribbean Race Relations: A Study in Two Variants* (New York: Oxford University Press, 1971).

3 For the sake of convenience, we shall speak of racially homogeneous societies where such a race problem does not exist.

4 Unfortunately, the English terms race and ethnic group are sufficiently elastic to allow inclusion of both racial (in the stricter sense of the word) and cultural groups. Problems of a widely different nature are thus sometimes lumped together in studies of courses on "ethnic relations." See Peter I. Rose, *The Subject Is Race: Traditional Ideologies and the Teaching of Race Relations* (New York: Oxford University Press, 1968).

racially heterogeneous societies that are not or have not been, culturally heterogeneous. (This is, of course, no law; it is no more than an observation.)

Thus, the conditions for cultural homogenization or assimilation must be different from those for racial homogenization. In agreeing with Van Lier, I call societies in which at the moment of their inception, racial and cultural heterogeneity coincided "segmented societies."[5] Comparative study of initially segmented societies can give better insight into the why and how of variations of biological and cultural homogenization. Biological homogenization means the historically observable trend whereby in an initially hetero-geneous society structural forces—often located in the racially mixed middle groups—make themselves felt, which try to realize an—unattainable—ideal, a racially homogeneous society, which ideal, at the same time, also becomes part of the collective (sub-) consciousness.

This trend toward homogenization may manifest itself in the following different ways: physical elimination of a segment, as exemplified in Haitian history and to which several "Back-to-Africa" movements of the nineteenth century (led by whites) aspired; efforts toward self-elimination of a segment, as in the Marcus Garvey movement and the present Ras Tafari cult in Jamaica; the tendency toward inhibition or displacement of a segment from the accepted societal image, as in the earlier U.S. custom—also among sociologists—to speak of Americans and Negroes in this society, in the perception and legalization of the Bantus as aliens in the Union of South Africa, or—to cite an inverse case—in Trinidad where creole whites are pitted against the "local population."[6] In all these cases we may observe either

---

[5] See R. A. J. Van Lier, *The Development and Nature of Society in the West Indies* (Amsterdam: Kon. Instituut voor de Tropen, 1950). I prefer the term "segmented" to "plural," because of the political and ideological connotations this latter term has acquired, especially in the United States.

[6] L. Braithwaite, "Social Stratification in Trinidad," *Social and Economic Studies* 2 and 3 (October 1953):91.

the cultivation of a fiction—which thereby is converted into a sociopsychological reality—of a racially more homogeneous society or of physical actions to come closer to such an ideal. Federalist, separatist, or other centrifugal movements might also be interpreted as an indication of this trend toward homogeneity, insofar as their essential motivation is the creation of sociopolitical units as homogeneous and autonomous as possible. All the enumerated ways toward racial homogenization could be summarized under the label of (physical or psychological) elimination. There is one other way that leads to homogenization via biological mingling, a long process in which the main precondition is: No group will want to preserve its own supposed racial homogeneity.

The processes toward cultural homogenization can be described in analogous terms, though it is hardly feasible that any group would succeed in its long-term cultural isolation, unless it were also geographically removed from the other groups. Where, as in the Caribbean, societies have existed for over four centuries, the mixing of the cultural heritage of the original groups must have advanced impressively. When even in such an advanced phase of cultural assimilation movements come to the fore that emphasize the cultural character (in the cultural anthropological sense) of a racial group, as is the case with the *Négritude* movement of the French-speaking islands, then there exists an ideology created by a culturally non-African intelligentsia; this ideology functions as a stimulant for the racial self-consciousness and is not the expression of a previously existing general collective conviction that racial heterogeneity always is, or ought to be, accompanied by cultural heterogeneity.

Those interrelated movements that can be placed under the heading "Black Is Beautiful," also are a paradoxical illustration of how far an initially segmented society has become culturally homogenized, since for generations cultural assimilation has led the black group to the inhibition of its own black somatic norm image and to the adoption of the white one. If the black groups had been isolated culturally, the beauty of blackness would have been a matter of course. Now the black intelligentsia needs missionary zeal to resuscitate this collective physical self-appreciation.

The Caribbean Experience in Racial and Cultural Variety

"Caribbean societies are among the most westernized of the modern world," writes Sidney Mintz, using the term westernization to refer to the effects of the length of contact, of the principal mode of economic organization, and of the elimination of the primitive from the culture of the Caribbean peoples. "Thus," he continues, "the Caribbean region makes clear what is well-enough known for retarded agricultural zones within more obviously western societies, as in the United States South: any absence of 'westernization' is in fact the by-product of the particular sorts of western control imposed on the inhabitants."[7]

The African, Amerindian, and European origins of Caribbean cultural elements while worthy of research, especially with regard to their unequal distribution per society and per social stratum, must not prevent the conclusion that in the majority of present-day Caribbean societies cultural and institutional diversity is not greater than in other predominantly agrarian societies with a fairly rigid social structure. The Maroons in Jamaica, the Bush Negroes in Surinam, and the culturally involuted Haitian rural population may still show—because of their long-lasting geographical isolation—an important measure of cultural anthropological uniqueness, but most Caribbean societies as a whole are less pluriform than Spain, Italy, or France in their language or folk customs.

Three societies form an exception to this generalization. In Trinidad, Guiana, and Surinam, as a result of the immigration of Asiatic groups in the nineteenth century, the racial and cultural heterogeneity became reemphasized to such an extent that these societies qua intensity of segmentation were moved back to a starting point. Small wonder that more than elsewhere in the area political party formation in these countries acquired a strongly segmentary character.

Initially, the East Indians, perceived as exotic and lower-class aliens, were kept outside the accepted societal image of the

---

[7] Sidney W. Mintz, "The Caribbean as a Socio-cultural Area," *Cahiers d'Histoire Mondiale* 9, no. 4 (1966):931–932.

Creoles. In Surinam, the term Surinamese was still applied only to the Creole segment, even when the East Indians already formed nearly half of the total population. But this period of pseudo homogeneity by inhibition has now ended. An increased political, economic, and numerical parity of Creoles and East Indians made competition between the two groups both possible and necessary; the initially horizontal lines of division became nearly vertical in the process. This present structure of vertical pluralism is potentially explosive. Only if the division of labor between the two groups, already existing in the lower strata, were to be extended and even institutionalized in the higher spheres of political authority and control in much the same pattern as that in Lebanon or The Netherlands could such a "pillarization" maintain itself for a considerable time. It would then only disintegrate after its *raison d'être* would have been undermined by the continuing biological and cultural intermingling of the two groups. If this intermingling does not occur at a rate sufficiently fast to create an awareness of a trend toward homogenization, then an alternative development might lead toward a new horizontal structure, this time with the East Indian group in the superior position. It is clear that such a reversal of power would not be achieved without serious conflict.

The impossibility of evaluating in these recently segmented societies all forces that influence their future development, such as differences in economic ethos and in numerical growth and the factors that determine biological and cultural homogenization (the latter still being called, significantly, creolization)—has led to an intensification of scholarly discussion.[8]

8 On the East Indians in Trinidad, see Morton Klass, *East Indians in Trinidad: A Study of Cultural Persistence* (New York: Columbia University Press, 1961); see further Donald Wood, *Trinidad in Transition: The Years After Slavery* (London: Oxford University Press, 1968); Ivar Oxaal, *Black Intellectuals Come to Power: The Rise of Creole Nationalism in Trinidad and Tobago* (Cambridge, Mass.: Schenkman, 1968); and Anthony P. Maingot, "From Ethnocentric to National History Writing in the Plural Society," *Carribbean Studies* 9, no. 3 (October 1969). On Surinam, see J. D. Speckmann, "The Indian Group in the Segmented Society of Surinam," *Caribbean Studies* 3, no. 1 (April 1963), and *Marriage and Kinship Among the Indians in Surinam* (Assen: Royal

In most other Caribbean societies, cultural variety is slight. However, some qualification is needed here. Both in linguistic and in religious respects there is a greater uniformity in the Spanish speaking areas than in those where English or Dutch is the official language. The French areas have a relatively widespread religious homogeneity as do Spanish speaking countries. In these latter societies, the central position of the Catholic Church, which saw itself as an all-embracing institution, led to results other than those where the official overseas Protestant churches saw themselves as an extension of the metropolitan institution and therefore maintained a certain hesitation and reluctance vis-à-vis the "alien" groups. The high degree of linguistic uniformity achieved only in the Spanish area must probably be ascribed to the more active function as cultural and social brokers of the colored middle groups in that area.

It is undoubtedly the racial rather than the cultural variety that strikes the observer in most Caribbean societies. Only a few tiny islands are inhabited exclusively by blacks or whites. Limiting the discussion for the moment to those societies where no Asian immigration has complicated the older structure, the classic hierarchy still maintains itself to a large degree: a small group of creole whites enjoying the highest social prestige, intermediate group of coloreds holding an intermediate position, and the numerically largest group—Negroes—occupying the lowest social position.

In some writings cultural diversity or pluralism means that the different positions of these racial groups in the social structure entail different role behavior and ways of life, mostly, though not exclusively, determined by economic circumstances.

In this sense it is possible to speak, as does M. G. Smith, of white, brown, and black cultures.[9] Such a terminology, however, is synonymous with that of upper-, middle-, and lower-class cultures

Van Gorcum, 1965); the Javanese in Surinam were studied in Annemarie de Waal Malefijt, *The Javanese of Surinam: Segment of a Plural Society* (Assen: Royal Van Gorcum, 1963).

[9] M. G. Smith, *The Plural Society in the British West Indies* (Berkeley: University of California Press, 1965), pp. 162 ff.

in societies that are not racially heterogeneous but that do have a socioeconomic structure similar to the ones described by Smith in the British Caribbean. Smith's terminology may further lead to the misunderstanding that it is the cultural heritage—in the cultural anthropological sense—of racial groups that keeps them separated, while he actually uses the concept of culture in its sociological meaning—a correlate of social position.

The sociological peculiarity of Caribbean society is not to be found, of course, in its socioeconomic structure where a great gulf exists between elites and landless proletariat, each with its own deviations from what is perceived as the cultural norm and ideal, but, rather, in that the social status of an individual and his potential frequency and distance of social mobility are determined to a very large extent by his somatic traits. As the Jamaican saying goes: "If you white, you all right; if you brown, stick around; if you black, stand back," or to quote a young Jamaican nationalist: "The accepted passport to preferment seems to be a physical appearance as near to that of the average European as possible";[10] this statement still has validity for the vast majority of people in the area.

In terms of racial and cultural heterogeneity, it is the former that attracts attention because of its stagnation, at least in the British, French, and Dutch areas. It is true that high civil service and political offices with their attendant occupational prestige are now mostly occupied by colored or black members of society, but, given the importance of somatic traits in the overall social ranking, it is the native whites who retain—because of these ascriptive traits—the highest prestige. Where, due to economic changes, these whites are no longer able to maintain the way of life associated with this prestige they emigrate, as has happened already on several smaller islands. Where, due to political forces, they are barred from the official public sector, they withdraw even more

---

[10] H. Orlando Patterson, *The Children of Sisyphus* (London, 1964), p. 115, quoted in David Lowenthal, "Race and Color in the West Indies," *Daedalus* (Spring 1967), p. 582. See also " 'Realism and Race' by a Young Jamaican Nationalist," in "The Views on the Problem of Race and Colour in Jamaica Today," *West Indian Economist* 3, no. 10 (April 1961):6, quoted in Lowenthal, "Race and Color," p. 581.

into an exclusive and intimate social network, of their own. This may lead to their finally being perceived, and perceiving themselves, as "aliens,"[11] at the same time seeing their former mother country ever more with the eyes of the prodigal son; all of these tendencies fit into a trend toward racial homogenization whereby, of course, the objective indications of this trend exist prior to their subjective impact.

In many present-day non-Hispanic Caribbean societies, the somatic type of the colored with light brown skin and Caucasoid traits is propagated as the aesthetically desirable model; this phenomenon is a plausible accompaniment of the just mentioned trends, which lead to a simplification of the social structure, whereby the colored group will gradually take over the position of the white creoles.

The dividing line between the Negroes, or blacks, or creoles, or Africans—all these terms have been tried in the Caribbean—and the coloreds is fluid; in the statistical data it is subject to the census taker's capriciousness.[12] But in all Caribbean societies there is a group of light coloreds for whom the adage (too often repeated by sociologists) "Every rich Negro is a mulatto, every poor mulatto is a Negro" is nothing less than social heresy. It is this group of light coloreds that has performed a crucial role in the development of race relations. In the major Caribbean societies, this group reached early—no later than the eighteenth century—a position of relatively high social prestige often backed by economic prosperity and a high level of education.

Where, as in Surinam, economic crises caused most of the native whites to leave the country already in the eighteenth century, these prestigious coloreds occupied from that early period the highest positions in the native social ranking order.

---

[11] Cf. the earlier cited remark on the Trinidad Creoles and the local population. Sudden upheavals and revolts, as in Curaçao in May 1969, seem to accelerate this process. See "30 Mei 1969: Rapport van de Commissie tot Onderzoek van de Achtergronden en Oorzaken van de Onlusten welke op 30 mei 1969 op Curaçao Hebben Plaatsgehad" (Aruba: De Wit, 1970).

[12] See Lowenthal, "Race and Color," p. 600 for some examples.

Where, as in Haiti, social discrimination against these prosperous slaveholding coloreds coincided with the bourgeois revolution in the metropolitan country, and its concurrent ideological
dissemination into the colonies, this colored group initiated its own
revolution, eliminated the white segment, and occupied its position
by force.[13]

Where, as in the other French and Dutch areas as well as in the
British West Indies, the native white groups stayed in the country
and in power, the colored group had to accommodate itself within
the system, even though in the Dutch Antilles a part of them rather
consciously assimilated the nearby South American culture in
order to be able to assume the role of "aliens," marginal to the
Dutch colonial structure.[14]

The accommodation of these light coloreds implied that in cases
of slave or Negro revolts they often readily aligned themselves with
the whites even though they were never recognized as the latter's
social equals. But this sophisticated group of coloreds also sometimes produced a nonconformist avant-garde, who took sides with
the poor black masses. Thus, in Haiti after the U.S. invasion
before World War II, mulatto elite authors who had been educated
in Europe, such as Carl Brouard, Jr., Emile Roumer, and Jacques
Roumain, provided the ideological and idealizing foundations for a
political emancipation movement of the blacks. This movement
under Duvalier seemed to lead to the elimination of the privileged
position of this same colored group; the last phase of the Haitian
homogenization process thus seemed to have begun.

In the history of the British, French, and Dutch areas, the group
of prestigious coloreds has played a much more complex and
unpredictable role—from revolt against whites to silencing of
blacks—than in the Spanish colonies.[15] This illustrates their more

---

[13] See J. G. Leyburn, *The Haitian People* (New Haven, Conn.: Yale
University Press, 1966).

[14] See H. Hoetink, *Het Patroon van de Oude Curaçaose Samenleving*: *Een
Sociologische Studie* (Assen: Royal Van Gorcum, 1958).

[15] Cahnman observed several years ago that "the main practical attitude
between Anglo-American and Latin-American race attitudes is in the
position of the Mulatto rather than the Negro" (W. J. Cahnman, "The

ambivalent intermediate position in the former territories. Coloreds were socially unacceptable to the whites, though they used them as their group of reference, and considered themselves socially superior to the Negroes, though they sometimes acted as their ally. Upward and downward their emotional reactions, whether affectionate or aggressive, were stronger than was the case *grosso modo* in the Spanish areas.

In 1887, when the (mulatto) politician Gregorio Luperón became a candidate for the presidency of the Dominican Republic, one of the leading (white) intellectuals of the period applauded him as follows:

The government that rules us . . . should begin to think seriously about the destiny reserved by Providence for the Negroes and mulattoes of America. From now on, this destiny is manifest, given the present numbers of this race; and I believe the island of Santo Domingo is called to be the nucleus, the model of its glorification and individuality in this hemisphere. And who better than you could begin to lay the groundwork, the foundation of this greatness? Who better than you could know how necessary the white race is for the achievement of this goal, but at the same time recognize the superiority of the combinations of this great race? And who better than you could melt, amalgamate and shape a homogeneous whole from the wisdom and ignorance of one and another family so that from today, we as a model of tolerance and restraint, may attract the benevolent gaze of the Universe and place ourselves, robust and free, in a highly enviable position?"[16]

Such a plea for amalgamation by a representative of the white group was and is unthinkable in the British, French, and Dutch multiracial societies though their numbers of whites were and are equally small. In these latter areas the whites might point to the necessity of alliances with and goodwill toward the coloreds, who could serve as a buffer between them and the Negroes, but the thought of biological assimilation of their own white group was

Mediterranean and Caribbean Regions: A Comparison in Race and Culture Contacts," *Social Forces* 22 [October 1943–May 1944]:210, n. 5).

[16] Gregorio Luperón, *Notas Autobiográficas y Apuntes Históricos,* vol. 3, 2d ed. (Santiago de los Caballeros: El Diario, 1939), p. 250.

anathema to them (sexual relations with Negro or mulatto women was something entirely different, since it left the white group intact).

The separation between white and colored was less strict in the Spanish Caribbean; the categories were less absolute; the definitions of who was or is white were more elastic,[17] at least with regard to the crucial group of light coloreds whose position was therefore less frustrating and less aggressive (for example, the Haitian light-colored refugee was accepted in the Dominican Republic as a white). In the Spanish area the colored group saw itself as a social broker and ascribed to itself an essential role in the process of biological homogenization. This perception of itself agreed with reality and, in its turn, also fostered cultural assimilation. This does not mean that racial prejudice and discrimination were ever absent in the Spanish Caribbean, but they did not lead to such a pronounced endogamy of the native whites as in the other areas. The ideology of total racial mixture thus received a boost from reality, which was virtually absent in the Northwest European Caribbean.

The wish for homogenization is certainly also present in the non-Spanish countries. Their national mottoes and flags emphasize it more than the Spanish speaking countries do (Jamaica: "Out of Many, One People"; Guiana: "One People, One Nation"). But precisely this strong emphasis betrays an uncertainty that is, perhaps unrealistically, absent from the Spanish Caribbean. Other influences make this difference even more pronounced. The greater linguistic and religious uniformity and the impact of patron-client and co-parenthood relations also contribute to a subjective notion of lesser racial separateness in the Hispanic areas.

The different position of the light coloreds in the Spanish Caribbean, as compared with the Northwest European variant cannot be caused by differences within the institution of slavery, first, because the character of master-slave relations was not a

---

[17] See Eduardo Seda Bonilla, "Dos Modelos de Relaciones Raciales: Estados Unidos y América Latina," *Revista de Ciencias Sociales* 12, no. 4 (Diciembre 1968):569–597.

constant factor in time in any society and, second, because the position of the prestigious coloreds became fixed not within, but outside the slavery system.

Nor can the different position of the coloreds in the two variants be explained by differences in numerical proportions of the different racial groups. Of the Spanish speaking areas the Dominican Republic has a proportion similar to the majority of the British, French, and Dutch areas. Nor were the whites in the Spanish colonies there to stay, while in the rest of the area they were there only as temporary inhabitants. The history of Curaçao and Barbados refutes this generalization. Nor, finally, did only the Spanish areas suffer from a lack of white women, so that the colonists had to marry coloreds. In several non-Spanish societies such shortages also existed, and for prolonged periods, but this did not lead to a complete social acceptance of the colored sexual partners of the white men.[18]

Although in both areas there existed a group in a similar intermediate position in the social, cultural, and economic structure, social acceptability of a marriage partner from the light coloreds apparently differed in each because more intimate factors influenced the selection of who was to bear one's socially recognized children, including socially determined aesthetics—a different perception of who is a white, a different somatic norm image. In its turn, the original white Spanish somatic image must have been influenced (darkened) in time because of the continual absorption of light coloreds into the white group. It goes without saying that one has to allow for variation in this process between the different Spanish Caribbean societies.

Because the whites in the Spanish Caribbean did not separate themselves so far from the light coloreds, biological homogenization has not only further advanced in that area but also the mood (that is, the sum of expectations concerning final racial assimilation) is more optimistic. The British, French, and Dutch areas, on

[18] This argument is again used in the otherwise admirable article by Peter Dodge, "Comparative Racial Systems in the Greater Caribbean" (New York: Columbia University Press, 1968).

the contrary, seem to strike a more dramatic note in this respect, as does the United States. In the latter country, however, the numerical proportions preclude the type of Haitian *chimère* that can be encountered more or less openly in the non-Hispanic area, and of which the following quotation from a column in the Jamaican *Gleaner* is a good example:

No country has ever profited by getting rid of white people. One of the first to try was Haiti, but after 300 years the black people there are still mainly in poverty, misery, and oppression—ruled by a black boss whom they dare not offend. . . . So the first main point is that Jamaica as a nation of mainly black people cannot succeed and achieve what it wants for those black people unless it maintains excellent relations and friendships with white people abroad. The second main point follows from this. Good relations with white people abroad cannot be maintained unless there are good relations with white people in Jamaica, whether resident or visiting.[19]

Such admonitions to the blacks, inspired by fear, are as yet unheard of in the Hispanic Caribbean, where the sense of social alienation of the Negro qua Negro is much less pronounced and where social conflicts so far have rarely tended to develop along racial lines. *Négritude* movements with strong political overtones are therefore less successful in the Spanish speaking areas. And in the United States, sons of immigrants from the British West Indies rather than from the Spanish Caribbean have become leading figures in the black movement.[20]

Yet, the social significance of the somatic factor in the Spanish Caribbean cannot be denied. As Mejía Ricart observed for the Dominican Republic:

The Dominicans have an ethnic complex. . . . Since racial purity is very rare and a mixture of the different variations prevails: white, near white, mulatto and Negro, the consequence is that one is constantly observing the differences in skin color, hair texture and more or less white origins. Such an importance ascribed to this aspect of the individual naturally produces the aspiration to improve their color on

[19] *Gleaner,* January 14, 1970.
[20] See Lowenthal, "Race and Color," pp. 609 ff.

the part of those who are nearly white, while those small groups who have all white ancestors aspire to preserve this gift which they consider a real family patrimony.[21]

And Pedro Andrés Pérez Cabral in his *La Communidad Mulata*[22] also writes extensively on the desire for what he calls arianization of the Dominican people, whose country he considers "the only mulatto nation of the world."

The socioracial situation in the Hispanic Caribbean is not different from that of the Northwest European variant of the area, insofar as higher social prestige is allotted to whites' than to Negroes' physical traits. The basic difference lies in the greater degree of mixing between the whites and the other socioracial strata and in the definition of whiteness related to this phenomenon. In the Dominican Republic the most recent available data show that well over 10 percent of all marriages take place between whites and mulattoes.[23]

In this context the observations made by North American visitors to Puerto Rico early in the twentieth century, when the island only recently had become a U.S. possession, are interesting. One of these observers feared that it would not be possible to impose a color line on the island, because race mixing already had progressed so far that a clear distinction between whites and Negroes (as defined in the United States) had become impossible.[24] Another visitor stated in the same period that according to census figures about three-sevenths of the Puerto Rican population was Negroid; the lighter coloreds, she observed, are accepted as

[21] M. A. Mejía Ricart, *Las Clases Sociales en Santo Domingo* (Ciudad Trujillo: Librería Dominicana, 1953), pp. 27–38.

[22] Pedro Andrés Pérez Cabral, *La Comunidad Mulata: El Caso Socio-Politico de la República Dominicana* (Caracas: Gráfica Americana, 1967).

[23] Estadistica Demografica de la República Dominicana, 1960, 1961, cited by Pérez Cabral, *La Comunidad Mulata,* p. 115.

[24] Eugene P. Lyle, "Our Experience in Porto Rico," *World's Week* 11 (1960), cited in T. G. Mathews, "La Cuestión del Color en Puerto Rico," unpublished manuscript, 1970.

whites and are not, as in the United States, considered as Negroes. If, she added, all mulattoes, quadroons, octoroons, quintroons, and other mixed bloods were labeled as Negro instead of white, the Negroes would form a large majority of the population.[25]

ECONOMIC STAGNATION AND RACIAL TRANQUILLITY

In Brazil the economic and social lot of the darkest population groups is deplorable. Their mortality is twice as high as that of the Brazilian whites. In Rio de Janeiro where 29 percent of the population is classified as Negro, 71 percent of these live in the *favelas,* the shanty towns, and their efforts toward social improvement are clearly undermined by the racist principles of selection characteristic of every multiracial society. Several authors[26] have published data that show how openly these principles are put into practice.

Prospective employers usually establish various prerequisites for new recruits, but the basic one is that of color. . . . Many of them specify that they will consider only "Portuguese" or "Spanish" applicants which means "white" in the code language. Many mulatto girls with other qualifications . . . have to work as domestics because few companies will hire them.

The American Negro girl's horizon, especially in big cities like New York, is much wider. . . . Even today, the advertising sections of leading newspapers are full of ads for domestic servants requesting "Portuguese" or "light" applicants and a few more bluntly specifying "white." . . . In 1962, a poll of 2000 white college students in Recife and São Paulo showed that only 54 percent of them would accept Negroes as fellow club members, 64 percent as neighbors, 58 percent as members of the same profession, and 62 percent as fellow citizens.[27]

---

[25] Margherita Arlina Hamm, *Porto Rico and the West Indies* (New York: F. Tennyson Neely, 1899), cited in Mathews, "La Cuestión del Color."

[26] For an excellent overview and analysis of Brazilian publications in this field, see John Saunders, "Class, Color and Prejudice: A Brazilian Counterpoint," in *Racial Tensions and National Identity,* ed. John Q. Campbell (Nashville: Vanderbilt University Press, 1972).

[27] Jean-Claude García-Zamor, "Social Mobility of Negroes in Brazil," *Journal of Inter-American Studies and World Affairs* 12, no. 2 (April 1970):242–254.

It seems not an effective line of defense merely to consider the presence of prejudice and discrimination in Brazil as an anachronism, as Florestan Fernándes does: "Archaic elements and factors sometimes continue to exist and to have an active effect long after their own historical period. They exercise negative influences on the development of culture and of society itself. This seems to be the case with São Paulo, even though it is the most modern and the most highly developed city in Brazil. It is still held in the clutches of the past in the field of racial relations." And elsewhere he speaks of a still-persisting traditionalism, a terminology suggesting that the phase in which the phenomena under discussion were functional has been surpassed by now and that there remain only fossilized survivals, which may be deplorable, but hardly indicative, of modern Brazil.

Fernándes summarizes his judgment as follows: "Generally speaking, the Brazilian racial difficulty resides more in the lack of equilibrium between racial stratification and the current social order than in specific ethnocentric and irreducible influences,"[28] but it is hard to see how this lack of equilibrium can ever be overcome, when in all social sectors there is a built-in mechanism operating in favor of the light colored or white, a mechanism that has survived many economical and technological changes without losing its vigor.[29] Rather, it has to be understood as a vital characteristic of any multiracial society past or present.

When, as in the period of Brazilian slavery, the whites and light coloreds could consider themselves de jure superior to the racially

[28] Florestan Fernándes, "The Weight of the Past," in *Color and Race,* ed. John Hope Franklin (Boston: Houghton Mifflin, 1968), pp. 292, 295, 299.

[29] "Discrimination is subtle and covert but in competitive situations when equality of qualifications exists between a white and a person of color, the latter is frequently handicapped. Cardoso reports that the totality of the Negroes and mulattoes he interviewed in Florianopolis stated that unless a job was open to public competition through examination, that is, unless that award of the position was based on objective criteria, that color was a limitation" (John Saunders, "Color and Prejudice," p. 29).

subordinated group of slaves, the need for such a racist mechanism of selection was even less than when in more recent times the barriers of legal inequality were abolished and those of social inequality had to be more emphatically stressed. "During the empire, the pressure of more vigorous liberal sentiment, the fact that the population was still 'new' . . . and the dispersion of the élite permitted rapid social ascension. . . . Social mobility for Negroes was easier at that time, and most of the isolated cases of individuals who broke through the color barrier date to this period. After independence . . . outstanding examples of individual mobility became rarer. The parliaments today are 'whiter' than during the empire."[30]

In several Latin countries, such as the Dominican Republic, Venezuela, and Cuba, a similar phenomenon can be observed; here the rapid social rise of clearly Negroid persons in the nineteenth century was also due to the many military and political upheavals in which the rural *cacique,* often of lowly social origins, could attain great political and economic power, even though it was often only for short periods. (See below, p. 150.)

When at the end of the nineteenth century the population in these countries had increased, the political situation showed signs of stabilization, and the social structure evidenced those of crystallization, rapid social rise for the dark skinned became considerably more difficult. As for the Dominican Republic, "it is probable that the sheer numerical growth and the increasing social consciousness of the national bourgeoisie increased the social relevance of the racial factor, if only because through it, the mechanism of social control could be manipulated more effectively. In the last decade of the nineteenth century, we find frequent use of such pejorative terms as *culebrón* for a social climber. Finally, urban growth in the 'eighties and the 'nineties may have caused more pronounced segregation, specifically between the Negroes and the other population groups. . . . Just as the new bourgeoisie founded its exclusive social clubs in these years, so, too, the dark-skinned groups started their 'social centers,' and in their statutes restrictive rules

[30] García-Zamor, "Social Mobility," p. 248.

abounded. One of the most prestigious of these clubs was . . . the 'Black Pearl.' "[31]

The Dominican Republic was, incidentally, the only country in the Caribbean where the full development of large scale sugar plantations took place as late as the last two decades of the nineteenth century; it was, consequently, the only country in that part of the hemisphere where slavery was abolished long before the sugar economy made its dramatic impact. The considerable immigration of (black) sugar workers from the surrounding Caribbean islands to the Dominican Republic in the eighteen eighties and nineties was, as far as can be ascertained, of an unorganized, "spontaneous" nature. Yet, also without slavery, the effects of the sugar plantation economy on the economic and socioracial stratification undoubtedly were those of both greater differentiation and distinctiveness of the different strata, without ever reaching, however, the type of white endogamy that we notice in the non-Hispanic areas.

This Dominican experience is important in that it once again denies the often postulated sociological causality between slavery and "racism." For Cuba, Franklin W. Knight,[32] in his excellent study, observes that in the course of the nineteenth century, when increased sugar production led to an increasing immigration of slaves, "racism" against the group of freemen also became more serious. This leads him to view the chronological sequence: sugar revolution–harsher slavery–increasing racism against freemen, as a general sociological causation, while in fact it is not more than a historical convergence, which took place, indeed, in most Caribbean plantation societies but not in all of them. There is, as we have tried to demonstrate earlier in this book, no sufficient causality between the change for the worse in the attitudes toward the free

---

[31] H. Hoetink, "The Dominican Republic in the Nineteenth Century: Some Notes on Stratification, Immigration, and Race" in *Race and Class in Latin America,* ed. Magnus Mörner (New York: Columbia University Press, 1970).

[32] *Slave Society in Cuba during the Nineteenth Century* (Madison, Wis.: University of Wisconsin Press, 1970).

blacks, and the mildness or harshness, or even the presence or absence, of slavery.

The causal link in Cuba, as well as in the Dominican Republic, was rather with the fear of the increasing number of blacks, by whom the "intermediate free colored population (especially in Cuba) was swamped," as Knight puts it. The sudden influx of thousands of blacks, which later caused the free "colored" population to be predominantly black rather than mulatto, traumatically upset the dimensions of the previously existing socioracial structure and made for increasing prejudice and discrimination in Cuba, and even led to severe riots in the early twentieth century. The difference between "Iberian" and non-"Iberian" racial attitudes is, as we have maintained, discernible rather vis-à-vis the light coloreds than towards the unequivocally black. Such an unfavorable development would also have occurred if the African immigrants in Cuba had not come as slaves, but on their own free will, and it would also have occurred if it had not been the nineteenth-century sugar plantation but, say, an expanding demand for unskilleds in the service sector of a twentieth-century industrialized society, which had attracted them. For the fear of a "spiraling black population," to use Knight's words, is, unfortunately, a phenomenon whose occurrence is *not* so neatly conditioned by a specific economic structure as is sometimes believed.

Yet, even in Cuba, the different racial groups worked surprisingly close together in the war against Spain at the end of the nineteenth century, and Knight is of the opinion that the war had a decidedly beneficial effect on race relations in general. This positive fluctuation in race *relations,* however, did not have an observable effect on the socioracial *structure* which in the course of the twentieth century grew ever more rigid within the Spanish American setting; not only the reasons just mentioned may have been responsible for this, but also the increasing impact of North American notions of "social race" in modern Cuba.

What was operating in these countries at the end of the nineteenth century was the phenomenon that in an expanding social structure as soon as it is controlled more by the newly reestablished economic interests than by the improvised military-rural elements, as soon as, in other words, the stabilizing prevails over the convulsive social element, the higher open positions in that structure are allotted to those who are somatically most akin to the traditional social elite. The expanding economy, if left to itself, prefers for these positions the poor white (native or immigrant) over the Negro, in the same fashion as Marvin Harris postulated for the United States: "In the United States, . . . the disproportion between white settlers and Negro slaves and the mulatto offspring of the Negro slaves has been further aggravated by the remarkably rapid rate of economic expansion and, hence, the rapid rate of the appearance of middle class positions which the whites have sought to monopolise for themselves."[33] However, in view of the foregoing evidence, Harris's opinion that "in both the highland and lowland Latin American regions racial conflict of a direct and overt sort has been kept to a minimum by virtue of the fact that *there has not been too much to fight over*" (my italics) is hardly tenable. Moreover, the theory behind this opinion is not very plausible: Why should economic expansion in itself, that is, less scarce—but not open—resources lead to greater racial troubles than economic stagnation?

It is generally more logical to defend the opposite idea: Where economic differentiation is slight or on the decrease, other possibilities for social distinction are going to be more emphatically used. In Haiti under President Pétion in the early nineteenth century, land reform, which reduced considerably the differences in economic power and prestige, led precisely to an increased emphasis on the social distinction between Negro and colored, in much the same way in which the poor whites in the U.S. South tended to attach a greater social value to their somatic characteristics vis-à-vis the Negroes than the upper class whites, who could point to so many more socially relevant differences.

Therefore, Harris's thesis should not be that "the price which the underdeveloped countries or regions in Latin America have paid for relative racial tranquility is economic stagnation."[34] It is

[33] Marvin Harris, *Patterns of Race in the Americas* (New York: Walker, 1964), p. 97.
[34] Ibid., p. 98.

not the expanding economy per se that may disturb the racial tranquillity but, rather, the presence or immigration of poor whites lured by this expansion, who are not objectively different from the other poor racial groups and hence tend to exploit their ascriptive distinctions *à outrance.*

Such a situation was not unique for the United States but occurred also in several expanding Latin American economies in the late nineteenth and early twentieth centuries, where the rapid social rise of poor white immigrants and their children was observed with bitterness and frustration by the dark-skinned groups. The "relative racial tranquillity" in these Latin American countries, in spite of earlier data on the overt discrimination against the darkest parts of their population and in spite of the latter's socioeconomic position—which objectively was no different, and perhaps worse, than their counterparts in the United States—has to be understood, not in terms of economic stagnation, but in terms of an already-existing socioracial structure in which blacks and whites are not two fundamentally distinct groups but, rather, flow toward each other via a great number of color gradations. The blacks' position is psychologically more tolerable in such a structure since they have relatives and friends in one of the contiguous or even further removed socioracial categories that no longer possess the social odium of blackness. They thus have the constant possibility of psychological escape and projection through identification with socially attainable, nonblack groups and individuals.

A logical consequence of the Latin American racial conceptualization is that, though the social distance between the opposite groups, such as whites and blacks, is considerable, the social distance between contiguous categories is not that remarkable. If we measure the social distance between *grifos* and *mulatos,* between *negros* and *grifos,* between *blancos* and *blancos con raja,* we will find that it is considerably less than between the two poles in the continuum. . . . As a result of the "tolerance" between contiguous categories, there is a marked tendency towards race-mixing between persons of contiguous categories so as to produce physical types with greater acceptability in society. Given the existence of racial prejudice, the hypogamic pressure is directed toward "whitening."[35]

[35] Seda Bonilla, "Dos Modelos," p. 577.

It is, therefore, incidentally, not entirely correct to explain the increasing portion of whites in the Latin American censuses solely as a result of white immigration. In countries such as Cuba and the Dominican Republic, the numerical effects of European immigration since the middle of the nineteenth century were more than canceled out by Negroid immigration from the surrounding Caribbean islands; yet, the censuses show a whitening there also, which can only be understood by the continuous absorption of light coloreds—as marriage partners—in the socioracial category of the whites and by the continuous numerical growth of the colored group through racial mixing—not necessarily on the basis of social equality and marriage—between the darkest and lighter skinned groups, a process called *"mulatización"* by Pérez Cabral.[36]

SOCIAL VERSUS RACIAL PREJUDICE

The existence of a socioracial continuum in the Latin countries, which means that the white group has not consistently tried to evade racial mixing with contiguous color gradations, has led some researchers to the opinion that in Latin America no racial prejudice exists, only a social prejudice.

Seda Bonilla strongly opposes this line of thought not only because racial prejudice against the darkest population groups in Latin America is by now undeniable or because any racial prejudice is of course sociologically determined but also, and especially, because he detects in it a curious tendency, above all among North American scholars, to monopolize the existence of racial prejudice for the United States since only in that country "pure" whites supposedly are to be found.

In Latin America, where "the number of racially pure whites without any admixture of Indian or other 'colored' factors is certainly very small,"[37] and where it is hard to ascertain "how much African blood flows in the veins of Mexicans, Peruvians, Brazil-

---

[36] Pérez Cabral, *La Comunidad Mulata,* pp. 71 ff.
[37] John Gillin, "Mestizo America," in *Most of the World,* ed. Ralph Linton (New York: Columbia University Press, 1949), p. 60.

ians, Cubans,"[38] the impurity of the whites, or so it would seem, makes their having racial prejudices ludicrous in the eyes of these researchers. Such an argument is correctly rejected by Seda Bonilla on two grounds. First, there is, of course, no question but that white racial purity in the United States is a myth.

In 1960, according to estimates of Robert P. Stuckert, the number of white North Americans with Negroid ancestry was 23 percent of the total white population; the number of persons yearly passing the color line was estimated by John Burma at 2,500.[39] These data, even if used as only crude indicators, are enough to dispel any notion about white purity, in itself, of course, an untenable concept in human biology. Seda's second argument is found in the virtually universal tendency in the Latin countries toward *blanqueamiento,* whitening—a somatic preference that would be inconceivable in an environment devoid of any racial prejudice.

The crucial difference between North American and Latin American prejudice is not, then, that one is racial and the other social but that the social definition of who are acceptable as whites is different in both areas, a difference in "social race," as Charles Wagley calls it.[40]

In this context it is worth noting that logically the black militants in the United States have adopted their society's definition of whiteness, with (in marginal and therefore doubtful cases) its heavy emphasis on genealogy rather than on physical appearance. The pride with which one of their adepts may state that Mozart or some other celebrity was really black is hard to understand by a

[38] Hubert Herring, *A History of Latin America* (New York: Alfred A. Knopf, 1960), p. 62, cited in Seda Bonilla, "Dos Modelos."

[39] Robert P. Stuckert, "Race Mixture: The African Ancestry of White Americans," in *Physical Anthropology and Archeology,* ed. Peter B. Hammond (New York: Macmillan, 1964), pp. 192–197; John H. Burma, "The Measurement of Negro Passing," *American Journal of Sociology* (1952), cited in Seda Bonilla, "Dos Modelos."

[40] Charles Wagley, *The Latin American Tradition* (New York: Columbia University Press, 1968), pp. 155 ff.

Latin American of any socioracial group, who only needs one practiced look at the man's portrait to deny the validity of such a statement within the context of his society's perceptions.

INTERNAL COLONIALISM

In turning to Indo-Latin America, it is surprising to see the number of parallels with the Latin Afro-American situation in spite of some obvious differences between the areas.

The most commonly observed difference is that in several Indo-American countries distinct indigenous communities exist with a social structure and culture sharply deviant from those considered to be the national norms. The Indian problem, as far as these isolated communities are concerned, is commonly analyzed in terms of lack of economic and cultural integration, and the solutions are couched in similar terms; the culturally desirable solution has vacillated in the course of time among three available options: westernization, cultural blending (*"mestizaje cultural"* or "ladinization"), and modernization-cum-retention of the autochthonous cultural character. This terminology can also be found in other parts of the world where autochthonous population groups, who in an earlier period would have been characterized as "primitive" (even though their pre-Conquest past may have been culturally glorious), suffered through colonization the ordeals of decimation and subordination.

In this respect the term internal colonialism, now frequently used in both Americas (vis-à-vis Negroes in North America and Indians in South and Central America and Mexico) in certain academic circles, is appropriate. It is appropriate in Indo-America because a subordinate autochthonous and culturally distinct population group exists; it is appropriate in North America since the black minority's principal characteristics are described in terms of racial and even cultural differences as well as economic ones. For, one of the unavoidable implications of the concept of colonialism is the recognition of the multicultural and/or multiracial character of the society to which the concept is being applied. The term is not used in cases of economic exploitation and subordination within culturally or racially homogeneous societies.[41] In this sense, the term internal colonialism is first a recognition (unintentional by most of its users) of the existence of racial and/or cultural diversity and its sociological relevance.

The term internal colonialism in regard to Indo-America is further used in some publications to emphasize either that the present isolation and lack of integration of indigenous communities in reality do not exist or that alternatively it is a product of a withdrawal process, caused by the exploitation of the colonial conquerors and their successors.

Those who deny the isolation point to the economic network, the markets and commercial relations, through which the Indian communities participate in regional and ultimately national economies, whereby the ladinos or mestizos generally function as urban or semiurban commercial brokers. The degree to which this is the case may vary from region to region and from country to country, but in general terms André Gunder Frank's opinion is acceptable: "The 'Indian problem' does not lie in any *lack* of cultural or economic integration of the Indian in society. His problem . . . lies rather in his very exploitative metropolis-satellite integration into the structure and development of the capitalist system. . . ."[42] Of course, with regard to the Indian communities, it is necessary to interpret Frank's use of the term cultural in its sociological sense, i.e., socially determined role behavior, and not in the anthropological sense, i.e., related to language, religion, customs, and so forth. In this latter sense, there is of course very little cultural integration in countries such as Bolivia, Ecuador, and Peru.

[41] See also Pablo Gonzáles Casanova, "Internal Colonialism and National Development," *Studies in Comparatve International Development* 1, no. 4 (1965):27–37.

[42] André Gunder Frank, *Capitalism and Underdevelopment in Latin America: Historical Studies of Chile and Brazil* (New York: Monthly Review Press, 1967), p. 142. The methodological shortcomings of Frank's main thesis have been put forward convincingly by Richard M. Morse, "Primacy, Regionalization, Dependency: Approaches to Latin American Cities in National Development" (paper presented at the III Jornadas de Historia Social y Económica, Buenos Aires, 1970).

It is here that the semantic misunderstanding in which Frank and his followers are enveloped emerges. They correctly emphasize the economic bonds among the different population groups and regions but at the same time incorrectly imply that such bonds deny the validity of the concept of the dual economy.[43] They then proceed to draw unwarranted conclusions from this with regard to the degree of cultural integration. For it is entirely possible to envisage a society in which one population economically dominates another, while nevertheless there exist considerable differences in cultural heritage between both groups.

The isolation in the cultural-anthropological sense of the Indian communities and hence their lack of integration in the national sociocultural framework need not at all be incompatible with their integration in regional or even national economic networks. Yet, it is entirely correct to complain, as do Frank and others, that many cultural and social anthropologists have neglected these economic, mainly exploitative, networks, absorbed as they were in the study of the exotic aspects of the autochthonous community; such complaints are loud echoes from similar and earlier criticisms in other colonial and ex-colonial areas, where also in the last decade or two a greater anthropological and sociological attention for the larger social units is trying to correct the earlier community biased approaches.

In comparing Spanish Indo-America's Indian communities, on the one hand (which differ culturally among themselves and from the norms of national culture), with Indian population groups, on the other (which have broken with their communal origins and have adopted the national cultural traits in terms of language, clothing, religion, and so on, or are in the process of doing so), it would be little more than a tautology to state that the transition from communal Indian to acculturated noncommunal Indian—under whatever names the latter may be known—is a matter of cultural rather than racial factors; racially, no change is involved; any

---

[43] The originator of this concept, Furnivall, believed that it was economic interdependence that kept a plural society together. See J. S. Furnivall, *Tropical Economy* (Cambridge: Cambridge University Press, 1945), p. 2. See also Frank, *Capitalism and Underdevelopment,* pp. 221 ff.

difference in status between the two Indian sectors, as perceived by any of them, is by definition culturally determined.

Such a cultural transition is, of course, not unique in the Americas; for example, in the cases of the Maroon communities in Jamaica, the Bushland Creoles in Surinam, and the Haitian rural dweller there exists a cultural-anthropological isolation, or a cultural involution, as the result of efforts to evade slavery and colonial exploitation (Jamaica, Surinam) or drastic economic change and deterioration after colonial exploitation had come to a violent end (Haiti). The migration of a Surinamese Bush Negro to the capital city of Paramaribo is comparable with the transition of a communal Indian to a noncommunal situation; in both cases the process is confined to the same socioracial stratum because there are no socially relevant somatic differences between the lowest urban strata and the rural immigrant; it is merely a matter of adaptation to different patterns of life and thought, to different modes of dress, language, and so forth. Of course, this does not mean to say that such a cultural adaptation is a simple process nor that its successful completion automatically entails social acceptance. Where the small scale of the community allows the persistence of social bias on the basis of genealogy, and where stereotypes about *indios* (or Maroons) are unfavorable, a social barrier may hinder complete acceptance during more than one generation.

However important for Indo-America the problem may be of the cultural differences between communal Indians—those who in their daily behavior demonstrate their membership in an autochthonous culture and structure—and national cultural norms and social organization, the racial components in intergroup relations can better be analyzed in situations where cultural homogenization has proceeded farthest, so that the racial variable can be isolated with more success. Much of the modern literature, however, is not very helpful in our task of evaluation of the racial variable. This is partly caused by what Seda Bonilla viewed as a tendency to deny the existence of a racial problem in Indo-American countries, where the upper stratum is supposed to be not purely white. Furthermore, among several researchers there exists a clear preference for analyzing the intergroup relations exclusively in socioeconomic terms and to concede the existence of a socioracial structure only in a hesitant and ambiguous manner or to dispel it immediately as an anachronism or anomaly.

The article "Classes, Colonialism and Acculturation: A System of Inter-Ethnic Relations in Meso-America" by the Mexican sociologist Rodolfo Stavenhagen,[44] while in many respects admirable, is an excellent specimen of this type of analysis, and should be critically examined. In this article about the Maya region of Altos de Chiapas in Mexico and Guatemala, Stavenhagen first discusses the relevant differences between Indians and ladinos. On the somatic differences between both groups he writes:

It is well known that biological factors do not account for the differences between the two populations; we are not dealing with two races in the genetic sense of the term. It is true, of course, that in a general way the so-called Indian population has biological traits corresponding to the Amerinds and equally, that the so-called ladino population has the biological traits of the Caucasoids. But even though ladinos tend to identify with whites, in fact they are generally mestizo. It is the social and cultural factors that distinguish one population from the other.[45]

It would seem that here Stavenhagen has adopted the North American preoccupation with racial purity. He dismisses the social relevance of biological factors, because, naturally, there are not "two races in the genetic sense" and because the ladinos in spite of their "Caucasoid traits" have sufficient Indian admixture to be "really" and "biologically" mestizos. Stavenhagen does not accept the fact that, in spite of these racial impurities, somatic differences among social groups may have a strong impact on structure and mobility.

Stavenhagen consequently has to reject Alfonso Caso's description of an Indian community as one in which "there exists a predominance of non-European somatic elements, where language is preferentially Indian, possessing within its material and spiritual

---

[44] In Irving L. Horowitz, ed., *Masses in Latin America* (New York: Oxford University Press, 1970), pp. 235–289.

[45] Ibid., p. 237.

culture a strong proportion of Indian elements and finally, having a social feeling of being an isolated community within surrounding ones, distinguishing it from white and mestizo villages"[46] because in Stavenhagen's opinion Caso introduces "racial considerations," and because in this definition the elements needed for a study of the relations between Indian and ladino are lacking. But it is impossible to refrain from observing that both groups first have to be defined socially and culturally in much the same way as Caso is trying to do in order to study these relations.

Stavenhagen rejects this common procedure and rather abruptly declares that "the importance attributed by ethnologists to cultural elements of Indian populations has long concealed the nature of socioeconomic structures into which these populations are integrated."[47] This thesis is in itself correct but creates impressive difficulties for Stavenhagen, who, in the course of his essay, tries to dissect the economic relations between two groups without having accepted any sociocultural description of each of these. If ladinos were always employers and Indians always laborers, both groups could be conceived as classes in a homogeneous society and could be defined exclusively in economic terms. Now we find statements such as: "In Jilotepeque (Guatemala), laborers constitute 90% of the active population, of which only 9% are *ladinos*"; "in Guatemala's coffee plantations compulsory labor for Indians existed until recently; . . . yet no *ladino,* even those possessing no land, was forced to perform this kind of work";[48] and "in Jilotepeque, a *ladino* laborer earns 50% more than an Indian laborer,"[49] and "the *ladino* owners generally possess more lands than the Indian owners."[50] All these statements make clear that within the economic categories of laborers, landless rural proletariat, and landowners

[46] Alfonso Caso, "Definición del Indio y de lo Indio," *América Indígena* 8, no. 5 (1948), cited in Stavenhagen, "Classes, Colonialism and Acculturation: A System of Inter-Ethnic Relations in Meso-America," in *Masses in Latin America,* ed. Horowitz.

[47] See Stavenhagen, "Classes, Colonialism and Acculturation," p. 238.

[48] Ibid., p. 243.

[49] Ibid., p. 244.

[50] Ibid, p. 252.

other observable distinctions exist between Indians and ladinos, which make it impossible to analyze their relations merely in terms of economic and class relationships.

This is not to deny that *grosso modo* there exists a dominant-subordinate relationship between the two groups, which may amount to exploitation of the Indians in the economic sphere of life. But because the economic dividing lines partly coincide with other differences of a cultural and somatic nature, intergroup relations and their mechanisms are complicated in a fashion completely absent in the ideal-typical Western homogeneous society, which unfortunately keeps producing the conceptual framework for the sociological analysis of completely different types of society.

It is to Stavenhagen's merit that after dealing with the land and "social relations" between Indians and ladinos (though without defining these groups) and analyzing these relations in economic terms he proceeds to pay attention to a "social stratification" apparently distinct from these social relations. He thus cautiously acknowledges the existence of not only a socioeconomic but also of a sociocultural and a socioracial structure.

He now observes that "Indians and ladinos represent two different cultural communities," each with its own value system. "To the extent to which the value systems of these two communities are different, so too their systems of stratification shall likewise be different. It is thus easy to distinguish social stratification in each of them."[51]

But such an analysis of a social stratification based on a cultural value system is in Stavenhagen's opinion only "valid when the analysis of social class is set aside"; the "culturalistic perspective," unlike the analysis in socioeconomic terms, does not in his opinion part from "the existence of the whole society, of a single socioeconomic structure in which these two groups perform differentiated roles, and which might be called the structuralist perspective."[52] It is this line of thought that enables the author to keep intact the primacy of the economic factor in the analysis of social structure

[51] Ibid., p. 257.
[52] Ibid., p. 256.

and to relegate the sociocultural variables to the subjective area of the value systems of both groups, limiting their analytical usefulness to other aspects of intergroup relations outside the scope of the "analysis of social classes." But, in spite of all this, Stavenhagen's description of interethnic stratification clearly shows that, in fact, the value system of the dominant group, as far as the relations between the groups are concerned, has been imposed upon and accepted to some extent by the subordinated group. In other words, while the internal stratification system of each group may indeed be related to their respective set of cultural values, the criteria that determine each group's relative rank in the total social system (i.e., the socioracial structure seen from a structuralist perspective) emanate from the dominant group: "Ladinos hold a higher position not only in the objective scale of socio-economic characteristics, but they also consider themselves, qua ladinos, superior to the Indians. They are contemptuous of the Indians as such. The latter . . . know that those traits which identify them as Indians place them in a position of inferiority with respect to the Ladinos." In fact, Stavenhagen goes on to write, the social system consists of only two strata characterized by distinct biological and cultural traits. Ladinos "make use of physical stereotypes to affirm their 'whiteness' in contrast to the darker Indians."

The ladinos may really be mestizos, yet "one of the most valued criteria among the higher ladino strata is that of their supposed 'Spanish blood.' " Colby and Van den Berghe observed that in the community they studied there existed a coincidence between the socioeconomic stratification and the biological continuum.[53]

From these and other data, furnished by Stavenhagen, it becomes clear that in social reality, as perceived by ladinos and Indians themselves, the economic differences are less weighty than the sociocultural and the somatic ones. The attributes of power are of a noneconomic nature; in order to gain economic power, its noneconomic attributes have to be acquired. Surely, in an environ-

[53] Ibid., pp. 262–263; see B. Colby and P. Van den Berghe, "Ethnic Relations in Southeastern Mexico," *American Anthropologist* 53, no. 4 (1961).

ment where a total reversal of the group positions is not easily envisaged, this is a most logical perception.

Thus, here also there is the prevalence of the socioracial/cultural structure (i.e., the image of stratification and its criteria, such as it is perceived by the component groups in a multiracial and/or multicultural society) over the socioeconomic structure (i.e., the stratification such as it can be constructed on the basis of economic indices). The greater objectivity of the latter stratification model is powerless against the greater subjective reality of the former, however irrational its indices may be.

Since the two stratifications do not perfectly coincide, in cases of inconsistency the position of an individual in the socioracial structure prevails over that in the socioeconomic one. As Stavenhagen observes: "a Ladino will always be a Ladino, low as he may fall in the socioeconomic scale."[54] The parallel is obvious with the poor whites in the U.S. South or with the coloreds in the Afro-American societies outside the United States. They will retain a higher position than a Negro in the socioracial (i.e., the prevailing) structure, however low they may fall in the socioeconomic scale.

But just as the racial dividing line between Negroes and coloreds in the Afro-American societies outside the United States is diffuse and fluid, so too is the demarcation line between ladinos and indios: "At the lowest level of the Ladino ethnic group, it is difficult to distinguish clearly a Ladino from an Indian."[55] Indians may therefore be absorbed into the lowest strata of the ladino group, provided they have acquired certain economic and cultural traits and preferably after they have moved away from their place of origin.

However, it is not possible to conclude from the existing literature that a prosperous, Spanish speaking individual with pure Indian somatic traits will easily be accommodated within the higher layers of the ladino group. As Pitt-Rivers observes:

[54] Stavenhagen, "Classes, Colonialism and Acculturation," p. 265.
[55] Ibid., p. 261.

"National unity demands that to be truly Mexican [the Mexicans] must have some Indian blood, but social aspirations require that they should not have too much."[56]

What makes the parallel with specifically the Spanish and Portuguese speaking Afro-American societies remarkable is the following: If Wagley's judgment is accepted, there is also in Indo-America a somatic continuum between the groups at the extremes of the socioracial structure. "There is an almost imperceptible gradation of physical appearance from Amerindian to Caucasoid running from the Indians to the whites." In terms not unlike those used for the Spanish Caribbean, Wagley states: "In Mexico inter-marriage between Indian and mestizo, mestizo and white, or Indian and white generally adds to the mestizo group. The off-spring of these unions are usually raised within the mestizo group and thus become mestizos. And this system promotes continued racial intermixture."[57] This is a process, then, of biological and cultural homogenization from which the whites, unlike those in the Northwest European variant of the Caribbean and the United States, do not exclude themselves.[58] A rough indication of this phenomenon can be found in the Mexican marriage statistics from 1930 to 1940 according to which approximately one-fourth of the white men married mestizo women.[59]

As for the differences between the socioracial situations of Indo- and Spanish Afro-America, Pérez Cabral puts forward the axio-matic conclusion that the somatic distance between Indians and Spanish whites is less than that between the latter and Negroes,[60] so that resistance against biological mixing on the basis of mutual

56 Julian Pitt-Rivers, "Race, Color, and Class in Central America and the Andes," in *Color and Race,* ed. Franklin, p. 269.

57 Wagley, *Latin American Tradition,* pp. 166, 168.

58 Wagley actually states that in all Caribbean societies there is a socioracial continuum between Caucasoid and Negroid. I do not agree: In the British, French, and Dutch areas the dividing line between whites and coloreds is much more strictly drawn and, hence, less equivocal than in the Spanish- and Portuguese-speaking areas. See also p. 100 ff.

59 Moisés González Navarro, "Mestizaje in Mexico During the National Period," in *Race and Class,* ed. Magnus Mörner, pp. 150–151.

60 Pérez Cabral, *La Comunidad Mulata,* p. 74.

social acceptance, as far as somatic-aesthetic factors are involved, would supposedly be less between white and Indian and mestizo than between white and Negro and, possibly, mulatto. Such inter-mixture is hindered, however, by the fact that Indo-America, of all multiracial societies in the Western Hemisphere, shows a maximum cultural heterogeneity, while Spanish Afro-America has achieved a high degree of cultural homogeneity and continuity. Some authors are inclined to believe that once the cultural barriers between ladinos and Indians will have shrunken to lesser proportions, Indo-America will show the characteristics of a homogeneous class society. The present social importance attached to somatic traits hardly seems to warrant such a point of view. Richard Adams observed that in a community with small cultural differences between Indians and ladinos the latter group actually was inclined to ascribe increased social significance to the somatic differences between the two groups.[61] Conversely, as long as and insofar as the Indian is being characterized in such striking fashion by his autochthonous culture and structure, there is little social need for the ladino to emphasize the somatic differences between the two groups.

Hence, also the easiness with which in some regions, especially in Peru, the term "white Indians" can be used. The cultural traits clearly prevail in those rare cases where there are phenotypically white Amerindians. But again, where the cultural differences are slight, as in Adams's community, or are in the process of becoming slight, as in the rapidly homogenizing environment of the large city, there somatic traits acquire ever more the function of *ad hoc* indicators of social status, complying with the dictates of the subjective socioracial structure. "The serious thing about racism in Chile," writes Mörner, "is that it seems to have influenced the social attitudes of the middle strata toward the lower-class *rotos,* whose skin is often a shade darker."[62]

---

[61] Richard N. Adams, *Encuesta sobre la Cultura de los Ladinos en Guatemala* (Guatemala: Editorial del Ministero de Educación Pública, 1956).

[62] Magnus Mörner, ed., *Race Mixture in the History of Latin America* (Boston: Little, Brown & Co., 1967), p. 141.

There is much to be said, therefore, for Julian Pitt-Rivers's opinion that "in the open society, appearance takes over the function of descent in allocating social status. In a world in flux, the fact that appearance cannot be dissimulated, recommends it above all other indicators. Clothing, speech, and culture are losing force as indicators of status in the context of expanding cities, but color is becoming ever more crucial."[63] This certainly seems valid for the large Indo-American cities where, through massive immigration of Indians and their absorption into the lower strata, on the one hand, and the influx of considerable numbers of Europeans in recent decades, who assimilate into the upper social strata, on the other, the "correlation between class and color is increasing rather than diminishing." Such an increasing polarization can also be observed in urban Afro-America, and may certainly slow down the process of biological homogenization in the Spanish and Portuguese speaking areas. The development of "new class structures, devoid of their ethnic content" seems therefore rather more remote than Stavenhagen believes it to be.[64] To be sure, it is not primarily the white upper classes but, rather, the lower ladino (mestizo) strata who view the growth of an urban, mobile, rapidly acculturating Indian lower segment as a social menace.

In Peru this phenomenon has recently been clearly described by Julio Cotler. Literacy and knowledge of Spanish enable these Indians, the *Cholos,* to move out from under the traditional mestizo patronage and to engage in occupations hitherto unaccessible to them, such as truckdriving, door-to-door sales, construction, and the like.

The Cholo is characterized by an incompatible status: due to his social origins and to the low prestige of his occupation, he resembles the Indian; yet in terms of his income and the occupational independence he enjoys with regard to the mestizo, he does not fit into these ethnic-social groups. His reference group is ambiguous for he maintains Indian cultural traits while adopting some of the mestizo's, impregnating them with an elusive element. . . . The Cholo adopts an aggressive and

[63] Pitt-Rivers, "Race, Color and Class," pp. 278–279.
[64] Stavenhagen, "Classes, Colonialism and Acculturation," p. 282.

mobile behavior which differentiates him from the polite mestizo and from the servile and apathetic Indian.[65]

In the Peruvian Department of Puno, this group recently developed political initiatives and obtained successes, which underline the emancipatory potential of this segment and seem to provide the Indian peasant mass with a future leadership; the social consequences of such a train of events could be far-reaching.

Although a few sectors of the lower-mestizo class appear to welcome the *Cholos'* mounting political prestige, others plus the somewhat higher situated provincial mestizos, small and medium-sized landowners, perceive it as a clear threat, which explains in part their increasing migration to the urban centers of the coastal area.[66] Thus, what Stavenhagen indicated for Mexico seems also valid for Peru: a clear concern among the ladinos (mestizos), especially their lower strata, to maintain the bases of ethnic stratification in order to prevent direct competition with the mobile noncommunal, partly acculturated Indians, a phenomenon in which there are some parallels with the poor whites' attitudes in the South of the United States.[67] It is the outcome of processes such as this so-called cholification that will contain the clue to the question whether and to what degree somatic considerations will also influence and complicate social stratification in the Indo-America of the future.

Assuming that such considerations will continue to exert their influence—possibly even in a somewhat stronger fashion than today—the Indo-American societies would be moving toward a type that would be fully comparable to Spanish and Portuguese Afro-America, as far as somatic continuity and the tendency

[65] Julio Cotler, "Internal Domination and Social Change in Peru," in *Masses in Latin America*, ed. Horowitz, pp. 436–437.

[66] Ibid., pp. 437–438.

[67] Stavenhagen, "Classes, Colonialism and Acculturation," p. 282. For a part of Bolivia many of the points raised here are discussed by Madeline Barbara Leóns, "Stratification and Pluralism in the Bolivian *Yungas*," in *The Social Anthropology of Latin America*, eds. Walter Goldschmidt and Harry Hoijer (Los Angeles: University of California Press, 1970), pp. 256–282.

toward biological and cultural homogenization are concerned. The parallels would be especially striking with those Latin American countries, such as Brazil and the Dominican Republic, where the overwhelming majority of the population belongs to one of the numerous gradations within the mixed intermediary groups. The *"mestizaje"* of Indo-America thus finds its counterpart in the *"mulatización"* of which Pérez Cabral writes.

Bogus Differences between Indians and Negroes

There is, however, a frequently mentioned difference between Indo- and Afro-America—the Indians are living in a country that once was exclusively their own while the New World Negroes supposedly do not possess the Indians' psychological attachment to and cultural roots in the areas to which they were moved only a few centuries ago. This difference, it is assumed, leads to a greater collective pride, a stronger self-assertion, and a more forceful tendency toward rejection of the whites by the Indian than by the Negro.[68]

Pitt-Rivers comes close to this point of view when he writes that the Indian, "far from wishing to be integrated into [the social system with the Hispanic population] desires only to be rid of the mestizos physically. For this reason, the aims of Indian rebellions are the opposite of the aims of [Negro] race riots. The former would like to separate once and for all the two ethnic elements; the latter are inspired by the resentment at the existence of a separation. Indians rebel to drive the intruders out of the countryside; Negroes riot in towns when they are not accorded full civic privileges."[69]

It seems that these lines of thought are not acceptable. In order to refute them, it is not necessary to point either to the recent separatist currents among the militant blacks in the United States or to the Black Power developments in parts of the Caribbean. It suffices to think of Haitian history, which gives us a prime example

[68] Pérez Cabral, *La Comunidad Mulata,* p. 74.
[69] Pitt-Rivers, "Race, Color, and Class," p. 276.

of a successful physical elimination of the white, colonial element and which qua goals and scenario was not too different at all from the "War of the Castes" in Yucatán during the mid-nineteenth century.

Moreover, not only historical facts but also psychological probabilities negate the alleged differences between Indians and Negroes. Until very recently the great masses of the Negroid Caribbean populations had hardly any clear ideas about their African heritage, and certainly there did not exist, nor does there exist now, any collective feeling of really being culturally displaced persons. Such knowledge and such psychological reactions are limited to a small number of intellectuals. To extend and extrapolate this so as to include the Negroes as opposed to the Indians is nothing more than a futile exercise in intellectual *Hineininterpretieren,* imposing historical interpretations upon an unaware population. For psychological and logical reasons, the Negroes by and large consider their present habitat as their cultural and psychological father- and motherland; a growing awareness of a historical relationship and even solidarity with Black Africa is not, as yet, contradictory or incompatible with this fact. Among the mulatto intelligentsia of the Dominican Republic in the nineteenth century, the opinion could be heard that climatological laws were producing within this mixed group new physical traits similar to those of the Indian aborigines, a clear effort to legitimize themselves as the real inhabitants of the country.[70]

Again, the need for such a legitimation was felt only by the cultured intelligentsia and not by the large masses, just as, conversely, the glories of the Inca or Aztec past will not be known to many contemporary *indios* unless it is the result of recent cultural campaigns conducted by the national elite. While it is true that the collective feelings of the Negroes' dignity have been corroded by their much-remembered slavery past, by their present generally low status, and—but this applies also and, perhaps, a fortiori to the colored and white groups outside the United States—by their

[70] Hoetink, "The Dominican Republic," pp. 117–118.

recent colonial past, as well as by the continuing international economic dependence of their countries, such humiliating feelings are shared by the Indians and by Indo-America generally.

Just as, on the one hand, slavery is perceived too much as a unique Negro experience, so that the essential similarity between all forms of unfree labor in the Western Hemisphere is overlooked, thus, on the other, the objective differences in historical experience between Indians and Negroes are emphasized, to the neglect of the similarities in their subjective perception of historical reality.

4
CULTURE, RACE, AND NATIONAL IDENTITY

INDIGENISMO VERSUS AFRICANISM

Indigenismo as a cultural phenomenon finds its parallel in Africanism. While the similarities in socioracial structure between Spanish Indo-America and Spanish and Portuguese Afro-America have been so far stressed, it now is time to observe that the origins and widest growth of Africanism must not be looked for in Iberian Afro-America. Comparatively speaking, this latter area is culturally fairly homogeneous. This, together with its socioracial continuum, has created an environment hardly propitious for movements directed toward Negroid cultural identity. The "Negroid" poems of a Guillén in Cuba or a Palés Matos in Puerto Rico were not much more than individual expressions of socially inspired emotions there, of exotic interests here. (The much earlier romantic sensual descriptions, in prose or poetry, of the attractions of black or colored beauties have nothing to do with *Négritude* [even though Frantz Fanon, in 1939, still thought they had] and have to be judged in a completely different social framework.) Nor did cultural *Négritude* movements originate in societies where the socioracial structure distinguishes three groupings—whites, coloreds, Negroes—and where the dividing line between the first two is rigid, as in the colonial British, Dutch, and French Caribbean areas. The colored elite in these countries was (and often still is) tied to its white and metropolitan groups of reference; a spontaneous reevaluation of the Negro or African part of its cultural

Adapted from "Culture, Race, and National Identity," in *Racial Tensions and National Identity,* ed. John Q. Campbell (Nashville: Vanderbilt University Press, 1972). I should like to express my gratitude to Sydney W. Mintz, Yale University, for his useful comments.

heritage, although sporadically occurring in individual and isolated cases, could therefore hardly acquire the characteristics of an innovative movement.

For good reason, the historical origins of Africanism as a cultural movement are to be found in Haiti. This country, formally independent since the beginning of the nineteenth century, had a socioracial structure comparable with the Indo-American *Indio-ladino* dichotomy, and in which *grosso modo* the lowest rank was occupied by Negroes, the highest by mulattoes. This meant that the somatic line of division between the two groups could not be rigid; there existed a socioracial continuum. The caste-like structure of which Leyburn writes in *The Haitian People*[1] found its legitimation not only in somatic preoccupations but also in a drastic cultural separation: the mulatto bourgeoisie, French oriented in life style, family organization, religion, and language; the black masses, Afro-Haitian in culture and organization. Hence, these parallels with Indo-America. Sovereignty, racial continuum, and cultural and social separation produced the conditions under which an intellectual avant-garde could convince itself that cultural and physical identification with white Europe responded to neither their own nor the national situation.

After the late nineteenth-century works of Anténor Firmin and Hannibal Price, who rejected the then fashionable notions of black racial inferiority, Jean Price-Mars definitively affirmed and consolidated the Africa-oriented trend.[2] Coulthard comments on the great similarities between Price-Mars's work and that of the post-revolutionary Mexican *Indigenista* writers:

The same ground is covered as in Gamio's *Forjando Patria:* rejection of racial inferiority, acceptance of a native cultural past, and a suggestion that it should be incorporated into the mainstream of Haitian

[1] J. G. Leyburn, *The Haitian People* (New Haven, Conn.: Yale University Press, 1966).

[2] See Firmin, Anténor, *De l'Egalité des Races Humaines* (Paris, 1885); and Hannibal Price, *De la Réhabilitation de la Race Noire, par la République d'Haiti* (Port-au-Prince, 1900); David G. Nicholls, "Biology and Politics in Haiti," *Race* 13 (July 1971–April 1972):203–214.

culture, an interpretation of Haitian religion, but not in comparison to Christianity, . . . an encouragement to writers and artists to look at the true (Afro-French) situation of Haiti; and finally, a criticism of the distortion of Haitian cultural life by the snobbish, prejudiced worship of European models.[3]

In French Martinique, on the one hand, there was to be found a wider and more intense communication with France and French Africa and, on the other, a colonial social structure in which the colored intellectual suffered from the social prejudices of the white dominant group instead of belonging to the dominant stratum as in Haiti. Here, in the context of a less African influenced folk culture than that of Haiti, Aimé Césaire and Frantz Fanon initiated at a somewhat later point a series of ideas that, though similar in intent and sentiment to those of the Haitian *Africanistes,* were more abstracted from the local situation and more consciously addressed to a metropolitan audience. They pronounced strong indictments against European colonialism and Western civilization, they analyzed colonial racism, and they proposed the mystical-racial idea of a general cultural *Négritude.*[4] In this fashion their intellectual movement acquired an international flavor that *Indigenismo* lacked: via Léopold Senghor, French Black Africa became part of it. In his later years, Frantz Fanon came to reject the concept of *Négritude* in which he saw the danger of cultural exhibitionism, and, focusing on the global consequences of Western colonialism, he broadened the basis of his potential followers by addressing himself to all *damnés de la terre,* whatever their color.

Not only is Fanon's life history—from psychiatrist in Martinique to participant in Algeria's struggle for independence—re-

---

[3] G. R. Coulthard, "Parallelisms and Divergencies between 'Négritude' and 'Indigenismo,'" *Caribbean Studies* 8, no. 1 (1968):31, 49, 57. (Several of the data are taken from this article, but the interpretation is my own); Manuel Gamio, *Forjando Patria* (Mexico, 1916).

[4] See respectively Aimé Césaire, "Discours sur le Colonialisme," *Présence Africaine* (1955); Frantz Fanon, *Peau Noire, Masques Blancs* (Paris: Editions du Seuil, 1953); and Aimé Césaire, "Cahier d'un Retour au Pays Natal," *Présence Africaine* (1947) (first published 1939).

flected in his works but also the two tendencies that commonly characterize every emancipatory movement: the emphasis on the cultural and psychic dignity of the group and the stress on the political and economic struggle that must lead to ultimate equality or even to a reversal of positions. Fanon's shift from the first to the second emphasis coincides roughly with the change in his personal role and position: from an (in his case, near-desperate) objectively analyzing observer and member of the upper-middle stratum in Martinique's socioracial structure to activist in a nonblack part of the third world, identifying himself completely with the role and position of his subject.[5]

It would seem that there exists some relation between the ideological (as distinguished from fashionable) preference for either the cultural or the political and economic aspects of emancipation and social position. It could be that the cultural aspects are generally somewhat more heavily emphasized by those whose socioeconomic position is relatively secure and who, as a group, are not bound to expect considerable advantages from radical structural changes; they generally belong neither culturally nor somatically to the group whose lot they describe and sympathize with. They invite comparison mutatis mutandis with the intellectual upper-stratum avant-garde of the European labor movement in the nineteenth and early twentieth centuries. Their solidarity with the emancipatory movement—however far-reaching in its consequences—is academic and romantic, and is supported by discontent, often highly personal, with their own immediate environment rather than by any social or cultural affinity with the milieu that receives their emotional preference. They are rarely able to bridge completely the distance between themselves and their subject. Into this roughly hewn category fall the early *Indigenismo* of members of the Mexican and Peruvian white and mestizo cultural elite and the *Africanisme* of the Haitian bourgeois

---

[5] Similar stages in the development of colonized intellectuals were described by Fanon himself in his essay "Sur la culture nationale," in *Les Damnés de la Terre* (Paris: Maspéro, 1961); see also P. ten Have, "Emancipation and Culture," *Mens en Maaischappij* (July–August 1970), pp. 246 ff.

mulatto.[6] This is the category, so to speak, of Frantz Fanon in his Martinique phase.

Those who feel more committed to the political and economic aspects of an emancipatory movement would seem to be socially more closely linked to the subordinated group; the intellectuals among them are sometimes marginal men, insofar as they or their families are concerned, precisely because their social origins prevented their acceptance as social equals in the higher (nonwhite) strata of society. The initially literary and subsequently political activities of the rural doctor François Duvalier in Haiti perhaps should be understood in this perspective: *"un Noir au pouvoir"* was the slogan of his friend Estimé in 1946. Also, the life history and actions, especially those in Jamaica, of Marcus Garvey fall into this category; in the depth of identification and subjectivism it reminds one of Fanon's Algerian phase.

There are at least two reasons why the political and economic emphasis on the Negro struggle was developed most strongly in the United States. First, in that country there exists no intermediate and socially separate category of coloreds to whom the social definition of Negro is not applicable (although within the Negro category there do exist differentiations based on both objective and somatic criteria), so that the intellectual of whatever nonwhite shade could feel an existential involvement with the Negro problem; no aristocratic distance comparable to that of his Mexican and Haitian counterparts separated him from his object. Further, given his categorization as a Negro, he did not entertain fears of radical change in the socioracial structure; and, finally, it was this unique, unambiguous social definition of the Negro group that made legal discrimination possible in the United States on a scale unknown elsewhere in the hemisphere and that presented a clear target for collective action.

In several Caribbean societies, on the other hand, the success of

---

[6] The early political thinking of the Peruvian politician Victor Raúl Haya de la Torre and his APRA party would fall into this category, as would the initial Mexican *Indigenista* experiments. See Magnus Mörner, ed., *Race Mixture in the History of Latin America* (Boston: Little, Brown & Co., 1967), p. 143.

political black movements in societies where the whites only form a small minority has not been as great as one would expect. The main reason seems to be that the colored groups (as opposed to the Negroes) are not eager to change their perception of the socioracial structure in which they traditionally have occupied an intemediate position, into one constructed along U.S. lines. The pamphlet literature in Curaçao in the wake of the riots of 1969 bears clear testimony to this reluctance, which can also be observed in Jamaica. The same phenomenon goes far to explain why in the latter island black activism has for a long period manifested itself in the escapist, messianic Ras Tafari movement.[7]

Comparatively speaking, a social rapprochement between coloreds and blacks is most probable in those Caribbean societies, such as Trinidad, Guiana, and Surinam, where roughly half of the population consists of descendants of indentured East Indian workers. The presence of such a large segment that is culturally, somatically, and in social organization different from the old Creole population seems at least to have mitigated somewhat the latter's formerly incisive color and class differentiation. This incipient solidarity, based on common (Euro-)African descent and culture, perhaps is being challenged by still newer alignments; in 1970, the black militants in Trinidad tried to involve the East Indian sugar workers in their protests against a third, common, and external adversary: the foreign based corporation. In this way the revolt, though it originated and became known as a black uprising against the "phony Afro-Saxon alliance" in government and economy, tried to include all *damnés de la terre* in Trinidad; the future success of these efforts seems doubtful.[8]

Although in the non-Hispanic Caribbean the cultural differences between the white and colored elites, on the one hand, and the

---

[7] See David Lowenthal, "Race and Color in the West Indies," in *Color and Race,* ed. John Hope Franklin (Boston: Houghton Mifflin, 1968), pp. 302–349 and 317. On the Ras Tafarians generally, see Leonard E. Barrett, *The Rastafarians: A Study in Messianic Cultism in Jamaica* (Río Piedras: Institute of Caribbean Studies, 1969).

[8] See David G. Nicholls, "East Indians and Black Power in Trinidad," *Race* 12 (July 1970–April 1971): 443–459.

mass of the population, on the other, are generally more pro-nounced than in the Hispanic Caribbean countries—we need only mention here the existing linguistic and religious differences—these are not as easily reducible to a cultural dichotomy of "Euro-pean" versus "African" as would appear to be the case in Haiti. The chances for a purely cultural Africanism in its anthropological sense are smaller, and, as was suggested already with regard to Martinique, the cultural notions of the black movement tend to be expressed in the less concrete, more mystical terms of *Négritude.*

Of course, this is a fortiori the case in the United States where, comparatively speaking, the cultural-anthropological heritage of African origin, insofar as it is characteristic of only the Negro population, is small and diffuse. In fact, the remarkable lack of cultural-anthropological diversity along white-black lines in the United States can only be compared to some Hispanic Caribbean societies. Yet, the latter have no black movements to speak of, while the United States has. This suggests that by itself the lack of pronounced cultural diversity along racial lines is no impediment to the development of a black emancipatory movement, provided that (as in the United States or, for that matter, in the non-His-panic Caribbean) the socioracial structure is discontinuous instead of (as in the Hispanic Caribbean) continuous. The cases of Haiti and Mexico would seem to show that a socioracial continuum can produce a pro-black (or pro-indigenous) movement, provided that cultural differences between the upper and lower socioracial strata are very marked.

The definition of Afro-American culture, of course, cannot be limited to elements of distinctly African origin confined to the Negro population.[9] At least two other "cultures" of the Negro group have to be taken into consideration. One is the culture, in a sociological sense, as the product of a long period of low status, be

[9] See also Sidney W. Mintz, "Foreword," in N. Whitten and J. Szwed, eds., *Afro-American Anthropology: Contemporary Perspectives* (New York: Free Press, 1970); and Sidney W. Mintz, "Summary and Commentary," in Armstead L. Robinson, Craig C. Foster and Donald H. Ogilvie, eds., *Black Studies in the University* (New Haven, Conn.: Yale University Press, 1969), pp. 202 ff.

it in slavery or in ghettoes. The other might be called the emancipatory culture, the creation of which serves the function of increasing the recognizability and solidarity among the militant minority of the Negro group: Certain hair styles, clothing, and language forms perform these symbolic and communicative functions, which no emancipatory movement can do without. Such a movement further needs, as part of its cultural apparatus, its own interpretation of history, its own heroes and martyrs, and its own social art to further foster internal cohesion, to convert the brothers outside the movement, and to undermine the self-assertiveness of the dominant adversary. The parallels with other historical emancipation movements are obvious. Yet, in spite of these parallels, it may be useful to take a closer look at the term emancipatory movement, which has been used rather loosely so far, and to determine whether the black movement, especially in the United States, can be said to be really of an emancipatory character.

Emancipation, it seems to me, aspires to a change in the position and roles of the members of a minority; the change of the social system as a whole is an unavoidable concomitant or consequence of such an emancipation. The point to be made here is that emancipation is directed toward, and stands for successful inclusion; once the goals have been reached, the movement loses its *raison d'être*. The rituals, group language, uniforms or "Schillershirts," hair styles, and fanatical poems of the socialist movement of the 1920s and 1930s were abandoned after the successful conclusion of the struggle, which made most West European workers bourgeois.

EMANCIPATION AND POLARIZATION:
THE PARSONS THESIS

Is such a course of events to be expected with regard to the black movement in the United States? Talcott Parsons thinks it is. In "The Problem of Polarization on the Axis of Color" he defends the interesting thesis that "the race relations problem has a better prospect of resolution in the United States than in Brazil, partly because the line between white and Negro has been so rigidly drawn in the United States because the system has been sharply polarized," for "sharp polarization seems in the longer run to be more favorable to effective inclusion than is a complex grading of the differences between components, perhaps particularly where gradations are arranged on a superiority-inferiority hierarchy."[10]

This bold and rather unexpected exercise in dialectics, whereby antithetical polarization leads to synthetical inclusion, is the result of Parsons's analysis of three important social movements in Western history: the Reformation, the Democratic Revolution, and socialism.

Paraphrasing, but hopefully not oversimplifying Parsons's argument: these three movements initially caused polarization, conflict, and antagonism, which in a later phase led to inclusion of the emancipating group in the total social system; this inclusion was accompanied by a differentiation or pluralization of social roles and functions, which in turn made the earlier polarization obsolete.

Parsons is so convinced of the parallel of these historical processes with the present race problem that he phrases his conclusion in the past tense and introduces the earlier processes as explanatory factors:

I have . . . suggested that the pattern established in the Caribbean and the southern states of the United States by predominantly Protestant English groups, though initially more severe than the "Latin" pattern to the South, was in the long run more favorable to the resolution of the color problem by means of inclusion and pluralization precisely *because* it imposed rigorous polarization, a man being *either* white or colored with no intermediate category. This inclination includes the fact that, since anyone with any "Negro blood" was classified as a Negro, the rigid categorization became increasingly anomalous and morally untenable with the growth of egalitarian ideas. For this to take effect at the level of social organization, however, it was necessary *both* for the cultural structure to change, in the direction taken by "liberal Protestantism" *and* for the social, political and economic structure to change in the direction of greater differentiation and inclusion. The change in Protestantism was thus the cultural prerequisite of the total change. The decline of aristocracy and its

10 In Franklin, *Color and Race*, p. 352.

replacement by political democracy and by pluralism in the system of occupation and stratification . . . constitute the social prerequisites.[11]

However, nowhere in the Caribbean, Protestant or otherwise, British or not, did or does there exist the rigorous socioracial dichotomy postulated by Parsons.[12] Whether and to what extent religion, the political system, and the economic structure influence the socioracial structure of a multiracial society, or other aspects of racial relations, cannot be discussed here.[13] But it should be noted that a unidirectional influence, such as suggested by Parsons, cannot be found in social reality.

By defining the Negro struggle as an emancipatory movement (without using this term, but enumerating the characteristics commonly ascribed to such movements in their first phase, such as polarization, antagonism, and conflict) Parsons suggests its ultimate success (inclusion) on the basis of the historical fact that other emancipation movements also have been successful.

History is, however, replete with efforts toward reformist or revolutionary emancipation that did not lead to inclusion and where the phase of polarization was succeeded by repression, elimination, or expulsion. Further, Parsons's implication that the three great and successful emancipation movements were mutually consistent, or may be perceived as mutually reinforcing evolutionary phases—which, in their turn, would make a fourth emancipatory struggle (the racial one) successful—is not easily acceptable, if only because the goals and intentions of the earlier movements in their pure forms were not that compatible; in some countries the results of political democracy (in the sense of the French Revolution) had to make place for those of the socialist emancipation, and

[11] Ibid., pp. 366–367.

[12] David Lowenthal's paper on the Caribbean, in the same book in which Parsons's chapter appears, makes this again very clear ("Race and Color," in *Color and Race,* ed. Franklin, pp. 302–348).

[13] See pp. 40 ff. of this book and H. Hoetink, *The Two Variants in Caribbean Race Relations: A Contribution to the Sociology of Segmented Societies,* trans. Eva M. Hooykaas (London: Oxford University Press, 1967), pp. 4 ff.

vice versa, an example, moreover, that demonstrates the temporary character of some conflict resolutions.

It is indeed correct to say that several modern societies have absorbed elements of the earlier emancipatory struggles in rather diluted form. But is it not true that this dilution, this willingness to compromise, was most obvious in those societies that did not themselves experience the acute polarization of the conflict? Reformation may have produced a type of liberal Protestantism, considered by Parsons to be beneficial to the United States, but the polarization that gave birth and growth to this religious type led to long and tragic wars between and within nations in Western Europe, the effects of which are still evident in some of its societies.

Similarly, the polarization in the struggle for political emancipation produced a bloody revolution in France; the unbloody compromises were introduced in the neighboring countries. Again, the laboring classes in Western Europe rapidly and peacefully profited from the willingness of the West European bourgeoisie to compromise, a willingness that was produced by the polarization *à outrance* in the Russia of 1917. Certainly, the final result was the inclusion of the social or religious minorities in most of these societies, both in those where the sharp polarization produced bloody conflicts and in those more peripheral ones where a more complex grading of the differences between components prevented violent convulsions from erupting but produced enough fear to reach a compromise. Parsons himself views Britain's failure to experience a French revolutionary polarization and the U.S. failure to experience a Communist revolutionary polarization so far as the favorable result of an attenuation of the polarization process in both English-speaking countries. But has not a similar attenuation of racial tensions progressed further in Brazil than in the United States, so that it can be said of the former country that a racial polarization "can no longer predominate in viable interpretations of the 'essential' interest of society?"[14] Such a conclusion would, however, be contradictory to Parsons's original thesis. The reason

---

[14] Talcott Parsons, "The Problem of Polarization on the Axis of Color," in *Color and Race,* ed. Franklin, p. 362.

for this is that, whereas Parsons correctly analyzes the attenuation of a religious polarization in (socio-)religious terms and of an economic polarization in economic structural terms, he does not concede that the attenuation of a polarized racial conflict has to be found primarily in a change (a pluralization) of the socioracial structure.

It is one thing to argue, as was done earlier, that because of its bipolar socioracial structure the political and economic black struggle developed most strongly in the United States, which means that the polarity of the structure was and is reflected in the polarization of the struggle. It is a different matter altogether to predict on the basis of such a polarization that the resolution will be favorable, i.e., leading to inclusion.

As Parsons acknowledges, "inclusion . . . presupposes some order of *common* value-commitment."[15] An escapist movement like the Ras Tafarians is not emancipatory; neither is Zionism. A struggle for civil rights against discrimination and for improvement of social conditions is emancipatory; a struggle for political independence or even autonomy is not. The desire for exclusion implies a self-perception so different from the dominant adversary that the goal cannot be equality with him, but only equivalence separate from him. In this context the terminology of internal colonialism is interesting because real anticolonial struggles are also aimed at self-determination, and colonial peoples commonly have a different self-perception from their colonizers, based on cultural and/or somatic factors. It seems clear that emancipatory and exclusionist elements are both present among black leaders in the United States, with the exclusionists gaining ground in recent years, which causes wonder whether increased polarization, at least in this case, does not diminish the chances for inclusion. The crucial element in all this, the self-perception of the struggling group and its closely connected vision of the future, brings us to another part of Parsons' argument that deserves special attention.

But first it is necessary to examine Edward Shils's three "pri-

[15] Ibid., p. 352.

mordial connection[s] with which human beings find it difficult to dispense": kinship connection, territorial location, and ethnic identification; Shils calls color identification a particular variant of the latter. He believes that "the need for connections or relationships of a primordial character will be endemic in human existence as long as biological existence has a value to the individual organism."[16]

Now, Parsons adopts this line of thought, applying it both to color identification and to aristocracy as a variant of kinship connection. He correctly observes that color serves as a potential category for all mankind, while aristocracy is always limited in numbers; but he then continues: "One primary aspect of [color's] primordial character is that it is completely ascribed, so far as the individual is concerned; it is no more subject to change by individual achievement than the leopard's spots. *This it shares with aristocratic or 'common' birth.*"[17]

In this equation the limited and static character of Parsons's famous variables takes its revenge. For while color and aristocracy (or being a commoner) may both receive his label *"ascribed"* because of their hereditary character, in reality these are sociologically two entirely different types of heredity: color is a biologically determined physical trait, which (in a multiracial society) generally tends to produce favorable or unfavorable social consequences for the individual. Being an aristocrat or a commoner is a favorable or unfavorable social position to which the prevailing social system has allotted a certain hereditary value.

Color indeed is as the leopard's spots: Only biological processes may change it. Aristocracy is rather like a leopard's skin: In some societies it is an indicator of an hereditary elevated status but can be laid down or torn off at any moment. Differences of a feudal nature can be abolished by society, differences in color per se cannot. The factors that determine the self-perception and the vision of the future of commoners in a polarized situation vis-à-vis

[16] Edward Shils, "Color and the Afro-Asian Intellectual," in *Color and Race,* ed. Franklin.

[17] Parsons, "Problem of Polarization," p. 365; my italics.

an aristocracy are therefore intrinsically of another nature than those of a subordinated racial group in such a relation vis-à-vis the dominant racial segment.

Skepticism about attaining social equality in a society in which the biologically determined marks of the different socioracial groups are going to persist pervades the subordinated racial group's vision of the future. This may lead to a greater tendency toward exclusion, be it in the form either of elimination of the dominant segment or of the subordinated group's own autonomy or separation, than is the case with other social movements. In societies where since the inception of its multiracial character, a principle of social selection has operated that largely depends on primordial racial solidarity, a great deal of confidence is needed in the ideology of human social equality, if one seeks to advocate inclusion rather than exclusion on behalf of the subordinated group. The common value system, as far as it exists and is relevant in this regard, is put under an immense pressure. One would estimate the chances for such a confidence and for such an inclusion to be greater when the line between white and Negro is less rigidly drawn and the system less sharply polarized.

NATIONAL SYMBOLISM AND SOCIORACIAL STRUCTURE

In reference to "the problems of national integration faced by those Caribbean societies whose populations appear today to be seriously divided by ethnic factors," Sidney Mintz writes:

The supposition that national identity is interdicted by the presence of large and seemingly unassimilable ethnic groups rests upon yet another supposition—that national identity hinges upon some sort of total social homogeneity or homogeneity of values. . . . Thus argued, those societies with the greatest sense of national identity will also be those whose populations are most homogeneous in their values. While this view has certain common-sense appeal, it is not supported by fact. Societies characterized by marked heterogeneity can exhibit a high degree of national identity, as long as individuals are able to align themselves on different issues on bases other than membership in particular ethnic or class groupings. In fact, to the extent that social movement can be randomized institutionally so that individual talents are rewarded differentially, a high degree of social heterogeneity may

contribute to greater, rather than lesser, national identity. An un-
qualified emphasis upon . . . homogeneity—either of population or of
values—implies that national integration increases as the number of
distinguishably different social groups within a society declines. Yet
both history and sociological theory qualify this view; not the number
of groups, but the extent to which they interpenetrate in the maintenance of communication and in the solution of national issues, may
be the critical factor.[18]

At first, these cautious remarks do not provoke disagreement.
However, it is useful to note that Mintz sees at least two conditions
for the beneficial effects of cultural and/or ethnic heterogeneity to
take place, conditions which in social reality may be considered to
be formidable obstacles: the ability of the members of society to
engage in social alignments, crosscutting the existing ethnic and
cultural boundaries, and the interpenetration of groups in order to
maintain communication and solve national problems. Will not, in
fact, these conditions only be present in a situation in which ethnic
and/or cultural group differences have been relieved of their social
significance?

Both conditions show some affinity with Parsons's concepts of
pluralization and interpenetration.[19] It seems not entirely acceptable to suggest, as Parsons does, that greater socioeconomic
differentiation and pluralization[20] in themselves will generally lead
to the improvement of race relations through the emergence of
solidarities other than racial group ones.

For it is not difficult to envisage a multiracial society in which
such a differentiation, as far as its sociological effects are concerned, is limited to its dominant racial group, especially when the

18 Sidney W. Mintz, "Caribbean Nationhood in Anthropological Perspec-
tive," in *Caribbean Integration: Papers on Social, Political and Economic
Integration*, eds. Sybil Lewis and Thomas G. Mathews (Río Piedras:
Institute of Caribbean Studies, 1967), pp. 141–155.

19 Parsons, "Problem of Polarization," pp. 351–352.

20 By which Parsons means that distinctions such as "between economic,
managerial, political, technical and cultural functions . . . by and large
[do] not [imply] generalized hierarchical status, but [rather] that . . .
qualitative differences [tend] to predominate in defining status" (ibid.,
pp. 351–352).

latter, as in the United States, forms a vast numerical majority. In the very specific case of the United States, at least three factors have fostered a satisfactory degree of interpenetration and cross-cultural solidarity among the different white population groups: (1) the common impact and challenge of the New World environment,[21] leading to specifically North American sociocultural innovations in which all groups were to participate; (2) their belonging to the white group in the overall socioracial structure; and (3) in complete accordance with Parsons's reasoning, their attainment of considerable mobility and increasing emphasis on achieved status effected by the industrial and technological expansion even though the ethnic or religious divisions preserved their social significance in many respects. Where, conversely, the dominant racial group is very small in number, increased socioeconomic differentiation does lead to a more complicated class structure within the subordinated segments, but not necessarily to a greater interpenetration among all segments.

A functional relationship between economic differentiation and the increase of interracial or intercultural solidarities may, rather, be expected in those societies where the dividing lines between the segments run vertically; in these societies, indeed, all horizontal solidarities, such as those based on economic position, foster inter-communication and may mitigate the existing cultural or racial antagonisms.

It is interesting that the modern societies that often are put forward as examples of reasonably well-functioning cultural heterogeneity, such as Belgium, Switzerland, Great Britain, and the Soviet Union, all have vertical cultural boundaries, to the point that their cultural segments even have territories of their own with a certain degree of cultural and sometimes political autonomy. Although European history shows many cases of repression, expulsion, or political elimination of such territorially limited cul-

---

[21] See also, for the psychological plasticity of new countries, Arnold J. Toynbee, *A Study of History*, vol. 4 (London: Oxford University Press, 1962), p. 292.

tural minorities, and although it would be naïve to underestimate the still-existing cultural and political tensions in countries like Belgium or Great Britain, it is correct to assume that a minimum of horizontal interpenetration and communication gives these systems a certain viability.[22] Countries where the cultural and somatic divisional lines between the main population segments run vertically (for example, Surinam, Guiana, and Trinidad) seem, therefore, best fitted for a quasi- or formal federative collaboration among these groups, provided that a minimum of interpenetration can be maintained.[23] Here, the question is whether, due to differences in demographic growth, economic ethos, and social mobility, one of these groups may achieve dominance in the long run, the vertical lines of division thus becoming horizontal once again.

In this context it may be appropriate to remember that in sixteenth-century Spanish America the colonial government, especially through its *Nuevas Leyes* of 1542, aspired to create a vertically divided dual society, in which the *res publica* of the Spaniards and that of the Indians would coexist separately, each maintaining its own cultural, social and territorial integrity, and both subject only to royal authority. It took, however, not a long time before the dividing line became horizontal rather than vertical, the Spaniards and their *criollo* descendants occupying the dominant position.[24]

---

[22] See Jonathan Pool, "National Development and Language Diversity," *Sociologische Gids* 17, no. 2 (1970):86–102.

[23] "[Ethnic] partition and communal representation was actually suggested by some Hindu leaders in Trinidad on the eve of independence, but those suggestions provoked far more hilarity and derision than serious discussion among the majority of the Negro and Muslim populations" (Wendell Bell and Ivar Oxaal, *Decisions of Nationhood: Political and Social Development in the British Caribbean* [Denver: University of Denver, 1964], p. 36). More recently, similar suggestions have been made in Guiana, Surinam, and Trinidad, but without official party endorsement.

[24] Cf. José Tudela, ed., *El Legado de España a américa,* 2 vols. (Madrid: Ediciones Pegaso, 1954), I, 47 ff.

In most other multiracial societies of the Western Hemisphere, the lines of socioracial division always have been and still are mostly horizontal. In such societies stimulation of solidarities based on economic or class position may have an aggravating effect on socioracial or cultural antagonisms rather than a mitigating one.

All governments attempt through the inculcation of nationalistic sentiments in school, the army, and so forth to diminish intranational divisiveness. Although it makes sense to distinguish, as Mintz also suggests, between national identity and political nationalism, there is some nexus between the two; an abundance of political nationalism often indicates a weakly developed sense of national identity. This is a logical correlation, for, if national identity is defined as the degree to which the historical experiences of the nation are perceived and transmitted as common experiences, then it is clear that acts of political nationalism in the past and the present may serve to strengthen this notion of commonness.

It is obvious that territorial chauvinism, using informal channels, can flourish without political independence. Many Caribbean islands attest to this; the insular sense of identity is nourished through comparison with neighboring islands, especially if these are in an equivalent but competitive position vis-à-vis the metropolitan patron state (for example, Jamaica versus Trinidad, Aruba versus Curaçao, Guadeloupe versus Martinique) and, further, through comparison with the metropolitan country itself and its local representatives, where the cultural differences are often marked.

In the same fashion, interterritorial or regional chauvinism may develop. In the Caribbean, the ideas of Hostos, Martí, Betances, Luperón, and others about the common destiny of the Greater Antilles, especially the Spanish-speaking of them, led in the 1870s and 1880s to plans for a confederation of these islands.[25] Also,

[25] See Thomas G. Mathews, "The Project for a Confederation of the Greater Antilles," *Caribbean Historical Review* 3–4 (December 1954): 70–107.

the ideal of Caribbean integration is still considered viable by many present-day young intellectuals of the region in spite of the failure of the attempt at federation of the English-speaking countries in the 1950s.

Finally, there are solidarities of an even wider scope: the Latin American awareness in Cuba, the Dominican Republic, and Puerto Rico; emotional and cultural bonds with Africa or India as in several other countries; a varying sense of pride and belonging in British, French, or Dutch (supranational) political frameworks; and, in a few groups, an incipient sense of solidarity—at least intellectually—with the third world. But it is clear that formal sovereignty with its own national symbols, with its international representation and activities, but above all with its institutionalized mechanism for inculcation increases and fortifies a territorial sense of identity. Seen in this perspective, the United States, Haiti, and the Latin American countries are at an advantage, ceteris paribus, compared to the recently created British Caribbean states and, even more so, to the French and Dutch areas and Puerto Rico. Ceteris paribus because there are, of course, other variables that determine the strength and extension of feelings of loyalty to a nation. (The term nation refers to the total society, whether politically independent or not.) First, there are objective variables: The infrastructure of a country may be insufficient and some population groups therefore so isolated that they hardly have any national consciousness at all. Their perspective is limited to their own community or region, and they are not nationally integrated. This phenomenon is well known in Central and South America but less so in the Caribbean or North America.[26] Then, there is the subjective variable: To what extent can national experiences be subjectively accepted as common?

In the vertically segmented societies of Trinidad, Guiana, and Surinam, the process of designing a national mythology in which heroes and memorable feats are carefully distributed over the cul-

---

[26] See Richard N. Adams, "Nationalization," in *Handbook of Middle American Indians,* vol. 6, ed. Robert Wauchope.

tural heritages of the two main groups could recently be observed;[27] it comes close to a contradiction in terms.

In the older horizontally layered societies, their traditional national mythologies allotted a high place to the king or president who signed the decree of the abolition of slavery; in colonies of monarchal mother countries, the royal family was always stressed as a loyalty symbol, often rationalized by certain historical actions of monarchs as wise arbiters in internal conflicts or, even better, in conflicts between colonials and metropolitans. Generally, in these traditional mythologies, the "good" dignitaries from the dominant segment achieved the status of national symbol: the noble priest, the governor with sympathy for the poor—in short, those who would have a maximum acceptability for the subordinated segments.

Only in the Latin American countries, whether independent or not, the nonwhite holy priest, the dark-skinned saint, and the institution of the national patron saints are found. Also, in many Latin American republics during the turbulent nineteenth century, men of nonwhite origins obtained the presidency (Juárez in Mexico, Paez in Venezuela, Heureaux in the Dominican Republic). Thus, Iberian Catholicism, both because of its national inclusiveness and through its creation of national religious human symbols, exerted a favorable influence on the awareness of national identity in the Latin American countries, while at the same time the early independence of these countries (except Cuba and Puerto Rico) led to political mobility, however chaotic, which had the useful effect of increasing the sense of participation of the lower socioracial strata in national politics.

The only comparable period in the United States is that of the Reconstruction after the Civil War, but here the phenomenon was not national, but regional, and included a strong retrogressive reaction.

In many Latin American countries, dark-skinned military men

[27] For the problem of rewriting history in such societies, see Anthony P. Maingot, "From Ethnocentric to National History Writing in the Plural Society," *Caribbean Studies* 9, no. 3 (October 1969).

and intellectuals played a sufficiently great role in the struggle for independence to become incorporated into the national pantheon, for example, Piar in Venezuela, Antonio Maceo in Cuba, and Sánchez in the Dominican Republic. Or would it be preferable to say that this incorporation, which significantly did not always come about without protest and delay, was rather the reflection of an already-existing and sufficient integration of the population groups than a consequence of an increase in such an integration as a result of their personal actions? Both points of view are plausible and are not incompatible.

The comparison with the War of Independence in the United States points to nearly symbolic differences. In this country the revolutionaries were initially reluctant to admit Negroes to their ranks, while the British were not. It was the colonial power, not the nationalists, who promised freedom to the slaves; and it was with the evacuating British that thousands of Negroes fled. Yet, in spite of this, there were also "hundreds of Negroes whose exploits are remembered for exceptional bravery and allegiance to the cause of the Revolution,"[28] though none of these became incorporated into the neotraditional mythology of the new republic.

Where the achievement of early formal independence was not accompanied by a fundamental change in socioracial structure— and the latter was the case only in Haiti—the new national mythology preserved its traditional traits as far as the recruitment of its heroes was concerned; only in Haiti were all of these nonwhite. In the United States they were all white; and in Latin America they were predominantly white with, however, at least one significant exception in nearly every country. It may be noted that in the portrayed, symbolic, countenances of these dark heroes there was a tendency to whiten them, even in Haiti, for a long time to come.[29]

The extent to which this traditional national symbolism subsequently came under attack and criticism, and to which alternative

[28] Melvin Drimmer, ed., *Black History: A Reappraisal* (New York: Doubleday, 1967), p. 133.

[29] Compare the same phenomenon in the portraits of the twentieth-century Puerto Rican political leader and nationalist Albizu Campos.

symbols were adopted or demanded correlates rather clearly with the variations in the emergence and success of *Indigenismo, Africanisme,* and *Négritude.* The Mexican Revolution, one century after the achievement of independence, led to a new national mythology proposed by an intellectual elite and accepted by the state in which Indian symbols are preferred over European ones (which may have been the result of a mestizo affirmation rather than a truly Indian nationalism).

In Haiti, an *Africaniste* ideology, strengthened within a predominantly mulatto avant-garde during the period of U.S. occupation in the 1920s and 1930s, has only more recently achieved the political backing that made it possible to place, though hesitantly and ambiguously, the vodun religion and the creole language on the altar of national dignity, some 160 years after independence.

In the United States, characterized not by a cultural but by a social pluralism between black and white,[30] the militant blacks now demand recognition of their own group symbols and culture, and some have begun to reject the traditional national symbols.

In the recently independent British Caribbean, as well as in the French and Dutch areas, a growing awareness of *Négritude* asks for its recognition on a national level but finds some resistance from the colored middle sectors and the white elite in the horizontally layered societies[31] and from the Asian population groups

[30] See Pierre L. Van den Berghe, *Race and Racism: A Comparative Perspective* (New York: Wiley & Son, 1967); and Milton M. Gordon, *Assimilation in American Life* (New York: Oxford University Press, 1964), who uses the term "structural pluralism."

[31] See Gordon K. Lewis, *The Growth of the Modern West Indies* (London: MacGibbon and Kee, 1968, p. 176), on the return in 1964 of Marcus Garvey's ashes to Jamaica, his "elevation by the Jamaican government to the status of official hero," and the controversies this produced. "At the time of independence, some Jamaicans were reluctant to accept the growing emphasis upon African origins and slavery in the interpretation of Jamaica's past. . . . Such resistance . . . reflected either the rejection of identity with the Negro racial stock . . . or the principle . . . that the symbols of the African origins and slavery were somehow degrading" (Bell and Oxaal, *Decisions of Nationhood,* p. 63). It is

in the vertically structured societies, the latter insisting on equal representation on the national symbolic level.

It would seem that only in the Afro-Latin societies has the traditional national symbolism (as far as it is relevant to inter-racial relations) remained reasonably free of observable tensions and unhampered in its functionality.

A word must be said here about Cuba. Though this country underwent a profound economic and political revolution, which, as far as can be ascertained, had some favorable consequences for the character of race relations, it did not undergo a fundamental change in its socioracial structure; movements to foster exclusively Negro oriented cultural or social goals do not seem to have been stimulated,[32] and some foreign black militants may be disappointed in the limited ideological usefulness of the Cuban Revolution for purposes of *Négritude*. On the other hand, the revolution was, of course, the creator of powerful symbols—Fidel, Che—for the struggle of Fanon's *damnés de la terre* against the capitalist exploiters (who are only accidentally white in their majority, much as is the Cuban cabinet). In Cuba itself, the concurrent use of

---

interesting to note that these authors express themselves forcefully against "the story of the rise of the enslaved black man from Africa" becoming "*the* history of Jamaica" because "some Jamaicans, perhaps all those who are not fairly dark-skinned Negroes, might be excluded from sharing in the new Jamaican history, perhaps from the new Jamaican society itself" (ibid., p. 64).

The authors praise Eric Williams, Premier of Trinidad and Tobago, for the emphasis (in *History of the People of Trinidad and Tobago,* issued on the first day of national independence) "on the common history of exploitation" of the two main population groups (p. 65). In Curaçao, the demands of some young intellectuals in 1967 to have streets in Willemstad renamed after leaders of the 1795 slave revolt met with sufficiently strong public opposition to be refused.

[32] There is no rejection of European culture in Afro-Cuban art, nor a search for anything specifically African, but rather a search for which is Cuban through the [Cuban] Negro" (Salvador Bueno, "African en América," *Casa de las Américas* 36–37 (1966), p. 186, cited in Coulthard, "Parallelisms and Divergencies."

older national symbols, such as José Martí, serves to stress the historical continuity with the national past.

Within horizontally layered multiracial or multicultural societies these Cuban symbols serve to emphasize the economic aspects of the stratification; within vertically structured societies they may serve to foment interracial or intercultural solidarity, and thus foster feelings of national solidarity within certain economic strata and their intelligentsia. The Cuban symbols may further stimulate national or nationalistic feelings of identity insofar as the nation as a whole may be represented—correctly or not—as the victim of foreign economic and political exploitation. Thus, it becomes understandable that the majority of Puerto Rican independence movements and parties have adopted the Cuban symbols. This must not lead to the conclusion that elsewhere in the Hemisphere nationalism is always accompanied by radical political or economic goals. Politically more conservative sectors certainly do not lack national fervor, which often expresses itself especially in the wish to preserve the traditional sociocultural patrimony.

If some correlation exists between national identity, on the one hand, and the satisfactory functioning for a prolonged period of time of one national symbolism (as far as its relevance for interracial or intercultural relations is concerned), on the other, it seems that the Afro-Latin countries show a greater stability in the symbolic expression of their avowed national unity than the others. This would mean that in the Afro-Latin countries the subjective acceptance by the socioracial strata of what are presented as common symbols is less critically scrutinized and less subject to doubts expressed along racial or cultural lines. Briefly, it means that national identity in those countries is stronger. Even if one wants to interpret this phenomenon in terms of brainwashing or oppression, and to view it as a lag in the process of becoming conscious of the black population groups in Afro-Latin America, there is still the obligation to look for factors that can explain the continuity and effectivity of this cultural domination and inculcation in that part of the Hemisphere.

To recapitulate and summarize the foregoing, the following observations can be made:

1. The change from colony to independent state does not necessarily lead to the inclusion of the subordinated racial group in the national symbolic pantheon.

2. Inclusion of the subordinated racial group in the national symbolic pantheon is not necessarily the consequence of, or concomitant with, a radical improvement of this group's position in the national power structure. The symbolic inclusion, as in Mexico and Haiti, may respond to a change in the identity awareness of an upper stratum culturally and economically removed from the subordinated group but linked with it through a socioracial continuum. This link makes it possible for the upper stratum to demand (or at least to accept) a replacement of European symbols by indigenous ones, without having to suffer from irreparable alienation as a consequence. (Where, as in Haiti, such a symbolic inclusion or even substitution is followed by harsh efforts to change the traditional socioracial structure, the resistance of the upper strata is of course predictable.)

3. Where there is no socioracial continuum, the substitution of the traditional symbolism by one representative of the lower racial segment leads to psychological exclusion of the creole-white (quasi-) endogamous population group, which lacks the subjective potential for identification with the new symbols. Where, as in most of the British, French, and Dutch areas of the Caribbean, the overwhelming majority consists of blacks, a wish for such a substitution is nevertheless understandable. In some of these countries, if flags and mottoes as a compromise now symbolize the racial diversity, it is really the racial or cultural discontinuity that is being symbolized, but it is being done in a fashion (equally large circles, equally wide stripes) suggesting the equivalence of the segments. Such a symbolism, then, is not a reflection of real power or numerical relations in the horizontally layered societies, but creates the fiction of a vertically segmented society where all segments are equally powerful.

In the United States where numerical proportions preclude a substitution of the traditional national symbolism by one, representative of the subordinated segment, such a divided pantheon of symbols would seem to be the only viable answer to the current wishes of the black group. Such a symbolism, with its suggestion of segmentation along vertical lines, would be representative of a division in racial groups as unequal (in power) but equivalent parts. Indeed, the United States is the only one of all societies under discussion where, as a result of its peculiar numerical proportions, black militants try to change the society from horizontal to vertical segmentation (often accompanied by claims on certain political, economic, and cultural autonomy) and where this change —short of exclusion—can be considered as a final goal.

4.   The foregoing two points warrant the conclusion that in the horizontally layered American societies the absence of a socioracial continuum is a greater obstacle than is a pronounced cultural diversity for the acceptance of any national symbolism, with the exception of the vertically divided type.[33]

5.   Where, as in Afro–Latin America, there exists both a remarkable cultural continuity and a socioracial continuity between the strata, there are absent by definition the objective and subjective conditions for clear-cut categorization and loyalty along racial or cultural lines.

In such a situation the question is not whether the Negro loses some of his militancy, as Talcott Parsons seems to suggest, but,

---

[33] Karl W. Deutsch (*Nationalism and Social Communication,* 2d ed. [Cambridge, Mass.: The Massachusetts Institute of Technology Press, 1966], p. 27) observes that "Most serious writers have agreed that nationality . . . has little if anything to do with race," which is, of course, correct in the sense that the formation of a national identity is not the privilege of the members of any race. But one only needs to read in his book the index references to intermarriage to conclude that Deutsch also considers intermarriage between distinctive units within a national territory an important factor in the growth of national identity. Where in multiracial societies one or more racial groups abstain from intermarriage, the negative effect of such a socioracial discontinuity on the "wide complementarity of social communication," which, according to Deutsch, is characteristic of "membership in a people" (p. 97), can hardly be denied.

rather, whether he qua Negro needs such militancy at all. Parsons's line of thought is ethnocentric based as it is on the North American socioracial structure.

While there is no need to dispute the objective fact of serious discrimination against the darkest strata in virtually all Afro-Latin countries, it makes a great difference subjectively whether the black stratum feels itself literally related to the higher strata or not. What García-Zamor says about Brazil is applicable for all Latin America: "It is often quite difficult to distinguish between a Negro and a mulatto, or between a mulatto and a white, solely on the basis of physical characteristics."[34] (This means that there are many gradations among the main socioracial categories, and not, as is sometimes believed, that an unequivocally Negroid person will be considered unequivocally white for social purposes, as soon as he has fulfilled certain socioeconomic prerequisites.)

Any North American who reads that "less than 2 per cent of all civil servants [in Brazil] are Negroes"[35] must take into account that Negroes here are defined as those whose somatic traits make it impossible to consider them as part of even the darkest strata of the mulatto group. It is clear that, if the North American definition of Negro were used in Brazil, the number of Negroes in professional organizations and governmental bureaucracies would be much higher.

With García-Zamor, it is possible to consider the Brazilian national ideology favoring racial miscegenation, which can also be found elsewhere in Afro–Latin America, with its emphasis on the whitening of the darkest part of the population "in itself a manifestation of [the whites'] latent or camouflaged prejudice against the *preto* [black] race,"[36] but the essential point is that there does exist an inclusionist ideology of interracial mixing and that it can exist because there is indeed a socioracial continuum. (The question whether demographic proportions really warrant the genetic

---

[34] Jean Claude García-Zamor, "Social Mobility of Negroes in Brazil," *Journal of Inter-American Studies and World Affairs* 12, no. 2 (April 1970):246.

[35] Ibid., p. 251.

[36] Ibid., p. 248.

feasibility of whitening the whole population is not relevant for the ideology and its social function.) The fact that in such an ideology emphasis is placed on the whitening or "bleaching" of the darkest part of the population is virtually unavoidable in a multiracial society where a racist ingredient in the mechanism of social selection (based on the dominance of the white somatic norm image) operates, as it were, by definition; under such circumstances the emphasis on whitening is functional for all groups involved. At the same time, one cannot deny that the operation of such a racist principle in all multiracial societies constitutes a source of social injustice and serious frustrations. It is for that reason that I have paid attention elsewhere to the pathology of such societies.[37]

But it is also clear that where the frequency of *connubium* among (often contiguous yet different) socioracial categories justifies the acceptance by all groups of an ideology of ultimate racial amalgamation, the vision of the future can be inclusion directed for the darker strata, even if their actual self-perception is being influenced negatively by what are, ideologically speaking, still-functioning racist principles of selection. Under those circumstances, efforts, often under external inspiration, toward greater exclusivity (blacks versus whites) have less chance of success in the Afro-Latin countries than in the societies where a socioracial discontinuity tends to foster an exclusion oriented vision of the darker strata.

Thinking once again of Parsons's idea that the problem of racial relations is closer to its solution in the United States than in Brazil, Cuba, or the Dominican Republic, it is possible to conclude that in reality there are here two very distinct problems, which tend toward two very distinct solutions. In the first case (to name but a few of the salient differences), there exists a discontinuous structure in which parts of both racial groups aspire to inclusion of the black population on the basis of an ideology of social equality, which is constantly undermined by social reality. But, in the other case, there exists a society that has a socioracial continuum in

[37] Hoetink, *Caribbean Race Relations,* pp. 148 ff.

which ultimate amalgamation is put forward as a national ideology, and which finds some justification in social reality.

As noted before in the Latin countries, dark heroes were incorporated into the national symbolic pantheon, or strengthened national awareness via national religious symbolism. Such incorporation intensified awareness of national identity among the lower strata though it is also possible to believe that such incorporation was made possible and admissible because of an already-existing consensus or ideology, which was rooted in the continuity of the socioracial structure. In turn, this consensus and this continuity were favorably influenced by the social mobility available to lower segments that accompanied political-military revolutions in many countries in the nineteenth century.

Other factors can similarly be seen as both cause and effect of socioracial continuity and national awareness. The remarkable cultural continuity in religion and language, for example, in the Afro-Latin countries was certainly facilitated by the channels of communication produced by the socioracial continuum while, conversely, these channels were widened and deepened by a common religion and language. Such communication further both facilitated and was itself enhanced by certain patterns of interaction, which lend themselves well for vertical contacts and which, therefore, survived easily their transplantation from the south European or Mediterranean culture area. Patron-client relations, extended blood and ritual kinship patterns, *personalismo* and patrimonialism must be mentioned in this context.[38]

Nearly all of these patterns concern individual relationships among social unequals with personal solidarities based on honor and loyalty and with complementary or reciprocal obligations. Because of a personal emotional charge, these relationships give to communication an urgent—some would say oppressive—character, a communication that has its structural parallel on the reli-

---

[38] See H. Hoetink, *El Pueblo Dominicano 1850–1900: Apuntes para su Sociología Histórica* (Santiago de los Caballeros: Universidad Católica Madre y Maestra, 1971).

gious level in the relations between believer and personal, regional, or national patron saint.

The functionality of these vertical patterns of interaction in horizontally layered multiracial societies, such as the Afro-Latin ones, is so great and their mutual interlocking so stable that it would be premature to dismiss their presence as the survival of an earlier socioeconomic stage, as some would like to. While some of these patterns also operate in the non-Hispanic areas, the impact of the total cluster can be found only in Latin America. Its culturally homogenizing effect seems clear.

It is interesting to observe how in the Spanish Caribbean societies where no Amerindians have lived for a very long time, a historical continuity with the aborigines is being postulated, which is completely absent elsewhere in the Caribbean. Coulthard observes that three of the best "Indianist" novels were written "in countries where Indians had long ceased to exist, Santo Domingo and Uruguay."[39] As noted before, in Santo Domingo at the end of the nineteenth century, an outstanding political leader claimed that certain climatological laws were changing the mulattoes' appearance into that of Indians. Today's children are often named after Indian *caciques*. The point here is not that this emphasis on the exotic Indian may serve as an escape from the complexities of present-day sociof racial relations but, rather, that such a search for historical continuity is hardly present outside the Spanish Caribbean.

The greater pride of the former Spanish countries in their colonial past may be seen as indicative of a greater measure of inclusivity and collective acceptability, which characterized the Spanish period in retrospect and which contributed to the present sense of national identity as compared with the non-Iberian areas —with the possible exception of the French—where the metropolitan country is much less perceived as a center of inclusive cultural expansion but, at best, as a faraway political arbiter and commercial senior partner.

Mintz also argues that the Spanish Caribbean countries (includ-

---

[39] Coulthard, "Parallelisms and Divergencies," p. 34.

ing nonindependent Puerto Rico) have "a more defined national identity" than the non-Hispanic. In this context he speaks of an already fixed "assimilation model" that made it possible for a country like Cuba to absorb over 100,000 Chinese and massive importations of African slaves in the nineteenth century and a quarter of a million Jamaicans and Haitians early in the twentieth century. Cuba was able "to maintain its ideological identity as a nation," while the same cannot be said of the non-Hispanic Caribbean areas where large-scale immigration recently took place.[40]

Mintz suggests as an important explanatory factor the "early emergence of a stable creole culture" in the Spanish areas, so that important sectors of the population early considered themselves Cuban, Puerto Rican, or Dominican as opposed to Spanish or metropolitan. This early cultural creolization was partly determined by "the very uneven development of the plantation system in the Hispanic Caribbean, the early growth of peasant or yeoman sectors, and the attenuated influence of the metropolis in the rural areas during the seventeenth and eighteenth centuries." He further pays attention to the development of different socioracial structures by observing that the Spanish areas were those "in which genetic intermixture proceeded most rapidly and in which the rise of intermediate groups of freemen was rapid and continuous," while such groups "achieved statuses much closer to those of the planter groups than to those of the slaves."[41] Mintz cautiously suggests that because in the Spanish areas "the masters came to stay, legitimized their unions with women of inferior status, and recognized their own alienation from the European past, creole culture in the most genuine, innovative sense could really begin to take shape."[42]

---

[40] Mintz, "Caribbean Nationhood," pp. 151, 152. Different estimates of Chinese immigration are given by Duvon Clough Corbitt, *The Chinese in Cuba 1847–1947: A Study* (Wilmore, Ky.: Ashbury College, 1971).

[41] Ibid., p. 148; although in the quoted text Mintz refers to Saint Domingue, it is clear from the context that he considers it valid for the Spanish Caribbean, too.

[42] Ibid., p. 147.

In a recent important essay,[43] Mintz has somewhat amended his views. He states that Spanish administrative control over its colonies "was more rigid than that of the French and English" and that it is precisely this greater rigidity that may have contributed to a full growth of creole identity of the white settlers.

Furthermore, in this essay Mintz mentions once again the factors that he holds responsible for the development of a stronger creole identity in the Spanish Caribbean: "the types of local economic development; the presence . . . of colonial institutions within which all colonists could participate; the relative proportions of different social groupings, particularly of slaves and freemen; the distinctions of privilege established by the metropolis to separate 'creoles' from 'homelanders'; and the sexual and mating codes and practices in each colony."[44]

In order to evaluate Mintz's stimulating and important suggestions, the hypothetical character of which he is careful to stress, it is necessary to observe that in his use of the concept of creole culture two different phenomena have to be distinguished: (1) the development of the cultural and social identity of the white settlers vis-à-vis the metropolitan country and its direct representatives and (2) the growth of a cultural and national identity, affecting all population groups. Though it is obvious that factor 1 may foster factor 2, there is no causal link between the two.

It is probable that a strong sense of white creole identity could not easily be formed in several non-Hispanic societies where the absenteeism of the plantation owners for long periods led to demographic instability among the whites. But there were also non-Hispanic colonies where over long periods of time such an instability did not exist. There is no doubt that the white population of Curaçao, for example, was subjected to both Latin and African

[43] Sidney W. Mintz, "Comments on the Socio-Historical Background to Pidginization and Creolization," in *Pidginization and Creolization of Languages, Proceedings of a Conference Held at the University of the West Indies,* ed. D. Hymes (New York: Cambridge University Press, 1971).

[44] Mintz, "Comments," p. 14.

cultural influences, which resulted in its "creolization."[45] Of course, this objective cultural adaptation has to be distinguished from the subjective awareness of it. While the Curaçaoan whites invoked their Dutch cultural role vis-à-vis the rest of Curaçaoan society and the neighboring countries, they came to recognize their cultural Creole-identity in their contacts with metropolitans; in turn, the latter reported vividly on these cultural deviations.

The creation of such a Creole cultural variant within the dominant segment is conditioned by the degree of permanency of the white settlers, be they public servants, plantation owners, or yeomen; the cultural content of the creole deviation is determined by the culture of the other population groups, by the contacts with the surrounding cultures, and by the peculiar social structure of the colony, which demands cultural innovations; the vigor and affirmative force of such a creole variant will be influenced by the distinctions of privilege between creoles and homelanders, as Mintz suggests.

Whether a strong all-inclusive awareness of cultural identity arose depended in part on channels of communication such as that constituted by the Catholic Church in the Spanish and French areas and within which indeed all colonists could participate; such was not the case with metropolitan religion in the Protestant areas.

Gordon Lewis shows how great an obstacle a discontinuous socioracial structure can be for the development of a national identity out of a Creole-white separate identity vis-à-vis the mother country. He suggests that one of the earliest indications of a Jamaican struggle toward nationhood can be found in "the efforts of the Jamaican settler-historians of the eighteenth century, particularly Long and Edwards, to give a coherent creole philosophical foundation to the struggle of the colonists against the absentee metropolitan power"; but he also notes that this movement "gradually [became] eroded as its wider and deeper growth within Jamaican soil was frustrated by the white distrust of the 'persons

---

[45] H. Hoetink, *Het Patroon van de Oude Curaçaose Samenleving: Een Sociologische Studie* (Assen: Royal van Gorcum, 1958), pp. 137 ff.

of color' and by the joint insensate distrust that both white and colored had for the black majority. Similarly, the localist loyalism of the great colored population of the later period was an expression, likewise limited, of the continuing struggle against the social supremacy of the whites after their legal supremacy had been broken."

For Barbados, Lewis notes a parallel development: Already in the mid-seventeenth century the local settlers were characterized by a "separate and equal Barbadian identity, which found its expression in political actions against the metropolitan power, and which showed how early in the colonization process a Creole society had been formed which, while not yet culturally homogenous, was already oriented in terms of separate colonial life. But with the development of a slave majority that theory of an English community . . . degenerated, inevitably, into a defense of the classes against the masses."[46]

The effects of the relative proportions of slaves, freemen, and whites on the development of national identity are not easy to evaluate. If it could be established that "generally speaking, the Hispano-Caribbean colonies were never dominated demographically by inhabitants of African origin,"[47] then even some causal relationship might be inferred. But several data would be at variance with such a conclusion. Cuba in the years 1817, 1827, and 1841 had a majority of Negroes (as distinguished from coloreds) over whites.[48] And, more importantly, because it affected the initial phases of culture contact, Santo Domingo had already in 1560 some 20,000 Negroes, 13,000 mestizos and mulattoes, and only 5,000 whites; around 1545, according to Benzoni, "the Negroes had multiplied in such a manner . . . that many Spaniards . . . did not doubt that within a few years this island would become the property of the Negroes."[49] This indi-

[46] Gordon K. Lewis, *Modern West Indies,* pp. 132, 168.

[47] Mintz, "Comments."

[48] Cf. Pedro Andrés Pérez Cabral, *La Comunidad Mulata: El Caso Socio-Político de la República Dominicana* (Caracas: Gráfica Americana, (1967), p. 101, and the literature cited there.

[49] Ibid., pp. 80, 81, 82.

cates that a relatively high degree of cultural homogenization in the Hispano-Caribbean societies could be achieved under sometimes adverse numerical conditions.

Whereas Mintz acknowledges that in the Spanish areas the socioracial continuum served as an important factor in the emergence of a creole culture, he clearly sees the latter as the more fundamental condition for the growth of national identity. In my view, however, national creole cultures can also emerge (though more slowly and cumbersome) in societies with a discontinuous socioracial stratification; but they then will not produce an all-inclusive awareness of national identity. The exclusivist endogamy at the basis of such a discontinuous structure corrodes the feelings of national solidarity. The Deep South, characterized by a remarkable cultural homogeneity, did not produce a social assimilation model comparable to the Hispanic Caribbean.[50]

Yet, it is indeed social assimilation that in the last instance leads to sentiments of common descent and destiny, to an awareness of internal social cohesion, and to the subjective acceptance of the commonalty of collective experiences. It is also social assimilation that, once a population has achieved a certain degree of objective cultural homogeneity, helps to elevate this to a level of subjective solidarity indispensable for a strong awareness of national identity.

In investigating the conditions that promoted social amalgamation in Iberian Afro-American multiracial societies, it is necessary to start with the fact that in all these societies, be it with a rhythm determined by economic and demographic conditions, very early in their history a socioracial continuum was already being formed, while in the non-Hispanic Caribbean and the United States—no matter what their economic, demographic, and cultural differences were and are—the white creole group consistently has tried to abstain from such a national amalgamation.

---

[50] Some fifty years ago, Max Weber wrote: "A common 'national sentiment,' as seen from the white group in the United States, hardly links these to the blacks, while yet the blacks had and have an American 'sense of national identity' (Nationalgefühl) at least in *mind,* when they claimed a right to it" (Weber, *Grundriss der Sozialökonomik,* Band 3, *Wirtschaft und Gesellschaft* [Tübingen: Mohr, 1922], p. 226).

5
CHANGES IN PREJUDICE: THE INFLUENCE OF NUMBERS ON PERCEPTIONS

MINORITIES AND PREJUDICE AS SOCIOLOGICAL CONCEPTS

Before investigating in the next chapter the factors that foster or hinder the emergence of a socioracial continuum, it first will be necessary to deal with a separate, though related, problem.

In the sociology of race relations, it has been fashionable for a long time to see prejudice as a central concept and to view it as a final cause of the attitudes toward culturally and/or somatically differing minorities. According to this line of thought, a consolidated attack against the prejudices of the dominant group, leading to their ultimate eradication, ipso facto would extirpate the problem. In this view, it was essentially irrelevant whether the minority in question differed from the dominant group only in cultural traits or, also, in somatic features. The prejudices in the United States against the white Italian or Irish population groups were considered to be of a sociologically identical nature as those against the Negro group, though the visibility of the Negroes was sometimes recognized as an additional, but strictly secondary, obstacle.

In the course of time, when the positions of the Italians or Irish in the total social structure were shown to have improved considerably and much more so than that of the Negro segment, it seemed logical and reassuring for the dominant majority to conclude the following: Since the Irish and Italians had proved that they were able to overcome the obstacles caused by prejudice, blacks ought to do the same. Thus, the dominant group attributed to the blacks the causes for their "failure." Deficient family organiza-

Adapted from "Change in Prejudice: Some Notes on the Minority Problem with References to the West Indies and Latin America," *Bijdragen tot de Taal-Land en Volkenkunde* 119 (1963):56–75.

tion, deviating economic ethos, and so forth were diligently ex-
plored as possible historical causes[1] of a destiny for which present
society at large, the dominant white majority, needs no longer feel
directly responsible, since the chances for social improvement had
been grasped by other—but basically similar—minorities.

This lumping together of all possible types of groupings under
the broad label of minorities (whose common characteristics were
zealously studied in the nation's schools) had several important
consequences.[2]

The wide variations between these groups obliged the social
scientist to formulate his generalizations about minorities on a high
level of abstraction, while the number of theoretical concepts
engendered by this approach remained poor in number and quality. Problems such as the differences in intermarriage rates between racially similar groupings and dissimilar ones could only be
dealt with in a superficial and theoretically unsatisfactory way. The
postulate of the essential sameness of all types of prejudice became
so deeply rooted that only recently—and then under influence of
black minority thinking itself—doubts have begun to be voiced
about it.

Could it be, it was hesitantly asked, that the social prejudice
against somatically very different groups is entirely distinct in its
long-term effects from that against somatically akin, though culturally somewhat differing, groups?

Therefore, can it be that the differences in social acceptance and
integration between Irish and Italians, on the one hand, and
Negroes, on the other, have to be phrased in terms of entirely
different types of prejudice?

An elementary distinction between racist and cultural prejudice
is not sufficient, however. For if it is true that in some multiracial
societies in the Western Hemisphere the white dominant group has
mixed with and absorbed more of the subordinated racial groups

---

[1] I do not want to deny entirely the significance of such causes; it would
be worthwhile to study more closely the question whether they, in
turn, are at least partly caused by the socioracial structure itself.

[2] See Peter I. Rose, *The Subject Is Race: Traditional Ideologies and the
Teaching of Race Relations* (New York: Oxford University Press, 1968).

than has been the case in others, is it not necessary, then, to speak of two different kinds of racist prejudice?

Some authors have indeed defended this idea. Thus, Nogueira speaks of a prejudice of origin in the United States and, by implication, in the Caribbean colonized by West Europeans and a prejudice of mark in Brazil and the Spanish part of Afro-America.[3] However, since it is hardly probable that the white North Americans or West Europeans would have been endowed by an act of God with one type of prejudice and the white Brazilians or Spaniards with another, the explanation of this difference must be found through comparative study of both societies.

In other words, prejudice is not an instinctive or final factor but only a shorthand indicator of a number of attitudes resulting from a particular sociological constellation. This means that prejudice can change in character, if and when certain ingredients in this constellation are also changing. It is not the pedagogical punishment of the symptoms—the prejudices—that will result in different group relations but rather the changes in these relations that will lead to other symptoms.

Some of the possible changes in a given socioracial constellation and the way they affect the prejudices involved will be discussed. In each of the situations the cultural and/or racial differences between the groups will be considered as given and unchangeable; and independent factors that may change existing prejudices, rather than acculturation or racial mixture and their social consequences, will be examined.

For the purpose of the discussion, it will be necessary to move to precisely that level of abstraction that has been criticized as too high—a level on which majority and minority are used as general sociological concepts.[4] The reason for doing so is simply that even on this level of abstraction a certain improvement in the conceptional apparatus may be achieved.

---

[3] O. Nogueira, "Skin Color and Social Class," *Plantation Systems of the New World* (Washington, D.C.: Pan American Union, 1959).

[4] Following the sociological usage, "majority" connotes a dominant, "minority" a subordinate position. The terms do not imply that the majority is necessarily larger than the minority. Often the reverse is true.

PSYCHOLOGICAL VERSUS SOCIOLOGICAL APPROACHES

There have been basically two approaches to the study of prejudice.[5] The psychological approach emphasizes its individual origin, trying to explain its presence with concepts such as the authoritarian personality, while the sociological approach emphasizes the function of power relations, of relative group positions, or of social conflict, all of which are seen as determining the prejudice of the members of a society divided into minority and majority. Carey McWilliams, defender of the latter viewpoint, writes:

Race relations are not based on prejudice; prejudice is a by-product of race relations—as influenced by other factors. Current psychological theories of race relations, however, are almost exclusively concerned with prejudice, which is discussed as though it were the cause of discrimination. . . . To make a theory of the function of prejudice in the psychic economy of the individual do double duty as a theory of group discrimination is to confuse different, if related, levels of meaning.[6]

In *Minorities in the New World,* Wagley and Harris reject the psychological approach on identical grounds; they state that the comparative study of the six minorities shows that it "is most useful to think of minority-majority relations as an ongoing social conflict."[7]

Again with similar arguments, E. K. Francis also rejects the emphasis on interpersonal relations in the study of minority problems and thinks that the really sociological approach needs to accentuate group relations.[8]

[5] For a more detailed analysis of both approaches and their convergence in some works, see Peter I. Rose, "The Development of 'Race Studies': Sociological Views and Expanding Horizons," *Race Amongst Nations,* eds. George Shepherd and Tilden LeMille (Lexington, Mass.: D. C. Heath, 1970), with an excellent bibliography.

[6] Carey McWilliams, *Brothers under the Skin,* rev. ed. (New York: Little, Brown & Co., 1951), pp. 315–317.

[7] Charles Wagley and M. Harris, *Minorities in the New World: Six Case Studies* (New York: Columbia University Press, 1958), pp. 255–256.

[8] E. K. Francis, "Variables in the Formation of So-called 'Minority Groups,'" *The American Journal of Sociology,* 60, no. 1, pp. 6–14.

Finally, Herbert Blumer clearly summarizes both approaches in "Race Prejudice as a Sense of Group Position."[9] There is no doubt, he says, that the extensive literature on race prejudice is being dominated by the notion that such prejudice has its basis in a feeling, or complex of feelings, rooted in the individual. Usually it is described as consisting of feelings like antipathy, hostility, hatred, intolerance, and aggressiveness. The scholarly research based on this premise has two tasks. First, there is the need to identify the feelings that produce racial prejudice and to examine both how they complement each other and how they are buttressed by other psychological elements, such as mythic representations. Second, there is the need to understand how this complex of feelings originates; some scholars want to reduce these feelings to inborn dispositions; others trace them back to personality characteristics, for example, the authoritarian personality; finally, others consider the feelings of prejudice as a product of social experience.

All these explanations commonly express that prejudice is located in individual feeling, and they can easily be found in the work of psychologists, psychiatrists, and social psychologists, as well as in the great majority of the sociological studies in this field. Unfortunately, Blumer continues, this common conception neglects and obscures the fact that racial prejudice essentially is "a matter of relationship between racial groups."

The existence of race prejudice automatically presupposes that prejudiced individuals view themselves as belonging to a specific racial group. It also means that they place others against whom they are prejudiced into different racial groups. Such an identification implies the formation of an image of their own and the other's racial group in terms of their mutual relations. This process of image formation is a collective process. It is the process of becoming conscious of one's position in the socioracial structure that, as a product of this phenomenon of collective characterization, forms the basis for racial prejudice.

[9] Herbert Blumer, "Race Prejudice as a Sense of Group Position," in *Race Relations, Problems and Theory,* eds. J. Masouka and P. Valien (Chapel Hill, N.C.: University of North Carolina Press, 1961), pp. 217–228.

It would seem that the sociological approach, as interpreted by Blumer, offers wider perspectives, especially for the comparative sociohistorical study of minorities, than the individual-psychological approach, although the latter must not be discarded as useless for differently formulated problems.[10] Clearly the definition of the concept of minority is also influenced by the psychological or sociological preferences of the author.

An extreme example of a psychological definition is that of Rose: ". . . the mere fact of being generally hated because of religious, racial, or nationality background is what defines a minority group."[11] The well-known definition of Louis Wirth, although showing a greater attention to the total social environment, also fits into this category: ". . . a group of people who, because of their physical or cultural characteristics, are singled out from the others in the society in which they live, for differential and unequal treatment, and who therefore regard themselves as objects of collective discrimination."[12]

While in these definitions stress is laid on the feelings of the dominant group versus the minority, in the sociological definitions there is, rather, an emphasis on the cultural and structural characteristics of the majority and the minority. For example, Schermerhorn conceives minorities as ". . . subgroups within a culture which are distinguishable from the dominant group by reason of differences in physiognomy, language, custom, or culture-patterns (including any combination thereof)";[13] and, also, Wagley and

[10] It is interesting to note that Blumer's opinions come very close to those that the Dutch sociologist Den Hollander, already in 1946, expressed concerning the general process of image formation. See A. N. J. Den Hollander, *Het Andere Volk: Een Verkenning van Groepsoordeel en Groepsbeeld,* oratie (Amsterdam, 1946).

[11] A. and C. Rose, *America Divided: Minority Group Relations in the United States* (New York: Alfred A. Knopf, 1948), p. 3.

[12] Louis Wirth, "The Problem of Minority Groups," in *The Science of Man in the World Crisis,* ed. R. Linton (New York: Columbia University Press, 1945), pp. 347–372.

[13] R. A. Schermerhorn, *These Our People: Minorities in the American Culture* (Boston: Heath, 1949), p. 5.

Harris view ethnocentrism and endogamy as the most important determinants of majority-minority relations.[14]

Yet, it is interesting to note that in both types of definitions there is only a difference in emphasis. The feelings of the majority toward the minority may or may not be the central focus. One may prefer to stress the hatred, the discrimination of one group against the other, or preference may be shown for a structural description from which the collective feelings can be derived as a secondary characteristic. However, there does not exist any difference of opinion about the *kind* of feelings of the majority vis-à-vis the minority. Wagley and Harris also speak only of repressive measures and of varying degrees of overt and covert hostility as typical indications of these feelings.[15] And Blumer, who so clearly links the process of collective and mutual image formation to the sense of social position of the respective group, and who even explicitly ascertains the changeability of this image formation,[16] nevertheless believes that in the racial prejudice of the dominant group four types of feeling are always present. These are: (1) a feeling of superiority, (2) a feeling that the subordinate race is intrinsically different and alien, (3) a feeling of proprietary claim on certain areas of privilege and advantage, and (4) a fear and suspicion that the subordinate race wants to conquer the privileges of the dominant race.[17]

Blumer's opinion that these types of feelings are always present causes some surprise, because he clearly understands that individual members of a dominant group may vary in the way in which they think and feel about a subordinate group. Indeed, some of them may be bitter and hostile, with strong antipathies and an exalted feeling of superiority; others may have philanthropic and protective reactions mixed with pity; others again will be conde-

[14] Wagley and Harris, *Minorities,* p. 258.
[15] Ibid., pp. 255–256. Cf. Michael Banton: "This emotionality and rigidity [of prejudice] are in practice, characteristic only of hostile dispositions" (*Race Relations* [London: Tavistock, 1967], p. 8).
[16] Blumer, "Race Prejudice," p. 218.
[17] Ibid., p. 219.

scending and show mild derision; while others yet will be inclined to politeness and correctness without a trace of aggressiveness. All these and still other patterns of feelings can be observed among the individuals of a dominant group. However, the consciousness of the social position of their group gives a common dimension to all these individual patterns. Whether the members are powerful or powerless, reactionary or progressive, rich or poor, educated or illiterate, Blumer says, "all are led by virtue of sharing the sense of group position to similar individual positions."[18]

The surprise is that this observation, which seems important and correct, has not been linked by the author in a more subtle way to the four types of feeling, which he discussed earlier. If it were assumed that at least one of these types of feeling were changeable (namely that of fear and suspicion), the conclusion would be immediately reached that there is a determinate changeability in the configuration of the individual patterns of feelings. If a given minority does not provoke the fear and suspicion that it harbors designs on the prerogatives of the dominant group, would not the most aggressive, hostile, and exalted individual reactions decrease in number and significance, and would not reactions like condescending benevolence, formal correctness, and so on become preponderant in this latter group?

In the next few pages, this situation will be seen as it presents itself in social reality. Although Blumer's hypotheses are correct, the four types of feeling are neither always present nor unchangeable, and there exists a relation between the constellation of these types of feeling and the configuration of the individual patterns of feeling in the members of the dominant group in a concrete situation.

Under what conditions will the majority form a subjective conception of the minority that will not imply the notion of menace? And how can a minority of the nonmenacing type develop into one of the menacing type (in the subjective conception of the dominant group) and vice versa? First, it is necessary

18 Ibid., p. 221.

to examine the existing classifications of minorities. At least three types can be distinguished: the finalistic, the mechanistic, and the situational.

Perhaps the best known classification is that of Wirth, which is based on the aspirations of the minority: The minority can be pluralistic, assimilationist, secessionist, or militant.[19] Simpson and Yinger devised a similar classification based on the objectives of the dominant group. They speak of six possibilities: assimilation (forced or permitted), pluralism, legal protection of minorities, population transfer (peaceful transfer or forced migration), continued subjugation, and extermination.[20] Unfortunately, the objectives of minority and majority are not always in harmony, and it must be considered a disadvantage of this kind of classification that the objectives (if they are formally proclaimed at all) are not always consistently adhered to. Thus, Wagley and Harris observe that "the traditional stated goal of the Jews in the United States has been pluralism, yet there is a marked trend toward assimilation in their actions."[21]

An interesting effort to devise a mechanistic classification has been undertaken by E. K. Francis in which he manipulates four variables (urban, rural, solidaristic, individualistic), and he relates them to the parent society, the host society, and the minority. By further using Znaniecki's four types of all-inclusive societies (tribal, folk, religious, and national), he succeeds in constructing an elaborate paradigm in which the degree of isomorphism between minority and host society seems to determine the fate of minorities.[22] Francis's aesthetically attractive classification seems

---

[19] Louis Wirth, "Minority Groups," pp. 354–363. A similar but somewhat more elaborate paradigm was suggested in Peter I. Rose, *They and We: Racial and Ethnic Relations in the United States* (New York: Random House, 1964). Unfortunately, R. A. Schemerhorn's recent study, *Comparative Ethnic Relations* (New York: Random House, 1970) was not available to me at the moment of writing.

[20] G. E. Simpson and M. J. Yinger, *Racial and Cultural Minorities: An Analysis of Prejudice and Discrimination,* rev. ed. (New York: Harper, 1958), p. 27.

[21] Wagley and Harris, *Minorities,* p. 286.

[22] Francis, "Variables."

to suffer from a shortage of variables, which causes his differentiation to become too crude and, therefore, his criterion of isomorphism to become too arbitrary.

Without denying the usefulness of these efforts, Cox's situational classification of minorities is the most interesting for our
purpose. He distinguishes seven situations:

1. Situations in which the colored person is a stranger in a white
society, such as a Hindu in the United States or a Negro in many parts
of Canada and in Argentina . . . the stranger situation;

2. Situations of original white contact where the culture of the
colored group is very simple, such as the conquistadors and Indians in
the West Indies, and the Dutch and Hottentots in South Africa—the
original contact situation;

3. Situations of colored enslavement in which a small aristocracy
of whites exploits large quantities of natural resources, mainly agricultural, with forced colored labor, raised or purchased like capital in
a slave market, such as that in the pre–Civil War South and in Jamaica
before 1834—the slavery situation;

4. Situations in which a small minority of whites in a colored
society is bent upon maintaining a ruling-class status, such as the
British in the West Indies or the Dutch in the East Indies—the ruling
class situation;

5. Situations in which there are large proportions of both colored
and white persons seeking to live in the same area, with whites insisting that the society is a "white man's country," as in the United
States and South Africa—the bi-partite situation;

6. Situations in which colored-and-white amalgamation is far
advanced and in which a white ruling class is not established, as in
Brazil—the amalgamative situation;

7. Situations in which a minority of whites has been subdued
by a dominantly colored population, as that which occurred in Haiti
during the turn of the eighteenth century, or the expulsion of whites
from Japan in 1638—the nationalistic situation.[23]

[23] Oliver C. Cox, *Caste, Class and Race* (New York: Doubleday, 1948),
pp. 353–354. The author calls these situations modern, because they
have to do with "aggressive whites [who] have sought most conveniently
and efficiently to exploit the human and natural resources of the colored
peoples" (p. 351).

Cox's classification gains in value if the dogmatic rigidity that permeates some of his explanatory remarks can be rejected. There is no reason to view his situations exclusively in terms of white and colored, and the situations are not as modern as the author assumes. By reducing Cox's seven situations to two key situations, attention will be mainly directed to the way in which the dominant group will be inclined to subjectively conceive the minority.

First, there is the nationalistic situation. As far as there is a realization of the objectives of the minority (as Cox suggests in his examples), this implies, at the same time, the end of the minority situation. The white quantitative minority was not subdued in Haiti; it was eliminated. If within the subordinated (colored) group there exists the wish to reach a nationalistic situation, then the constellation is similar to that of the ruling-class situation.

In discussing this latter situation, Cox shows that he is thinking of colonial multiracial societies. He commits the error, however, of believing that in such societies all whites always are metropolitans who "seldom set their roots in the area."[24] In the British West Indies, which he mentions as an example, there does exist a considerable group of native whites who consider Trinidad, Barbados, and Jamaica as their respective homelands. These and other Caribbean societies would better be placed under the heading of the bipartite situation, where large proportions of different races try to live together in the same area. For, if Cox considers the Negro group in the United States numerically large enough to speak of a bipartite situation in that country, he may concede that the—admittedly lower—percentage of native whites in the major Caribbean countries is still sufficient for the prevalence of the same situation there.

Second, there is the amalgamative situation. In defining it as it exists in Brazil, Cox suffers from too strong an emphasis on biological data, an emphasis that he attacks so vehemently elsewhere in his book; the definition of who is white in Brazil (and in the rest of Iberian Afro-America) is different from that in the United States. The idea that in Brazil "a white ruling class is not estab-

[24] Ibid., p. 360.

lished" is, therefore, not acceptable without qualification; this is not to deny, however, that the process of biological homogenization has progressed considerably in the latter country while it has not in the United States.

The slavery situation, which Cox considers the purest form of established race relations, is rather to be conceived as a phase in the development of the (colonial) ruling-class situation during which phase a juridical and economic system of unfree labor prevails.

Finally, in the original contact situation, Cox recognized that there is not so much question of a type as of a phase in the process of the development of a more or less stable pattern of race relations. It is also difficult to establish how very simple the culture of the colored group must be in order to fit into this category.

EXOTIC AND REAL MINORITIES

Thus, it may be allowed for our purposes to reduce Cox's classification to a dichotomy: the stranger situation, on the one hand, and the real minority situation, on the other. Historically speaking, this latter situation can ideally be subdivided into different phases, each of which can be denoted with one of Cox's terms. After the original contact situation, there may follow a colonial period in which the inhabitants of metropolitan origin constitute the ruling class; these metropolitans may then create a slavery situation that after some generations may develop into a multiracial bipartite society; under certain conditions, a process of biological and social amalgamation of the native whites and the other groups may get under way; finally, subordinated nationalistic groups may produce the elimination of the dominant group. All these phases tend to have in common the recognition that there is a real minority in the sense given to this concept by the authors who were quoted before; in all these phases there are normally present in the dominant group, in greater or lesser degree, all of Blumer's types of feeling, including fear and suspicion and the feeling of menace, provoked by the presence of the minority.

One of the merits of Cox's work is that it pays attention to the stranger situation. In those cases, he says, where the number of colored people in the total population is so small that they "can neither be expected to compete with whites, nor serve any considerable purpose as a labor force," there will usually be little racial antipathy shown toward them—unless or until they, perhaps, try to penetrate into the higher strata of society where competition is keener. As examples, he mentions the Negro in Canada and the Hindu in the United States, where each is still a romantic figure.

Cox further points out that the numerical factor is not always decisive in the creation of this situation; if a colored individual arrives in a society where a negative attitude against him was already present—for example, a white community in the South of the United States—then even his minimal numerical strength will not function as a guarantee against signs of racial antagonism.[25]

While, on the one hand, Cox correctly ascertains that paucity alone does not always lead to a stranger situation, he appears, on the other hand, not to be fully aware that such paucity does not always need to be a condition for the creation of this situation.

The essential characteristic of the stranger situation is neither the actual strength nor the potential power of the minority, but the subjective conception that the dominant group possesses of this minority. In this conception the factor of the menace has been pushed to the background or is even completely absent. Although it is obvious that the numerical factor will often play an important role in the process of image formation, it is nevertheless conceivable that under specific conditions this factor becomes less important in this process. Just as one Negro in a white community in the Deep South can readily provoke defensive reactions, so it is possible to think of situations in which the members of a numerically important group in a society are considered as racial strangers.

Thus, contrary to the prevailing opinion that attributes to the dominant group an exclusively negative attitude toward the minority (antipathy, hatred, collective discrimination, overt and covert hostility), Blumer's point of view in which the individuals of this

[25] Ibid., pp. 354–355.

dominant group may have a varied range of feelings vis-à-vis the minority, from aggressive hostility to pitiful philanthropy is accepted.

However (deviating from Blumer), there are certain minority situations in which the bitterness, the exalted hostility, may prevail among the individual members of the dominant group, whereas in other situations a mild benevolence, a condescending philanthropy, may predominate. In the former case the collective image formation of the dominant group is influenced by a notion of fear and suspicion of, and menace by, the minority; in the latter situation this notion (which Blumer assumes to be an ever-present type of feeling) will be less pronounced or even absent.

The members of this latter kind of minority can be called cultural and/or racial strangers. However, the term exotic group is preferred here. Elsewhere, it has been defined as a group "deviating in somatic and/or cultural respects, without being conceived subjectively as a menace to the existing social order."[26]

EVOLUTION OF MINORITIES AND OF PREJUDICES

A minority can evolve in the course of its existence from exotic group to real minority or vice versa. It must be stressed again that the attention here is not directed toward processes such as biological and cultural homogenization. Nor is the construction of so-called cycles of racial relations, as were designed by Park, Bogardus, and others in which a certain regularity in the process of accommodation, assimilation, and amalgamation is postulated, of interest here.[27] The primary objective is to understand the conditions under which the process of change in prejudice and in image formation can present itself in the course of given majority-minority relations.

[26] H. Hoetink, *The Two Variants in Caribbean Race Relations: A Contribution to the Sociology of Segmented Societies,* trans. Eva M. Hooykaas (London: Oxford University Press, 1967).

[27] Robert E. Park, *Race and Culture* (Glencoe, Ill.: The Free Press, 1949), p. 150; see also E. S. Bogardus, "A Race-Relations Cycle," *American Journal of Sociology,* 35, no. 4 (January 1930):613.

Earlier, it was seen that Cox considered the numerical weakness of the minority as the condition for the creation of a stranger situation. Consequently, a minority might evolve in the course of its existence from an exotic group to a real minority because of a relative numerical growth, just as an evolution in the reverse direction could present itself as a consequence of a relative numerical decrease. These evolutions can indeed be observed in social reality. However, as indicated, numerical strength is not the only factor that determines the type of prejudice.

Thus, a minority can be numerically strong and yet still be conceived as an exotic group because it is not sufficiently integrated in an objective sense in society or because, subjectively, it is marginal to the "societal image" of the dominant group.[28]

Certain concrete minority situations seem to lend themselves to a diachronic study in terms of the evolution between the two polar minority situations—the exotic group and the real minority situation.

The development of the relations between the Creole (Euro-African) sociological majority and the East Indian minority in societies like Surinam and Trinidad is a case in point.

In Surinam, the East Indians were aliens even in the legal sense

---

[28] It is on these grounds that I have ventured to state that, if we conceive the world at large as one society, the minorities of "the World" (which form a quantitative majority) will be viewed by "the West" as exotic groups, as long as they are not subjectively comprised within the societal image of the West. As soon as these minorities are viewed as integrated societal parts, they will be conceived as real minorities, and the range of attitudes of the dominant group concerning them will be significantly changed. Cf. Hoetink, *Caribbean Race Relations*, p. 226 ff. (The terms "the World" and "the West" are used here in the sense attributed to them by Arnold J. Toynbee, in *The World and the West* [London: Oxford University Press, 1953].)

It might be useful to add that the attitudes of the majority vis-à-vis an exotic group are, of course, not to be seen as static; within the indicated range of attitudes, fluctuations will present themselves. In definite periods of crisis, e.g., in the case of a conflict between the host society and the homeland of the exotic group, the latter may abruptly become drawn into the center of the societal image of the dominant group, temporarily being subject to bitterly aggressive reactions.

of the word from 1873, when their immigration began, until 1927, when the Surinam-born East Indians were declared to be Dutch subjects. And apparently this was how they themselves felt for in the beginning they were very reluctant to stay in the country as plantation laborers after the end of their contract. Only when the government offered them parcels of old plantations for lease and lots of the government domain for sale under special conditions did the number of those willing to stay begin to increase steadily. "These immigrants did not stay," writes Speckmann, "on account of a growing solidarity with their new country or because of an increased identification with Surinam society, but rather because the official provisions for settlement appealed to their highly opportunist mentality.[29]

In the 1930s, when the East Indians were already more than 25 percent of the total population of Surinam, they still found themselves sociologically in a stranger situation. They were considered to be a group of foreigners. They kept themselves "apart from the political activities of the Creole lower class population."[30]

It is true that two decades before, at the time of the so-called Killinger affair, the newspapers observed disquietedly and characteristically that in the discovered plot were involved, among others, "some natives and British Indians," but later it became clear that only one of the latter "had been an active participant in the conspiracy."[31] In 1933, the radical politician De Kom depended heavily on the Javanese masses, which he attracted in significant numbers by spreading rumors that they would be allowed to return without cost to their homeland. It is uncertain whether the few groups of East Indians who, according to Van Lier's description, also participated in several of De Kom's activities were not driven by a similar appeal to their nostalgia.[32]

[29] J. D. Speckmann, "The Indian Group in the Segmented Society of Surinam, *Caribbean Studies* 3, no. 1 (April 1963):3–17.

[30] R. A. J. Van Lier, *Samenleving in een Grensgebied: Een Sociaal-Historische Studie van de Maatschappij in Suriname* (The Hague: Martinus Nijhoff, 1949), p. 379.

[31] Ibid., p. 365.

[32] Ibid., p. 379.

The process of increasing integration of the East Indians into Surinamese society was not without fluctuations. The shift from plantation labor to small farming originally caused a lessening of their social isolation, for "the East Indian now came more into touch with other population groups."[33] However, for several reasons the urge toward urbanization increased among the Creole groups, and, consequently, it was possible to speak once again of a "concentration of the ethnic groups in separate areas. The country districts became more and more the preserve of the immigrant population."[34] This geographic segregation became only a little less perfect when during World War II the tendency toward urbanization became more pronounced among the East Indians. The social and economic development after the war finally led to a pronounced acceleration in the westernization, or rather creolization, of the East Indian group, while at the same time their level of ambition heightened, projecting itself on the sector of the "free professions and official positions. The Creole group [saw] this as a threat since it is precisely this sector which has always been a Creole preserve."[35]

When speaking of the process of increasing integration of the East Indians into Surinamese society, as above, there is the danger of trespassing the limits of objectivity and of becoming a victim of the image formation of the creole population group. For if processes of cultural and biological homogenization are abandoned, and attention is directed only to the strictly social function of the East Indians, it can easily be maintained that they were integrated socially since their arrival in Surinam. As plantation laborers and small farmers, they were never an unsocial group; they always had an acknowledged, useful, and specialized function in Surinam society as a social and economic whole, just as the creole groups had other integrated functions.[36]

On the purely social level in the last decade, an increasing

---

[33] Speckmann, "The Indian Group," p. 11.

[34] Ibid., p. 11.

[35] Ibid., p. 15.

[36] For a similar discussion on the degree of integration of the Amerindians in Indo-America, see pp. 116–117.

frequency of interaction between East Indians and creoles on the same socioeconomic levels and, hence, in the same socioeconomic markets has presented itself. It is not a greater integration (at least not in the conventional sense of the word), but a greater competition that can be observed, and which is conceived ever more clearly by the creoles as a threat and menace. The use of the term integration for this process means a reasoning within the subjective conception that the creole group has of Surinam society. What presented itself was a process whereby the East Indian group came within the creole world, within the creole societal image, as a menace-provoking element. It is a process of subjective integration of the East Indian group within the social reality as conceived by the creole group, a process which is functionally related to the factually increased social competition. The feeling of menace is maintained and enforced both by this increasing competition and by the faster numerical growth of the East Indian element.

As far as objective processes of integration are concerned, it could as well be stated that the creole group has the task to integrate itself into the new societal system, since this was created because of the Asian immigration, as maintained that the Asian population groups have to integrate themselves into Surinamese society, of which they numerically comprise more than half. Generally, the latter point of view is preferred because "seniority of territorial occupation . . . for the group that . . . has the advantage, is an important emotional factor in aspiring to impose its own norms and wishes on the others."[37]

Undoubtedly, soon after the arrival of the East Indians, the creole group coined unfavorable stereotypes of them.[38] It would

---

[37] Lou Lichtveld, *Suriname's Nationale Aspiraties* (Amsterdam: N. V. De Arbeiderspers, 1953), p. 28. It goes wihout saying, also, that accultura- tion (Surinamization, the creation of a truly Surinam culture) and biological homogenization (the creation of a typical Surinam somatic type) are essentially two-way processes that cannot be controlled ef- fectively by any of the participant groups. See Jan H. Adhin, "De Culturele Invloed van de Aziatische Bevolkingsgroep op Suriname," *Vox Guyanae* (November 1954–January 1955).

[38] Speckmann, "The Indian Group."

seem, however, that in the range of emotional attitudes of the members of the dominant layers of the creole segment vis-à-vis the East Indian population group there has been a gradual shift from more benevolent condescending to more bitterly aggressive reactions as the East Indians became more integrated into their societal image and were more keenly perceived as a threatening element.

The fact that the creole group used to speak of itself as Surinamers, excluding the East Indians and Javanese, is a typical indication of the exotic character attributed to those groups. Where today this term is still used with the same exclusiveness, there exists wishful thinking or, perhaps, a lag between the present reality of the East Indians as a real minority and the still-persisting subjective condition of this group as an exotic one. The situation, then, is analogous to that of the bipartite situation, which Cox erroneously supposes only to exist between colored and whites, and which has been called the pseudohomogenous phase elsewhere.[39]

For the same reason that either the United States or the Union of South Africa was or is sometimes referred to as a "white man's country," the creole group in Surinam showed its understandable but unrealistic wish for immediate cultural and biological homogeneity by devising a cultural and somatic definition of a Surinamer that excluded more than half of the actual population.

While Trinidad and Surinam are, as far as the relation between creole and East Indian is concerned, in a similar position, in Guiana a situation exists where an evolution of the East Indians from exotic group via real minority to sociological majority presented itself. The term evolution here must not be taken in a strict sense. Not only is a regression of the East Indians' majority position possible[40] but also (it goes without saying) a relatively faster population growth and an intense social integration on the national level do not automatically lead from a sociological minor-

---

[39] Hoetink, *Caribbean Race Relations,* p. 111.

[40] In the political, though not in the economic, sector such regression did indeed take place in the early 1960s.

ity to a majority position; in a case like British Guiana, factors such as difference in economic ethos and cultural heritage between creoles and East Indians as well as their specific relations to the external centers of political and economic power play a decisive role.[41] The term evolution, then, is certainly more justifiable (because it implies a greater degree of inevitability) if the discussion is limited to the transition from an exotic group to a real minority situation.

Where a constellation exists in which the exotic group grows faster than the dominant majority or in which the former already is a quantitative majority and the dominant group sees it as an exotic group, the following prediction can be made: The majority will consider the group a real minority as soon as the objective and subjective integration of this minority will have proceeded sufficiently. The term prediction is justified, because there only needs to take place a subjective recognition of a structure that objectively already exists or that is in the process of being formed.

From this point of view, it is possible to speak of the inevitable evolution of the Amerindian minorities in the so-called Indo-American countries. Quantitatively, the autochthonous groups in several of these countries always have constituted a majority, yet sociologically speaking their position in almost all of these societies has been, and often still is, that of an exotic group, which generally is not conceived as a menace by the dominant majority, because it seems to occupy only a peripheral position within this majority's societal image, at least on the national level and in the highest strata. (However, entirely different group relations may exist on lower levels.)

It is hardly debatable that an objective social and cultural (as distinguished from economic) integration of the rural autochthonous masses has not progressed very far.[42] The lack of subjec-

---

[41] Bradley speaks of "the frequently noted East Indian capacity for the skillful husbanding of available educational opportunities" (C. P. Bradley, "The Party System in British Guiana and the General Election of 1961," *Caribbean Studies* 1, no. 3 [October 1961]).

[42] See W. J. Goode, "Illegitimacy, Anomie, and Cultural Penetration," *American Sociological Review* 26, no. 6 (December 1961):910–925.

tive integration, manifesting itself in a social inhibition on the part of the dominant group, is nicely reflected in an observation of Métraux, who writing about what he calls a "racial pessimism" of the creole intelligentsia says that this pessimism "manifests itself also in the uneasiness or shame which these leading classes show with regard to the existence of natives in their country. When they cannot deny it, they at least try to waive aside its importance."[43]

It was the intellectuals of the *Indigenista* movement, initially especially strong in Mexico, who began to attack this "racial pessimism" and who saw as their task "the integration of the native masses into the rest of the population of the different countries."[44]

This shift from the pessimistic and inhibitive to the optimistic and encouraging attitude of the dominant intelligentsia is reflected in the literature on the Amerindians, in which a romantic idealization of the state of nature in the earlier *Indianista* novels made place for a romantic encouragement of the struggle for emancipation in the more recent *Indigenista* works of literature.[45] However, at least for the moment and in several of these countries, the *indígenas* maintain their subjective status as an exotic group on the national level. To the degree in which their emancipation will be successful, their position as a real minority may come to stand out more clearly.

An evolution in the reverse direction, from real minority to

---

[43] Alfred Métraux, "Problemas Raciales en América Latina," *Courier de l'UNESCO* (October 1960), cited in Juan Comás, *Relaciones Interraciales en América Latina: 1940–1960* (Mexico, 1961), p. 38.

[44] Métraux, "Problemas Raciales," p. 39.

[45] G. R. Coulthard, "A New Vision of the Indian in Mexican Literature of the Postrevolutionary Period," unpublished manuscript; see also the brief but excellent discussion of *Indigenismo* in Magnus Mörner, *Race Mixture in the History of Latin America* (Boston: Little, Brown & Co., 1967). See further Concha Meléndez, *La Novela Indianista en Hispanoamérica* (Madrid, 1934); and María José de Queiros, *Do Indianismo ao Indigenismo nas Letras Hispanoamericanas* (Belo Horizonte, 1962).

exotic group, is most likely to take place when a significant proportional decrease in numerical strength of the minority reflects itself in a qualitative change in the dominant group's attitudes.

In the Caribbean area, it might be interesting to investigate whether the black population group in Puerto Rico might not serve as an example. According to the available census material, the percentage of nonwhites in this island has been halved during the last hundred years. This is due partly to the immigration of whites and partly to a continued absorption of light mulattoes in the group defined as white. This process of whitening out,[46] linked to the historical process of biological mixing between white and Negro on a basis of social inequality, has led to a situation in which the group of decidedly dark-skinned persons already seems to possess the characteristics of an exotic group on the national level.

Such a process would be similar to that which occurred in countries such as Uruguay and Argentina. In Uruguay, 26 percent of the population in 1803 was colored, and in Montevideo, in 1843, this percentage was 19; today, no more than 2.3 percent are nonwhites. Of course, this change is due in great part to the massive European immigration, although it must not be forgotten that Uruguay's proximity to Brazil led to a continued immigration of Afro-Brazilians also. In the context of the national society, Afro-Uruguayans have acquired the characteristics of an exotic group. The *sociedades de negros* no longer perform their earlier political and religious functions but participate merely in Carnaval. Today, although prejudices are not absent, they are generally subtle. In the 1930s, however, they were apparently still strong enough to produce the Autochthonous Negro party, inspired by a similar movement in Brazil; it soon withered away. The whitening of the Afro-Uruguayan group is demonstrated by the fact that in 1954 only 13 percent were considered blacks (as opposed to

---

[46] The term "whitening out" is used by Preston James in *Latin America* (New York: Odyssey Press, 1942); T. Lynn Smith speaks of a bleaching process in *Brazil, People and Institutions* (Baton Rouge: Louisiana State University Press, 1946).

coloreds), whereas a century earlier, this percentage had been about 50.[47]

In Argentina, the blacks and coloreds (who in 1852 together numbered 125,000 out of a population of 816,000 and formed 34 percent of the population of Buenos Aires) have now completely disappeared as a social group: Here, the biological homogenization came to its final conclusion.[48] In Chile, a similar evolution from real minority via exotic group to disappearance by amalgamation came about in an even earlier historical phase: Between 1590 and 1620, this country had more Negroes and mulattoes than whites.[49]

It goes without saying that any of the discussed changes in the position of the minority vis-à-vis the majority will reflect itself not only in the attitudes of the dominant group toward the minority but also in the self-perception of the minority and its attitudes toward the majority. Speckmann's research on the East Indian's attitudes toward other Surinam population groups clearly shows the aggressive self-assertion of the erstwhile racial strangers toward the dominant creoles; the latter are accused of wanting to boss them, of suppressing them, of wanting to destroy them culturally and racially, while at the same time they are seen as lazy, untrustworthy, and so forth; these are no longer utterances of an exotic group that is conscious of its lack of power and marginal position in Surinamese society. However, both creoles and East Indians show a condescending sympathy toward the Javanese, who have maintained their quality of exoticism until today both because of their smaller number and their low socioeconomic status.[50]

[47] Carlos M. Rama, *Los Afro-Uruguayos* (Montevideo: El Siglo Ilustrado, 1967), pp. 74 ff.

[48] Ralph Beals, "Indian, Mestizo, White Relations in Spanish America," in *Race Relations in World Perspective,* ed. Andrew Lind (Honolulu, 1955), p. 415.

[49] Rolando Mellafe, *La Introducción de la Esclavitud Negra en Chile: Tráfico y Rutas* (Santiago de Chile, 1959), p. 252.

[50] See J. D. Speckmann, "De Houding van de Creoolse Bevolkingsgroep in Suriname ten Opzichte van de Creolen," and H. C. Van Renselaar, "De

A curious case of evolution of prejudice limited to the members of the minority can be found in the northeastern part of the Dominican Republic. The descendants of Protestant American Negro freemen, who immigrated in 1824 to the peninsula of Samaná and preserved much of their language and religion during the past 140 years, have always been considered by the dominant group on the national level as exotic, intriguing, and harmless, and referred to with condescending benevolence. However, because of the increasing integration of their formerly isolated peninsula into the national whole during the last three or four decades, this minority has had to revise drastically its range of attitudes toward the national majority. While at the end of the former century the societal image of the Samaná Americans did not comprise much more than their own peninsular society in which they formed a quantitatively sufficiently powerful and culturally sufficiently cohesive group to allow themselves a decidedly superior attitude toward the "idle natives" who "have no schools," the younger generation of today, instead of being proud of their North American origins, were found to worry about the English accent in their Spanish, because they feared the subtle ridicule of the nationally dominant group. The increasing integration also tends to accelerate conversion to Catholicism, which is now more clearly recognized as socially superior.[51]

Here, then, is a case in which decreasing isolation brought about a change in the attitudes of the minority toward the majority, while the latter did not need to change its evaluation of the former. The position of the minority, as conceived by itself, changed from a majority position on the regional level (which was the only level relevant to them) to an exotic group position on the national level (which became the more relevant level to them). As a result of

---

Houding van de Creoolse Bevolkingsgroep in Suriname ten Opzichte van Andere Bevolkingsgroepen (in het Bijzonder ten Opzichte van de Hindustanen)," *Bijdragen tot de Taal-Land- en Volkenkunde* 119, no. 1, 1963.

[51] H. Hoetink, " 'Americans' in Samaná," *Caribbean Studies,* 2, no. 1 (April 1962):3–22.

increasing integration, the minority came to see itself in the same position in which the national majority had always seen it. Given the paucity of the Samaná Americans in Dominican society, it is clear that only the process of cultural and biological assimilation already in motion will make their exotic group character disappear.[52]

MINORITY-MAJORITY STRUCTURES

By taking into account the objective majority-minority structure as well as the position of each group as it is conceived by itself and the other, a classification might be devised not of minorities per se but of minority-majority structures. The study of the objective and subjective relations between both groups would enhance the predictability of their future developments.

It is of importance to emphasize that such a study within one society would have to deal with very different social contexts. A group that on the national level shows the characteristics of an exotic group may be a real minority on the regional level and a dominant majority on the local level. On each of these levels the same actions of this group will be evaluated in entirely different fashion, because the expectations vary accordingly. Conversely, the members of the group will tend to act differently to the extent that they are conscious of the type of role behavior corresponding to each social context.

A similar differentiation has to be applied with regard to the different levels of social stratification within the sociological majority. Within one social stratum, the competition and sociopsychological threat of the minority may be perceived as very real, while, within another social layer of the same majority, the actions of the minority may be viewed as entirely exotic. (In New York, the recent social invitation extended by Leonard Bernstein to some

---

[52] Dr. J. J. Parsons was so kind to inform me that a similar change in attitudes presents itself among the population of the Colombian islands of San Andrés and Providencia. See J. J. Parsons, *San Andrés and Providencia: English-Speaking Islands in the Western Caribbean* (Berkeley and Los Angeles: University of California Press, 1956).

Black Panthers showed that to a milieu aspiring to be socially, culturally, and intellectually exclusive, these black militants represented an exotic value, probably not dissimilar to that of the first black slaves in that city.)

In several West European countries, the changing prejudices vis-à-vis their recent resident Negro minorities may also be best understood in terms of an evolution from exotic groups to real minorities on the regional level, and for specific native social strata. It is clear that *grosso modo* the attitudes toward these minorities are more favorable to the degree that they are less numerous. The reputation for tolerance that Great Britain enjoyed twenty years ago, and The Netherlands ten years ago, has been hurt in the meantime and transplanted to a country such as Sweden. This again shows how unfounded it is to consider prejudice as an unchangeable entity or to explain its local or national absence or benign character as a result of factors other than those that flow from the specific circumstances surrounding the encounter between majority and minority.

There is no doubt that a minority perceived as an exotic group has more chances of cultural and/or racial assimilation (quite apart from the question whether it desires these) than a real minority with the same cultural and/or racial traits. This does not mean that all exotic groups, no matter what their characteristics are, have those chances to the same extent, nor that all real minorities suffer from exactly the same barriers in this respect.

The distinction between exotic groups and real minority intentionally did not deal with the measure of cultural and/or racial differences between majority and minority. As soon as attention is directed to the varying magnitude of these differences, their influence on prejudice, and on the process of amalgamation or elimination, it will be necessary to descend to a lower level of abstraction, the same one on which our earlier comparisons within the Western Hemisphere were made.

6

SOMATIC FACTORS AND RACISM

Just as racial prejudice is inherent in every multiracial society and only its tone and volume vary in accordance with the constellation within which the social encounter among two or more racial groups takes place, so, too, every multiracial social system is racist in the sense that in its mechanisms of social selection and mobility a general preference is shown for individuals who more than others correspond to the social definition of race that the dominant group applies to itself.

Although the concrete manner in which this preference operates and the concrete content of the racial definition of the dominant group may vary, the function of the racist principle is the same in all these societies—it serves to preserve the characteristics of the dominant group, to wit its dominance as such and the somatic traits that make it recognizable qua dominant group.

In this context it is not very relevant whether through quasi-scientific theories the innate superiority of the dominant racial group is postulated. Such theories and their popularization are only a symptom: The legitimizing function of such ideologies must not be confused with the causes of social racism in every multiracial society; therefore, these theories must not be taken as a starting point for a sociological definition of racism.[1] For similar reasons it is also *theoretically* irrelevant here whether the racist

---

[1] As Van den Berghe, I believe, is inclined to do (*Race and Racism: A Comparative Perspective* [New York: Wiley & Son, 1967], p. 11) and also as implied by Michael Banton, *Race Relations* (London: Tavistock, 1967), p. 8.

aspects of social selection and allocation of positions are supported by legal measures, because the absence of such measures does not imply an absence of societal racism. Racism, then, is an attribute of a specific type of society, one in which there is a racial problem, and racial prejudice is an individual attribute from which no one in such a society can escape.

Seen from this point of view, such frequently heard opinions according to which only the present North American society is racist (as distinct from other or earlier multiracial societies) are hard to accept. The conviction, found in many sociological works, that race prejudice and racism within a multiracial society are closely related to a specific socioeconomic structure is not based on plausible evidence. Earlier it was shown that some Brazilian sociologists, such as Florestan Fernándes, believe that their country is moving toward an open-class system, and that the present racial prejudice must be viewed as a survival from an earlier socioeconomic phase. Such an evolutionistic line of thought parts from the idealistic premise that a multiracial society (and here the processes of homogenization, with which these authors generally do not occupy themselves, are not taken into account) is sociologically compatible with an open-class system, a premise that, so far, is contradictory to experience. In fact, the concept of an open-class system is one of many borrowed from classical sociology. It was elaborated for racially homogeneous societies, and its application to multiracial social systems ought to be subject to methodological debate. Of course, specific aspects of Brazilian society can be studied fruitfully with the help of classical sociological concepts; however, research exclusively based on such concepts cannot lead to a fruitful analysis of Brazil as a multitracial social system.

Socioracial and Socioeconomic Stratification

For analytical purposes it seems indispensable to clearly distinguish socioeconomic stratification from socioracial stratification in a multiracial society. Part of the racially dominant group are those who are economically weak but who, as a consequence precisely of the racist mechanisms of selection, cling to the conviction that their potential possibilities for socioeconomic upward mobility are greater than those of the member of the subordinated segments. This is one of the reasons for the opinion that in multiracial societies the socioracial stratification "prevails" over the socioeconomic one. Such an opinion is perfectly compatible with the sociological adage that a group's social consciousness and vision of society are predominantly determined by its social position. Here the argument is: In a multiracial society this sense of group position seems to be determined more by considerations of socioracial cohesion than by those of socioeconomic cohesion, which do not entirely overlap.

The analytical distinction between the two kinds of stratification further facilitates research into the question: In which strata of society may racial prejudices be expected to be especially volatile and hostile? As far as the dominant group is concerned, a provisional answer suggests itself: in those sectors whose position in the socioeconomic stratification is incongruent with that in the socioracial stratification or who find themselves on the border of such incongruity.

As was observed previously, the socioracial stratification as perceived by the dominant segment (and in a static situation also gradually internalized by the subordinated groups) finds its ultimate origin in differences in power just as any other stratification. What makes a given stratification sociologically interesting, however, are the criteria according to which this power is allocated and distributed. Economic possession is one of the important attributes and instruments of power, but the ways in which these possessions are distributed often correspond to criteria of a noneconomic character—criteria connected with differentiations in kinship, religious, sociogeographical, and even more informal social network lines, including social race. (The need for "achievement" or capability can be met within each of these networks.) The possible correlations with these latter types of criteria convert the socioeconomic stratification of a society from a mere statistical contraption into a sociological phenomenon. In a multiracial society, social race tends to be seen both as a paramount criterion for the distribution of economic possessions or positions and as an attribute of social prestige. This social prestige is *also* claimed by those members of the dominant racial group who occupy a low socioeconomic position, and it is denied those members of the subordinate racial group who are "allowed" to attain high positions in the socioeconomic stratification. Methodologically speaking, in an "ideal" model of a multiracial society, the correlation between membership in a racial group and socioeconomic characteristics might be assumed to be perfect. It is from such a model that the economic determinists derive their arguments to the point even of considering that the socioracial structure is nothing but the reflection of the socioeconomic stratification. (Similarly, cultural determinists argue that racial conflict is nothing but the reflection of cultural differences.) Hence, they assume that in a multiracial society socioracial solidarity is less than economic—or cultural—solidarity. Social reality, however, only seems to allow for such a line of thought if unverifiable concepts such as "false consciousness" are frequently introduced in the analysis. This is not to deny that such an analysis can be successfully applied to (parts of) societies that are racially or culturally homogeneous, in our sense of those terms. It was for those societies that the economic deterministic analysis was initially devised.

Nor can it be denied, of course, that the demand for a fundamental overhaul of the socioeconomic structure can be seen as desirable both by those who focus mainly on the many nonracial defects of the present one and by those who see this structure as the cause of societal racism.

During the search for parallels and divergencies between the multiracial societies of the Western Hemisphere, two remarkable differences were found in socioracial structure. The first one was the two-tier stratification in the United States in contrast with the three-tier hierarchy everywhere else in the Hemisphere. The second difference was the one between the existence of a socioracial continuum in the societies under Portuguese and Spanish influence in contrast with a socioracial discontinuity in all other societies in which the white dominant group clings much more determinedly to its endogamy. The present critical racial situation in the United States would seem to find its basic causes in the circumstance that in this country, the exception in the Hemisphere, two unfavorable variants of socioracial structure happen to coincide—a two-tier stratification and a socioracial discontinuity.

The latter factor is even more important than the former, because it is crucially significant for the development of an awareness of inclusive cultural and national identity, and because it seems to be a decisive factor in the question whether or not group conflicts tend to be verbalized and perceived in racial terms.

Now it is hard to see how and which differences in the socioeconomic structure or cultural heritage between the Spanish and Portuguese influenced areas, on the one hand, and the North American, British, French, Danish, and Dutch areas, on the other, could account for the emergence of a socioracial continuum in the former and its absence in the latter.

Whether directing attention, in the earliest or in later phases of the colonial period, to factors such as growth, fall, or even absence, of plantation economies; to numerical proportions between white men and women, among masters, freemen, and slaves, or among whites, coloreds, and Negroes; to religion; or to considerations of military or political security; it is always possible to find exceptions within one of the two main areas which invalidate the general explanatory value of any of these factors.

This should not cause any real surprise, for the answer finally must be found in psychological motivations, not economic and demographic situations, since the fundamental question is: Why are there differences among whites in their willingness to engage in the type of sociosexual unions with members of the contiguous nonwhite strata that imply the social recognition of its offspring?

Thus, it would seem as if a difference in racial prejudice between Iberian and Northwest European whites exists that expresses itself in the former's greater willingness to enter into sexual relations on a basis of social acceptance with persons from the lighter colored middle groups. But the concept of prejudice as a final cause is entirely unacceptable, and it is necessary to explain the observed difference in prejudice in other terms.

Elsewhere, the usefulness of the concepts of somatic norm image and somatic distance has been advocated.[2] There is a slight difference between Iberians and Northwest Europeans as to their respective social definitions of whiteness, and consequently, the somatic distance between Iberians and light coloreds is less than that between the latter and white Northwest Europeans. Existing research material went far to prove this point, and my conviction of the fundamental usefulness of both concepts as tools for a better understanding of the differences in rates of interracial sexual unions with social acceptance is still completely intact.

Critics have argued that the concept of somatic norm image is racist. If racism is defined as a belief in the hereditary superiority of one race, such an accusation is, of course, utterly absurd. But if it is meant to imply that, by using this concept, an explanatory value is assigned to sociosomatic factors in problems of interracial relations, such a charge has validity. Economic, demographic, or cultural factors, however important, are not sufficient to explain certain specific aspects of such relations. In a critique, M. G. Smith has correctly noted that, since race is defined as every group which, in principle, has a somatic-norm image of its own, "every dominant segment that has a distinctive rate of interracial assimilation constitutes a distinct 'race' and every 'group' changes its 'race,' whenever its interracial assimilation ratio changes."[3]

Of course, a group does not change its interracial assimilation ratio at will. The somatic norm image of the native whites in the non-Hispanic Caribbean and the United States has for three centuries prevented the absorption of what they define as colored people in socially significant numbers. In the Hispanic Caribbean, however, where such an absorption—but without that definition—did take place, it is plausible to assume that it led to a slow change in the somatic norm image of the dominant group; this change in turn tended to facilitate this absorption even more. In this case, exactly as Smith implies, a change in biological-racial composition

[2] H. Hoetink, *Caribbean Race Relations: A Study of Two Variants* (New York: Oxford University Press, 1971).
[3] M. G. Smith, review of H. Hoetink, *Caribbean Race Relations* in *Race* 10, no. 1 (July 1968):136.

was accompanied by a change in somatic norm image. But the interracial assimilation ratio may also change without there being an immediate, concurrent change in the biological composition of the group. Certain groups of white Puerto Ricans in the United States tend to abandon their Iberian-Caribbean somatic norm image and to adopt the dominant North American one.[4] This means that they no longer recognize certain persons as white who previously had fallen within their definition of whiteness. Such an adoption of a new somatic norm image does indeed mean that the race of the group in question has been redefined; sociologically speaking, they are now members of a slightly different race. Ultimately, this will also result in another biological composition, since the selection of marriage partners will operate on a different and more limited basis. This will finally lead to a renewed correlation between somatic norm image and somatic traits, both of which will have then changed.

Franklin W. Knight thinks that in Cuba since the end of the nineteenth century the social impact of the North American somatic norm image has also been discernible.[5]

A few Jamaican sociologists have argued that their society falls into the same category as the Iberian area, as far as the existence of a socioracial continuum is concerned. M. G. Smith believes that in the British West Indies generally, "interracial marriages are frequent, relative to the numbers of resident whites," and Orlando Patterson even "strongly suspects" that relatively more white Jamaicans have married light-skinned or "high-brown" people than is the case in the Iberian variant.[6] It proves extremely difficult to find proof of these opinions in the existing literature. British

---

[4] Eduardo Seda Bonilla, "Social Structure and Race Relations," *Social Forces* 40, no. 2 (December 1961).

[5] Franklin W. Knight, "The Role of the Free Black and the Free Mulatto in Cuban Slave Society," in *Neither Slave nor Free: The Freedman of African Descent in the Slave Societies of the New World,* eds. J. Greene and D. Cohen (Baltimore: The Johns Hopkins University Press, 1972).

[6] Smith, "Review"; H. Orlando Patterson, "Review," in *Caribbean Quarterly* (December 1967).

West Indian sociologists have hardly occupied themselves with the non-English speaking Caribbean.

Many years of observation in both the Hispanic and non-Hispanic areas have shown that in both areas there is a difference in intermarriage rates between those who are defined as whites and light coloreds in the non-Hispanic areas, the latter often being defined as whites in the Hispanic Caribbean. Such a difference is reflected in the socioracial structure, which in virtually all relevant literature is defined as discontinuous in the British, French, Dutch, and U.S. areas, and as continuous in the Iberian areas.[7] Although in both main regions there is a general socioracial division into whites, coloreds, and blacks (except for the U.S. mainland), the gradations between white and colored are perceived as much more varied, subtle—and more frequent within families—in the Hispanic than in the non-Hispanic region. Knight, who certainly does not draw too rosy a picture of Cuban race relations in the nineteenth century, observes:

With a light skin color and certain favorable circumstances—especially progeny, economic solvency, or female delicacy, guile and attractiveness—it was possible for the free person of color to move upward onto the white, privileged élite. Indeed, rich mulattoes of either sex— *in sharp distinction from rich blacks*—offered an efficacious way for the white peninsular, especially from the lower orders of the bureaucracy to secure or recoup a fortune to bolster their social position.[8]

In the Dominican Republic, the frequency of similar unions in the same period is equally striking,[9] and in Brazil and Puerto Rico the relative frequency of what in non-Iberian America would be described as interracial marriage has also been well documented. Yet, no similar documentation exists for the French, Dutch, and

---

[7] Philip Mason (*Patterns of Dominance* [London: Oxford University Press, 1970], pp. 126 ff) considers that Jamaica became a "racially fluid" society after recently attaining its independence, thus distinguishing it from all other British West Indian societies; his main reason for this seems to be that there are now so few whites.

[8] Knight, "Role of the Free Black" (my italics).

[9] H. Hoetink, *El Pueblo Dominicano 1850–1900: Apuntes para su Sociología Histórica* (Santiago de los Caballeros: Universidad Católica Madre y Maestra, 1971).

British areas. Neither does one find in the latter areas the whitening phenomenon reflected in their population statistics, nor is there any inclusive racial amalgamation ideology.

It cannot be overemphasized that the Iberian socioracial continuum is favored over the non-Hispanic discontinuity, not because of some a priori preference for a melting-pot ideology in the North American sense—which, for that matter, never included the blacks —but because of the favorable impact that such a continuum has on a wide range of issues.

ARCHETYPE OF BEAUTY AND IDEAL PERSONAGE

The terms somatic norm image and somatic distance are no more than convenient concepts to tackle the sociopsychological aspects of race; they facilitate a more objective and relativistic perspective. They are neither an invention (which does not exist in the social sciences) nor a discovery (the same phenomena have been described many times before in other terms). Thus, G. Rogler nearly thirty years ago wrote an article in which he used the term race distance, though without defining it, and, recently, Pérez Cabral started to employ a similar terminology.[10]

The Spanish sociologist Francisco Ayala, of the University of Chicago, has written more extensively and thought more deeply than others about the sociological significance of aesthetic factors.[11] In his *Tratado de Sociología*, Ayala begins by observing that the "archetypes of beauty, related to the human figure" always relate to sexually adult but not old figures, predominantly female; from this he concludes that the ideal of human beauty seems to be connected with love, the latter defined as "an independent cultural structure, built on the sexual-physiological function." Although in art other human forms may also be experienced as beautiful, this

[10] G. Rogler, "The Role of Semantics in the Study of Race Distance in Puerto Rico, *Social Forces* 22 (October 1943–May 1944); Pedro Andrés Pérez Cabral, *La Comunidad Mulata*: *El Caso Socio-Político de la República Dominicana* (Caracas: Gráfica Americana, 1967), p. 74.

[11] Francisco Ayala, *Tratado de Sociología* 3d ed. (Madrid: Aguilar, 1968), pp. 444 ff. When writing in 1959 the Dutch text of *Caribbean Race Relations,* Ayala's work was unknown to me.

latter beauty is perceived through archetypes, distinct from that corresponding to society's specifically aesthetic ideal, which latter has a decisive sexual component.

In the chapter "El factor de la tensión politico-social en la constitución de los arquetipos de belleza,"[12] Ayala deals extensively with what has been called elsewhere the one way transference of the dominant somatic norm image.[13] He observes that "the tension between racially distinct groups, to which, originally, corresponds the political contrast between dominance and subordination, is reflected in the . . . esthetic ideals"; in general, these are "based on the racial characteristics of the dominant group." By way of illustration Ayala refers to Indo- and Afro-America, where although "because of *mestizaje,* social evolution, and revolutionary movements, the relation between dominant and subordinated group has lost its earlier racial connotation . . . the ideal of human beauty, such as it emerged from this [formerly dominant group], persists, as something worthy in itself, with entire objectivity." He explains this phenomenon correctly in terms of the social prestige of the dominant group, reminding his readers of Thorstein Veblen's observations on the connection between social prestige and aesthetic preferences. Ayala further tries to show that precisely in a racially stratified society the erotic component of the aesthetic ideal of the dominant group in its predominantly female form is reinforced, because in such societies the dominant group is normally numerically weaker than the subordinate one, thus increasing the scarcity value and the erotic attraction of those women who come nearest to the prevailing aesthetic ideal.

In some cases, however, the woman from the dominant group, "in idealizing her figure . . . [cultivating] her beauty, emphasizing her features in agreement with the existing esthetic archetype," may become subject to such an extreme alienation that "precisely the person in whom the archetype is most perfectly reflected, becomes an object of spiritual or platonic love, or even of quasi-religious veneration: with respect to her, all sexuality becomes

12 Ibid., pp. 447 ff.
13 Hoetink, *Caribbean Race Relations,* pp. 133 ff.

offensive: the esthetic ideal has become objectified with regard to all sexual experience."

This latter phenomenon,[14] the elevation of the white woman onto an almost unattainable pedestal in the multiracial American societies, has previously been associated by several authors with the psychological influence of the subordinated racial group on the dominant group (for example, nursing mammies' influence upon the small white boy) or subconscious fears of the white man for the rape of the white woman by a Negro, and similar explanations. It is interesting to note how the same phenomenon is interpreted by Ayala as an extreme consequence of the heightened and more conscious awareness of the somatic norm image in a multiracial society.

Ayala then proceeds to discuss a socioaesthetical phenomenon that has to be distinguished clearly from the physical ideal of beauty, though it has some traits in common: This is the ideal personage as it is defined in different historical periods. While the somatic norm image in origin and principle is linked to a specific biological type (although it can be transferred to others), the characteristics of the ideal personage are by definition subject to direct and changeable cultural and social influences, as Taine already observed.

Thus, in a period and a society in which the nobleman-soldier is a central figure, the ideal male personage may be characterized by military posture, relative height, and youth, and there is an emphasis on corporal rather than facial expression.[15] A society in which

---

[14] Obviously, this phenomenon is linked to the easy accessibility of women from the subordinated group as objects of sexual relations, whose attractiveness is heightened by considerations of erotic curiosity and whose sensuality is more appreciated to the degree that the woman from the dominant group becomes more of a platonic than an erotic object. Ayala sees this quite clearly, but pays less attention to the social imperative among the men from the dominant group that their socially recognized progeny preserve the features of the dominant racial group. Hence, the often quoted saying in several Afro-American societies that a *mulata* is the most attractive erotic partner but that the spouse has to be white.

[15] Ayala, *Tratado de Sociología,* p. 450.

a courtly and decadent nobility dominates will shape its ideal personage accordingly; in this fashion it is possible to describe intellectual, romantic, businesslike, pioneering, and many more ideal personages, who might well coexist in a particular society, and whose images may compete for social preference. It is clear that in these images the erotic connotation is much less or even absent and that men and women may have their own ideal personages according to the idealized role of each sex group in a particular society.

"In Britain," Patterson observes, "the pallid, bosomy, long haired, broad shouldered, undulating expanse of womanhood [of Edwardian times], is far removed from the skinny, sun-tanned, closely cropped working-class Twiggy of today."[16] But Patterson errs if he thinks that he is dealing with anything else but the culturally induced and physically minimal variations permitted by a given somatic type; what he describes are variations of the ideal personage, which, as far as physical traits are concerned, do not allow for the nearly inexhaustible choices postulated by Patterson. These choices are even so limited that it is advantageous to try to list them: Hair can be worn long or short, straight or undulating, or hidden by a wig; society may make an individual want to gain, or to lose, weight.[17] Only in exceptional cases will surgery be undertaken, although the term "nose-job" reminds us that in the United States such operations are not altogether uncommon. In societies where part of the population is subjected to the penetrating influence of a somatic norm image, which does not at all correlate with its own physical type, surgical treatment of visible parts of the human body may become even more fashionable: For example, there are an increasing number of operations in Japan and other countries in the Far East to eliminate the Mongoloid eye split. Such a phenomenon, if sufficiently common, as is still the case with the efforts to bleach the skin and straighten the hair (Afro-America) or, conversely, to make the hair more wavy (Indo-America), may be labeled sociopathologic, because it re-

16 Patterson, "Review."
17 Werner J. Cahnman, "The Stigma of Obesity," *The Sociological Quarterly* (Summer 1968), pp. 283–299.

sults from the frustrating impossibility of having one's own physical type agree in a satisfactory manner with the imposed somatic norm image.

Nevertheless, within the general ideal of physical beauty adopted by a particular society, a certain margin exists for the slightly different. Thus, in a society where blond people predominate, the black-haired individual, assuming that his other physical traits fall within the prevailing somatic norm image, will have a certain scarcity value; conversely, France traditionally sings *"Auprès de ma blonde."* Similar appreciation of the exotic within the acceptable made Roman women put red barbarian locks in their hair.

The stimulation of curiosity, especially its erotic variety, may further lead to the fostering of favorable prejudices vis-à-vis exotic groups with sharply different somatic traits from the majority. This may lead to a higher rate of intermarriage between the two groups than would be the case if the minority would lack such an exotic quality, especially since in the latter case the dominant group would be more conscious of its own somatic norm image.[18]

DRESS AND STRUCTURAL POSITION

Next to the somatic norm image and the ideal personage there remains one other socioaesthetic influence on the perception of human beauty—the influence of clothing. It is most subject to change and has the greatest variability. Anyone, no matter his race, color, or, in most cases, creed, may dress in Japanese kimonos, Russian hats, or Edwardian suits in order to comply with the momentary sociocultural dictates of fashion. In social reality the three influences just mentioned are, of course, not operating separately, but are imposing themselves in combination.

Now, for the members of a subordinated racial group, the dominant somatic norm image is the most difficult to approximate; the ideal personage somewhat less difficult, as far as posture and expression are concerned; and the temporarily preferred type of clothing the easiest. It is therefore tempting to assume that the individual's interest in the social dictates of clothing fashion will

[18] See Hoetink, *Caribbean Race Relations,* pp. 131 ff.

increase to the extent that the aesthetic demands on his physical type are more difficult to comply with. Errol L. Miller confirmed this hypothesis in an investigation among 475 secondary school pupils in Kingston, Jamaica.[19] They were asked to respond to requests such as "Describe your idea of a handsome boy (or a beautiful girl)," "Describe what the average Jamaican looks like," and "What do you like about your body?" The pupils were classified according to color groups, and their answers were analyzed and compared by group. The more Negroid the respondents, the more frequently was dress mentioned in defining their idea of a handsome boy or a beautiful girl. Among the girls,

only 4.6 percent of the light-colored group records the fact that the beautiful girl should be well dressed. Ten percent of the Brown group, 13.4 of the Dark group and 33.3 of the Black group make this observation. . . . This is basically the same pattern that was observed when the concept of the handsome boy was discussed. Dress, it would appear, increases in importance in the groups in which there is the least number of ideal features [and] is probably a form of compensation for a lack of desirable features.[20]

TRANSFERENCE OF THE SOMATIC NORM IMAGE

What are the ideal or desirable features as conceived at present by these Jamaican youngsters?

[19] Errol L. Miller, "Body Image, Physical Beauty and Colour Among Jamaican Adolescents," *Social and Economic Studies* 18, no. 1 (March 1969):72–89.

[20] Ibid., pp. 83, 85. Since Miller's schools and pupils were selected at random, he implicitly dismisses the economic variable; yet, it would be worthwhile to investigate whether a poorer economic background of the darker-skinned children leads them to consider dress as more desirable. On the other hand, the considerable emphasis on dress, also among dark-skinned of higher economic strata, can easily be observed and must be explained in Miller's terms. It is notable that, at least until recently, the lower-strata blacks in many Caribbean societies did not follow consciously the directives of upper-stratum fashion but adhered to a subcultural fashion in which certain colors (purple and red) and certain tissues (silk, embroidered lace, or their surrogates) were clearly preferred among the female part of the group.

The data obtained indicate that all subjects, including the Chinese, perceive and cathect themselves within the *same* frame of reference. Although these adolescents have been growing up at the time in a society when public attitudes are not discriminatory and in fact actively support the "idea of the equality of the races," they still associate Caucasian features with the desirable and Negroid features with the undesirable. In the case of Chinese subjects, typically Chinese features that closely approximate to Caucasian features are positively regarded, while those features which differ from Caucasian standards are negatively cathected.[21]

While the ideal features are unequivocally Caucasoid, the ideal physique, described as "well-built, good, and muscular" is, according to Miller, "the only aspect of the Negro stereotype . . . accepted . . . as being a desirable feature"; the preferred skin color is described as "one or two shades removed from white," and is compared to the Spanish stereotype. Both physique and skin-color preferences, it would seem, point to the athletic, bronzed outdoor type. Insofar as the results of research done by Kerr[22] and Henriques[23] in the 1940s implied a preference for a pale-white skin color, Miller would be correct in assuming that

some changes have taken place since that time in the way in which skin-color is conceptualized. However, subjects' conceptions of other physical features, e.g. hair and nose, have remained basically the same [and] their concept of beauty is to a great extent congruent with the ideas of beauty reported by Henriques and Kerr during the 1940s when color discrimination was commonly evidenced.[24]

Miller's research convincingly illustrates the one-way transference of the dominant somatic norm image in Jamaican society, resulting in "the concept of the average Jamaican [being] very far removed from the concept of the handsome boy or beautiful girl."[25] If this is so in the native country of Marcus Garvey, overwhelmingly inhabited by black and colored citizens, it may be

---

21 Ibid., p. 78 (my italics).
22 Madeline Kerr, *Personality and Conflict in Jamaica* (Liverpool: Liverpool University Press, 1952).
23 Fernando Henriques, *Family and Colour in Jamaica* (London: Eyre & Spottiswoode, 1953).
24 Miller, "Body Image," pp. 88–89.
25 Ibid., p. 87.

safely assumed, especially since it is supported by a substantial literature, that the phenomenon is common in American multiracial societies.

Those groups, increasing in numbers, who want to convince the black man in these societies of his own dignity and beauty—that is, to restore the original somatic norm image suppressed for generations—have therefore taken upon themselves a useful, but extremely difficult, task, made more so because the dominance of the white somatic norm image in these societies is a function not only of the internal socioracial structure but also of its international dominance, manifesting itself through the internationally active communications media. With these obstacles, it is doubtful whether the awareness of the beauty of Negroid features will ever become an utterly natural—as opposed to artificial and militantly affirmative—experience in a society where, at the same time, with more frequency and accompanied by more internal and international social prestige, the white ideal physical type is presented without the necessity of belligerent or deliberate emphasis.

Somatic Norm Image and Marriage in Homogeneous and Multiracial Societies

What is the plausible connection between socially conditioned ideals of human beauty and marriage—or to phrase it more generally, sexual unions on the basis of social acceptance? First, this question will be placed in the context of a racially homogeneous society, where no racial problem complicates matters.

In such a society, too, criteria for physical beauty exist without which physical vanity would be unthinkable. These criteria pervade all sectors of life—literature, the pictorial arts, advertising, the cosmetics industry, etc.,—but are not as widely and consciously formulated and discussed on all social levels as is the case in multiracial societies. Granted this general difference, it is nevertheless clear that the female population of a racially homogeneous society shows a relatively greater personal interest in approximating the ideal of female physical beauty than do most men with regard to the male ideal. The cosmetics and related industries attest to this, and the reason is obvious: The competition between females on the marriage market (and to a lesser degree in other markets) is in large part based on considerations of physical beauty. The connection between the ideal of physical beauty and love, as postulated by Ayala, thus finds its confirmation in everyday life. Dress, as a complementary or compensatory element of beauty, is for similar reasons more heavily emphasized by the female part of a racially homogeneous society than by the male element. The female, as nominally passive potential marriage partner, is subjected to greater pressures to conform to the current demands of fashion. (Where this traditional female role is changing, a greater emphasis on male dress may be expected.)

Here, the parallel between the traditionally disadvantaged position of the female vis-à-vis the male in a racially homogeneous society and the situation of the young men and women from the darkest-skinned strata vis-à-vis the lighter colored in the Jamaican multiracial society, as depicted by Miller, is striking. In both cases there is a competitive need to comply as much as possible with the demands of what is considered to be beautiful or handsome, and a tendency on the part of the more disadvantaged to rely more heavily than the others on dress as an accessible complementary element.

It may be true, as numerous investigations have demonstrated, that in a racially homogeneous society the selection of a marriage partner generally takes place within a geographically, (sub-)culturally, and socioeconomically narrowly limited circle, but no one will conclude from this evidence that in modern society the individual selection of such a partner merely responds to geographical, socioeconomic, and the like, criteria. Within the statistically limited potential marriage market, a selection process takes place that in the final instance is (socio-)psychological rather than sociological; a selection in which considerations of physical attraction undoubtedly play their part.

Multiracial Societies

If all this is plausible with regard to a racially homogeneous society, why should the same reasoning be less acceptable if it is applied to multiracial societies?

If in one category of societies the racially dominant group tends to abstain from marriages with even those defined as light coloreds, whereas in another group of societies marriages with persons of that somatic type are evident and not insignificant in numbers, is it then not altogether probable that these differences in the rate of interracial marriages may be understood in terms of a somewhat different somatic norm image, which in turn correlates visually with the undeniable, though slight, differences in average physical features between northwestern and southern Europeans? In both categories of societies some socioeconomic strata are found to which different socioracial groups belong. Why do more marriages between whites and "light coloreds" take place within such a stratum in one type of society than in the other if not because of a different definition of whiteness and socially desirable physical traits?

Pitt-Rivers observes for Indo-America:

Political or commercial alliances are not the same as alliances through marriage. Their products are of a different order. Profits are colorless, children are not. Hence, phenotype may not matter in commercial dealings, but it is never more important than in marriage. . . . Individual motivations are ordered to produce conformity with an ideal image of ethnic class. This tends to reinforce the original image. . . . Color . . . is not something that can be altered in the individual's life, but it is something that can be put right in the next generation. For this reason, the wives of the well-to-do tend to look more European than their husbands. In the lower classes, paler siblings are sometimes favored at the expense of their more swarthy siblings; their potential for social mobility is greater.[26]

If it is true that in multiracial societies generally there is a racist ingredient that influences the mechanisms of social mobility, it would indeed be hard to understand why such a mechanism would not function in the selection of marriage partners. If, in spite of this general contention, there are significant differences in the frequency of interracial partner selections among two or more so-

---

[26] Julian Pitt-Rivers, "Race, Color, and Class in Central America and the Andes," *Color and Race,* ed. John Hope Franklin (Boston: Houghton Mifflin, 1968), pp. 277–278.

cieties, it seems perfectly permissible to investigate the possibility of a difference in socially determined esthetic criteria of selection. Such a procedure is certainly academically more rewarding than to postulate that by an act of Providence some societies are less racist than others as far as intermarriage is concerned.

The problems of intergroup relations are serious in all multi-racial societies of America. They appear to be more serious where no socioracial continuum exists and where, consequently, the dividing lines between socioracial groups are abruptly drawn. Only comparative research can try to understand the causes of such differences. Only comparative research can, further, demonstrate the character of the relationship, if any, between systems of involuntary labor and the complexities of interracial relations.

Only after such causes and such supposed relationships are more fully understood can any individual society hope to become better aware of the direction into which it is moving and of the chances, if any, of changing its course.

BIBLIOGRAPHY

Acosta Saignes, Miguel. *Vida de los Escalavos Negros en Venezuela.* Caracas: Hespérides, 1967.

Adams, Richard N. *Encuesta sobre la Cultura de los Ladinos en Guatemala.* Guatemala: Editorial del Ministerio de Educación Pública, 1956.

————. "Nationalization." *Handbook of Middle American Indians,* vol. 4. Edited by Robert Wauchope.

Adhin, Jan H. "De Culturele Invloed van de Aziatische Bevolkings-groep op Suriname." *Vox Guyanae* (November 1954–January 1955).

Arcaya, Pedro M. *Insurrección de los Negros de la Serranía de Coro.* Caracas: Instituto Panamericano de Geografía e Historia, 1949.

Ayala, Francisco. *Tratado de Sociología,* 3d ed. (Madrid: Aguilar, 1968).

Banton, Michael. *Race Relations.* London: Tavistock, 1967.

Barnet, Miguel. *Biografía de un Cimarrón.* Barcelona: Ariel, 1968.

Barrett, Leonard E. *The Rastafarians: A Study in Messianic Cultism in Jamaica.* Río Piedras: Institute of Caribbean Studies, 1969.

Beals, Ralph. "Indian, Mestizo, White Relations in Spanish America." *Race Relations in World Perspective.* Edited by Andrew Lind. Honolulu, 1955.

Bell, Wendell, and Ivar Oxaal, *Decisions of Nationhood: Political and Social Development in the British Caribbean.* Denver: University of Denver, 1964.

Blumer, Herbert. "Race Prejudice as a Sense of Group Position." *Race Relations: Problems and Theory.* Edited by J. Masouka and P. Valien. Chapel Hill, N.C.: University of North Carolina Press, 1961.

Bogardus, E. S. "A Race-Relations Cycle." *American Journal of Sociology* 35, no. 4 (January 1930).

Bosch, Juan. *Composición Social Dominicana: Historia e Interpre-tación.* Colección Pensamiento y Cultura. Santo Domingo: Julio D. Postigo e Hijos, 1970.

Bradley, C. P. "The Party System in British Guiana and the General Election of 1961. *Caribbean Studies* 1, no. 3 (October 1961).

Braithwaite, L. "Social Stratification in Trinidad." *Social and Economic Studies* 2 and 3 (October 1953).

Brinton, Crane. *Anatomy of Revolution,* rev. ed. (New York: Random House, 1957).

Bueno, Salvador. "Africa en América." *Casa de las Américas* 36 and 37 (1966).

Burma, John H. "The Measurement of Negro Passing." *American Journal of Sociology* (1952).

Cahnman, Werner J. "The Mediterranean and Caribbean Regions: A Comparison in Race and Culture Contacts." *Social Forces* 22 (October 1943–May 1944).

———. "The Stigma of Obesity." *The Sociological Quarterly* (Summer 1968).

Campbell, John Q., ed. *Racial Tension and National Identity.* Nashville: Vanderbilt University Press, 1972.

Caso, Alfonso. "Definición del Indio y de lo Indio." *América Indígena* 8, no. 5 (1948).

Césaire, Aimé. "Cahier d'un Retour au Pays Natal." *Présence Africaine* (1947) (first published 1939).

———. "Discours sur le Colonialisme." *Présence Africaine* (1955).

Colby, B., and P. Van den Berghe, "Ethnic Relations in Southeastern Mexico." *American Anthropologist* 53, no. 4 (1961).

Coleman, J. Winston. *Slavery Times in Kentucky.* Chapel Hill, N.C.: University of North Carolina Press, 1940.

Comás, Juan. *Relaciones Interraciales en América Latina, 1940–1960.* Mexico, 1961.

Corbitt, Duvon Clough. *The Chinese in Cuba 1847–1947. A Study.* Wilmore, Ky.: Asbury College, 1971.

Cotler, Julio. "Internal Domination and Social Change in Peru." *Masses in Latin America.* Edited by Irving L. Horowitz. New York: Oxford University Press, 1970.

Coulthard, G. R. "A New Vision of the Indian in Mexican Literature of the Postrevolutionary Period." Unpublished manuscript.

———. "Parallelisms and Divergencies between 'Négritude' and Indigenismo." *Caribbean Studies* 8, no. 1 (1968).

Cox, Oliver C. *Caste, Class and Race.* New York: Doubleday, 1948.

Dalton, Margarita. "Los Depósitos de Cimarrones en el Siglo XIX." *Etnología y Folklore* 3 (enero–junio 1967).

Davie, Maurice A. *Negroes in American Society*. New York: McGraw-Hill, 1949.

Davis, A., B. Gardner, and M. R. Gardner, *Deep South*. Chicago: University of Chicago Press, 1941.

Davis, David Brian. *The Problem of Slavery in Western Culture*. Ithaca, N.Y.: Cornell University Press, 1966.

Degler, Carl N. *Out of Our Past*. New York: Harper & Row, 1959.

Den Hollander, A. N. J. *Het Andere Volk: Een Verkenning van Groepsoordeel en Groepsbeeld*. Amsterdam, 1946.

de Queiros, María José. *Do Indianismo ao Indigenismo nas Letras Hispanoamericanas*. Belo Horizonte, 1962.

Deutsch, Karl W. *Nationalism and Social Communication*, 2d ed. Cambridge, Mass.: The Massachusetts Institute of Technology Press, 1966.

de Waal Malefijt, Annemarie. *The Javanese of Surinam: Segment of a Plural Society*. Assen: Royal Van Gorcum, 1963.

Dodge, Peter. "Comparative Racial Systems in the Greater Caribbean." New York: Institute of Latin American Studies, Columbia University, 1968.

Drimmer, Melvin, ed. *Black History: A Reappraisal*. New York: Doubleday, 1967.

Elizabeth, L. "The Free Black and Mulatto in the Slave Societies of the French West Indies." *Neither Slave nor Free: The Freedman of African Descent in the Slave Societies of the New World*. Edited by J. Greene and D. Cohen. Baltimore: The Johns Hopkins University Press, 1971.

Elkins, Stanley M. *Slavery: A Problem in American Institutional and Intellectual Life*. Chicago: University of Chicago Press, 1959.

Fahrenfort, J. J. "Over Vrije en Onvrije Arbeid." *Mensch en Maatschappij* 19 (1943):29–51.

Fanon, Frantz. *Les Damnés de la Terre*. Paris: Maspéro, 1961.

———. *Peau Noire, Masques Blancs*. Paris: Editions du Seuil, 1953.

Fernándes, Florestan. "Immigration and Race Relations in São Paulo." *Race and Class in Latin America*. Edited by Magnus Mörner. New York: Columbia University Press, 1970.

———. "The Weight of the Past." *Color and Race*. Edited by John Hope Franklin. Boston: Houghton Mifflin, 1968.

Firmin, Anténor. *De l'Egalité des Races Humaines*. Paris, 1885.

Foner, Laura, and Eugene D. Genovese, *Slavery in the New World:*

A Reader in Comparative History. Englewood Cliffs, N.J.: Prentice-Hall, 1969.

Francis, E. K. "Variables in the Formation of So-called 'Minority Groups.'" *American Journal of Sociology* 60, no. 1.

Frank, André Gunder. *Capitalism and Underdevelopment in Latin America: Historical Studies of Chile and Brazil*. New York: Monthly Review Press, 1967.

Franklin, John Hope, ed. *Color and Race*. Boston: Houghton Mifflin, 1968.

Furnivall, J. S. *Tropical Economy*. Cambridge: Cambridge University Press, 1945.

Gamio, Manuel. *Forjando Patria*. Mexico, 1916.

García-Zamor, Jean-Claude. "Social Mobility of Negroes in Brazil." *Journal of Inter-American Studies and World Affairs* 12, no. 2 (April 1970):242–254.

Genovese, Eugene D. "The Free Negro in the Slave States of North America." *Neither Slave nor Free: The Freedman of African Descent in the Slave Societies of the New World*. Edited by J. Greene and D. Cohen. Baltimore: The Johns Hopkins University Press, 1972.

Gillin, John. "Mestizo America." *Most of the World*. Edited by Ralph Linton. New York: Columbia University Press, 1949.

Glazer, Nathan. "Blacks and Ethnic Groups: The Difference, and the Political Difference It Makes." *Key Issues in the Afro-American Experience, Vol. II*. Edited by Nathan I. Huggins, Martin Kilson, and Daniel M. Fox. New York: Harcourt Brace Jovanovich, Inc., 1971.

Goffman, Erving. *Asylums*. New York: Aldine, 1961.

Goldschmidt, Walter, and Harry Hoijer. *The Social Anthropology of Latin America*. Los Angeles: University of California Press, 1970.

Gomez Acevedo, Labor. *Organización y Reglamentación del Trabajo en el Puerto Rico del Siglo 19*. Río Piedras: Editorial Universitaria, 1970.

Gonzales Casanova, Pablo. "Internal Colonialism and National Development." *Studies in Comparative International Development* 1, no. 4 (1965):27–37.

Gonzalez Navarro, Moisés. "Mestizaje in Mexico During the National Period." *Race and Class in Latin America*. Edited by Magnus Mörner. New York: Columbia University Press, 1970.

Goode, W. J. "Illegitimacy, Anomie, and Cultural Penetration." *American Sociological Review* 26, no. 6 (December 1961):910–925.

Gordon, Milton M. *Assimilation in American Life*. New York: Oxford University Press, 1964.

Greene, J., and Cohen, D. eds. *Neither Slave nor Free: The Freedman of African Descent in the Slave Societies of the New World*. Baltimore: The Johns Hopkins University Press, 1971.

Hamm, Margherita Arlina. *Porto Rico and the West Indies*. New York: F. Tennyson Neely, 1899.

Hammond, Peter B., ed. *Physical Anthropology and Archeology*. New York: Macmillan, 1964.

Harris, Marvin. *Patterns of Race in the Americas*. New York: Walker, 1964.

Henriques, Fernando. *Family and Colour in Jamaica*. London: Eyre & Spottiswoode, 1953.

Herring, Hubert. *A History of Latin America*. New York: Alfred A. Knopf, 1960.

Hoetink, H. " 'Americans' in Samaná." *Caribbean Studies* 2, no. 1 (April 1962):3–22.

———. *Caribbean Race Relations: A Study of Two Variants*. New York: Oxford University Press, 1971. Pocket edition.

———. *The Two Variants in Caribbean Race Relations: A Contribution to the Sociology of Segmented Societies*. Translated by Eva M. Hooykaas. London: Oxford University Press, 1967.

———. "Change in Prejudice: Some Notes on the Minority Problem, with References to the West Indies and Latin America." *Bijdragen tot de Taal- Land- en Volkenkunde* 119, no. 1 (1963).

———. "The Dominican Republic in the Nineteenth Century: Some Notes on Stratification, Immigration, and Race." *Race and Class in Latin America*. Edited by Magnus Mörner. New York: Columbia University Press, 1970.

———. "The Free Black and Mulatto in the Slave Societies of The Netherlands West Indies." *Neither Slave nor Free: The Freedman of African Descent in the Slave Societies of the New World*. Edited by J. Greene and D. Cohen. Baltimore: The Johns Hopkins University Press, 1972.

———. "The New Evolutionism." *Structure, Function, Process*. Edited by A. F. J. Köbben. Assen: Royal Van Gorcum, 1973.

———. *Het Patroon van de Oude Curaçaose Samenleving: Een Sociologische Studie*. Assen: Royal Van Gorcum, 1958.

———. *El Pueblo Dominicano 1850–1900: Apuntes para su Socio-*

logía Histórica. Santiago de los Caballeros: Universidad Católica Madre y Maestra, 1971.

Horowitz, Donald R. "Color Differentiation in the American Systems of Slavery." Unpublished manuscript, 1969.

Horowitz, Irving, ed. *Masses in Latin America*. New York: Oxford University Press, 1970.

Hymes, D., ed. *Pidginization and Creolization of Languages*. Proceedings of a conference held at the University of the West Indies. London and New York: Cambridge University Press, 1971.

Ianni, Octavio. *As Metamorfoses do Escravo*. São Paulo, Brazil: Difusao Europeia do Livro, 1962.

International Labour Organization. "Report on the Fourth Conference of American States' Members of the International Labour Organization. Conditions of Life and Work of Indigenous Populations of Latin American Countries. Geneva, 1949. "Report of the Joint Bolivian-United States Labour Commission." *Labour Problems in Bolivia*. Montreal, 1943.

James, Preston. *Latin America*. New York: Odyssey Press, 1942.

Jordan, Winthrop D. "American Chiaroscuro: The Status and Definition of Mulattoes in the British Colonies." *William and Mary Quarterly* 19, no. 2 (April 1962):183–200; reprinted in Laura Foner and Eugene D. Genovese, eds., *Slavery in the New World: A Reader in Comparative History*. Englewood Cliffs, N.J.: Prentice-Hall, 1969.

Kelso, Louis O., and Hetter, Patricia. *Two-Factor Theory: The Economics of Reality*. 1970.

Kerr, Madeline. *Personality and Conflict in Jamaica*. Liverpool: Liverpool University Press, 1952.

Klass, Morton. *East Indians in Trinidad: A Study of Cultural Persistence*. New York: Columbia University Press, 1961.

Klein, Herbert S. "The Colored Freedmen in Brazilian Slave Society." *Journal of Social History* 3 (Fall 1969).

Kloosterboer, W. *Involuntary Labour Since the Abolition of Slavery: A Survey of Compulsory Labour Throughout the World*. Leiden: E. J. Brill, 1960.

Knight, Franklin W. "The Role of the Free Black and the Free Mulatto in Cuban Slave Society." *Neither Slave nor Free: The Freedman of African Descent in the Slave Societies of the New World*. Edited by J. Greene, and D. Cohen. Baltimore: The Johns Hopkins University Press, 1972.

————. *Slave Society in Cuba during the Nineteenth Century.* Madison, Wis.: University of Wisconsin Press, 1970.

Köbben, A. F. J., ed. *Structure, Function, Process.* Assen: Royal Van Gorcum, 1973.

Kuper, Leo, and Smith, M. G., eds. *Pluralism in Africa.* Berkeley: University of California Press, 1969.

Larrazabal Blanco, Carlos. *Los Negros y la Esclavitud en Santo Domingo.* Santo Domingo: Julio D. Postigo e Hijos, 1967.

Leons, Madeline Barbara. "Stratification and Pluralism in the Bolivian Yungas." *The Social Anthropology of Latin America.* Edited by Walter Goldschmidt and Harry Hoijer. Los Angeles: University of California Press, 1970.

Lewis, Gordon K. *The Growth of the Modern West Indies.* London: MacGibbon and Kee, 1968.

Lewis, Sybil, and Mathews, Thomas G., eds. *Caribbean Integration: Papers on Social, Political and Economic Integration.* Río Piedras: Institute of Caribbean Studies, 1967.

Leyburn, J. G. *The Haitian People.* New Haven, Conn.: Yale University Press, 1966.

Lichtveld, Lou. *Suriname's Nationale Aspiraties.* Amsterdam: N. V. De Arbeiderspers, 1953.

Linton, Ralph, ed. *Most of the World.* New York: Columbia University Press, 1949.

————. ed. *The Science of Man in the World Crisis.* New York: Columbia University Press, 1945.

Long, Edward. *The History of Jamaica.* London: T. Lowndes, 1774.

Lowenthal, David. "Race and Color in the West Indies." *Daedalus* (Spring 1967).

Luperón, Gregorio. *Notas Autobiográficas y Apuntes Históricos,* vol. 3, 2d ed. Santiago de los Caballeros: El Diario, 1939.

Lyle Eugene P. "Our Experience in Porto Rico." *World's Week* 11 (1906).

Maingot, Anthony P. "From Ethnocentric to National History Writing in the Plural Society." *Caribbean Studies* 9, no. 3 (October 1969).

Mason, Philip. *Patterns of Dominance.* London: Oxford University Press, 1970.

Masouka, J., and P. Valien, eds. *Race Relations: Problems and Theory.* Chapel Hill, N.C.: University of North Carolina Press, 1961.

Mathews, T. G. "La Cuestión del Color en Puerto Rico." Unpublished manuscript, 1970.

―――. "The Project for a Confederation of the Greater Antilles." *Caribbean Historical Review* 3 and 4 (December 1954):70–107.

McVeigh, Frank J. "The Life Conditions of Afro-Americans." *Afro-American Studies* 1, no. 1 (May 1970).

McWilliams, Carey. *Brothers under the Skin,* rev. ed. New York: Little, Brown & Co., 1951.

Mejía Ricart, M. A. *Las Clases Sociales en Santo Domingo.* Ciudad Trujillo: Librería Dominicana, 1953.

Melendez, Concha. *La Novela Indianista en Hispanoamérica.* Madrid, 1934.

Mellafe, Rolando. *La Introducción de la Esclavitud Negra en Chile: Tráfico y Rutas.* Santiago de Chile, 1959.

Métraux, Alfred. "Problemas Raciales en América Latina." *Courier de l'UNESCO* (October 1960).

Miller, Errol L. "Body Image, Physical Beauty and Colour Among Jamaican Adolescents." *Social and Economic Studies* 18, no. 1 (March 1969):72–89.

Mintz, Sidney W. "The Caribbean as a Socio-cultural Area." *Cahiers d'Histoire Mondiale* 9, no. 4 (1966).

―――. "Caribbean Nationhood in Anthropological Perspective." *Caribbean Integration: Papers on Social, Political and Economic Integration.* Río Piedras: Institute of Caribbean Studies, 1967.

―――. "Comments on the Socio-Historical Background to Pidginization and Creolization." *Pidginization and Creolization of Languages. Proceedings of a Conference Held at the University of the West Indies.* Edited by D. Hymes. New York: Cambridge University Press, 1971.

―――. "Foreword." *Afro-American Anthropology: Contemporary Perspectives.* Edited by N. Whitten and J. Szwed. New York: Free Press, 1970.

―――. "Labor and Sugar in Puerto Rico and in Jamaica, 1800–1850." *Comparative Studies in Society and History* 1, no. 3 (1959).

―――. "Review of *Slavery: A Problem in American Institutional and Intellectual Life,* by Stanley M. Elkins." *American Anthropologist* 63, no. 3 (1961).

―――. "Summary and Commentary." *Black Studies in the University.* Edited by Armstead L. Robinson, Craig C. Foster, and Donald H. Ogilvie. New Haven, Conn.: Yale University Press, 1969.

Mörner, Magnus, ed. *Race and Class in Latin America.* New York: Columbia University Press, 1970.

————. *Race Mixture in the History of Latin America.* Boston: Little, Brown & Co., 1967.

Morse, Richard M. "Primacy, Regionalization, Dependency: Approaches to Latin American Cities in National Development." Paper presented at the III Jornadas de Historia Social y Económica, Buenos Aires, 1970.

Nañez, Falcón, Guillermo. "Paul Dieseldorff: German Entrepreneur in the Alta Verapaz of Guatemala, 1889–1937." Ph.D. dissertation, Tulane University, 1970.

Nicholls, David G. "Biology and Politics in Haiti." *Race* 13 (July 1971–April (1972):203–214.

————. "East Indians and Black Power in Trinidad." *Race* 12 (July 1970–April 1971):443–459.

Nieboer, H. J. *Slavery as an Industrial System: Ethnological Researches.* The Hague: Martinus Nijhoff, 1900.

Noel, Donald L. "A Theory of the Origin of Ethnic Stratification." *Social Problems* 16, no. 2 (Fall 1968):157–172.

Nogueira, O. "Skin Color and Social Class." *Plantation Systems of the New World.* Washington, D.C.: Pan American Union, 1959.

Oxaal, Ivar. *Black Intellectuals Come to Power: The Rise of Creole Nationalism in Trinidad and Tobago.* Cambridge, Mass.: Schenkman, 1968.

Park, Robert E. *Race and Culture.* Glencoe, Ill.: The Free Press, 1949.

Parsons, J. J. *San Andrés and Providencia: English-Speaking Islands in the Western Caribbean.* Berkeley and Los Angeles: University of California Press, 1956.

Parsons, Talcott. "The Problem of Polarization on the Axis of Color." *Color and Race.* Edited by John Hope Franklin. Boston: Houghton Mifflin, 1968.

Patterson, H. Orlando. "Review." *Caribbean Quarterly* (December 1967).

————. *The Children of Sisyphus.* London, 1964.

————. *The Sociology of Slavery.* London: MacGibbon and Kee, 1967.

Péréz Cabral, Pedro Andrés. *La Comunidad Mulata: El Caso Socio-Político de la República Dominicana.* Caracas: Gráfica Americana, 1967.

Pitt-Rivers, Julian. "Race, Color, and Class in Central America and the Andes." *Color and Race.* Edited by John Hope Franklin. Boston: Houghton Mifflin, 1968.

Pool, Jonathan. "National Development and Language Diversity." *Sociologische Gids* 17, no. 2 (1970):86–102.

Price, Hannibal. *De la Réhabilitation de la Race Noire, par la République d'Haiti.* Port-au-Prince, 1900.

Price-Mars, Jean. *Ainsi Parla l'Oncle: Essais d'Ethnographie.* Port-au-Prince, 1928. (New York: Parapsychology Foundation, 1954, new ed., unchanged.)

Rama, Carlos M. *Los Afro-Uruguayos.* Montevideo: El Siglo Ilustrado, 1967.

" 'Realism and Race,' by a Young Jamaican Nationalist," in "The Views on the Problem of Race and Colour in Jamaica Today." *West Indian Economist* 3, no. 10 (April 1961).

Robinson, Armstead L., Foster, Craig C., and Ogilvie, Donald H., eds. *Black Studies in the University.* New Haven, Conn.: Yale University Press, 1969.

Rogler, G. "The Role of Semantics in the Study of Race Distance in Puerto Rico." *Social Forces* 22 (October 1943–May 1944).

Rose, A. and C. *America Divided: Minority Group Relations in the United States.* New York: Alfred A. Knopf, 1948.

Rose, Arnold. *The Negro in America.* London: Martin Secker and Warburg, 1948.

Rose, Peter I. "The Development of 'Race Studies': Sociological Views and Expanding Horizons." *Race amongst Nations.* Edited by George Shepherd and Tilden LeMille. Lexington, Mass.: D. C. Heath, 1970.

———. *The Subject Is Race: Traditional Ideologies and the Teaching of Race Relations.* New York: Oxford University Press, 1968.

———. *They and We: Racial and Ethnic Relations in the United States.* New York: Random House, 1964.

Saco, José Antonio. *Historia de la Esclavitud de la Raza Africana en el Mundo Nuevo y en Especial en los Países Americo-Hispanos.* 4 vols. Havana: Editorial Cultural, S.A., 1938.

Saunders, John. "Class, Color and Prejudice: A Brazilian Counterpoint." *Racial Tension and National Identity.* Edited by John Q. Campbell. Nashville: Vanderbilt University Press, 1971.

Schermerhorn, R. A. *Comparative Ethnic Relations.* New York: Random House, 1970.

———. *These Our People: Minorities in the American Culture.* Boston: Heath, 1949.

Seda Bonilla, Eduardo. "Dos Modelos de Relaciones Raciales: Estados

Unidos y América Latina." *Revista de Ciencias Sociales* 12, no. 4 (Diciembre 1968) : 569–597.

————. "Social Structure and Race Relations." *Social Forces* 40, no. 2 (December 1961).

Shibutani, Tamotsy, and Kwan, Kian M. *Ethnic Stratification: A Comparative Approach.* New York: Macmillan, 1965.

Shils, Edward. "Color and the Afro-Asian Intellectual." *Color and Race.* Edited by John Hope Franklin. Boston: Houghton Mifflin, 1968.

Simpson, G. E., and Yinger, M. J. *Racial and Cultural Minorities: An Analysis of Prejudice and Discrimination,* rev. ed. New York: Harper, 1958.

Smith, M. G. "Institutional and Political Conditions of Pluralism." *Pluralism in Africa.* Edited by Leo Kuper and M. G. Smith. Berkeley: University of California Press, 1969.

————. "Review." *Race* 10, no. 1 (1968).

————. *The Plural Society in the West Indies.* Berkeley: University of California Press, 1965.

Smith, R. T. "Social Stratification, Cultural Pluralism and Integration in West Indian Societies." *Caribbean Integration: Papers on Social, Political and Economic Integration.* Edited by S. Lewis and T. Mathews. Río Piedras: Institute of Caribbean Studies, University of Puerto Rico, 1967.

Smith, T. Lynn. *Brazil: People and Institutions.* Baton Rouge: Louisiana State University Press, 1946.

Speckmann, J. D. "De Houding van de Creoolse Bevolkingsgroep in Suriname ten Opzichte van de Creolen." *Bijdragen tot de Taal- Land- en Volkenkunde* 119, no. 1 (1963).

————. *Marriage and Kinship Among the Indians in Surinam.* Assen: Royal Van Gorcum, 1965.

————. "The Indian Group in the Segmented Society of Surinam." *Caribbean Studies* 3, no. 1 (April 1963).

Spencer, Herbert. *Industrial Institutions,* Part VIII of *The Principles of Sociology.* New York: Appleton-Century-Crofts, 1880–1896.

Stavenhagen, Rodolfo. "Classes, Colonialism and Acculturation: A System of Inter-Ethnic Relations in Meso-America." *Masses in Latin America.* Edited by Irving L. Horowitz. New York: Oxford University Press, 1970.

Stedman, J. G. *A Narrative of a Five-Years Expedition against the Revolted Negroes of Surinam.* 2 vols. London, 1813.

Stuckert, Robert P. "Race Mixture: The African Ancestry of White Americans. *Physical Anthropology and Archeology.* Edited by Peter B. Hammond. New York: Macmillan, 1964.

Tannenbaum, Frank. *Slave and Citizen.* New York: Alfred A. Knopf, 1947.

Ten Have, P. "Emancipation and Culture." *Mens en Maatschappij* July–August (1970).

"30 Mei 1969: Rapport van de Commissie tot Onderzoek van de Achtergronden en Oorzaken van de Onlusten welke op 30 mei 1969 op Curaçao Hebben Plaatsgehad." Aruba: De Wit, 1970.

Toynbee, Arnold J. *A Study of History.* London: Oxford University Press, 1962.

————. *The World and the West.* London: Oxford University Press, 1953.

Tudela, José, ed. *El Legado de España a América,* 2 vols. Madrid: Ediciones Pegaso, 1954.

"U.S. Message from the President, Transmitting Report of the Secretary of State with Accompanying Papers Concerning the Alleged Existence of Slavery in Peru." *Slavery in Peru.* Washington, D.C.: U.S. Government Printing Office, 1913.

Van den Berghe, Pierre L. *Race and Racism: A Comparative Perspective.* New York: Wiley & Son, 1967.

Van Lier, R. A. J. *The Development and Nature of Society in the West Indies.* Amsterdam: Kon. Instituut voor de Tropen, 1950.

————. *Samenleving in een Grensgebied: Een Sociaal-Historische Studie van de Maatschappij in Suriname.* The Hague: Martinus Nijhoff, 1949.

Van Renselaar, H. C. "De Houding van de Creoolse Bevolkingsgroep in Suriname ten Opzichte van Andere Bevolkingsgroepen (in het Bijzonder ten Opzichte van de Hindustanen)." *Bijdragen tot de Taal- Land- en Volkenkunde* 119, no. 1 (1963).

Wagley, Charles. *The Latin American Tradition.* New York: Columbia University Press, 1968.

Wagley, Charles, and Harris, M. *Minorities in the New World: Six Case Studies.* New York: Columbia University Press, 1958.

Wauchope, Robert, ed. *Handbook of Middle American Indians,* vol. 4. Austin: University of Texas Press, 1966.

Weaver, Robert C. *Negro Labor a National Problem.* New York: Harcourt, Brace, Jovanovich, Inc., 1946.

Weber, Max. *Grundriss der Sozialökonomik.* Band 3, *Wirtschaft und Gesellschaft.* Tübingen: Mohr, 1922.

Weller, Judith Ann. *The East Indian Indenture in Trinidad.* Río Piedras: Institute of Caribbean Studies, 1968.

Whitten, N., and Szwed, J. eds. *Afro-American Anthropology: Contemporary Perspectives.* New York: Free Press, 1970.

Williams, Eric. *Capitalism and Slavery.* Chapel Hill, N.C.: University of North Carolina Press, 1944.

Wirth, Louis. "The Problem of Minority Groups." *The Science of Man in the World Crisis.* Edited by R. Linton. New York: Columbia University Press, 1945.

Wood, Donald. *Trinidad in Transition: The Years after Slavery.* London: Oxford University Press, 1968.

Woodward, C. Vann. *The Strange Career of Jim Crow.* New York: Oxford University Press, 1959.

INDEX

73 74 75   12 11 10 9 8 7 6 5 4 3 2 1